BEYOND FEAR

BEYOND FEAR

A Harrowing Journey Across New Guinea
Through Rivers, Swamps, Jungle, and the Most Remote
Mountains in the World

Joel P. Kramer

THE LYONS PRESS

Guilford, Connecticut
An imprint of The Globe Pequot Press

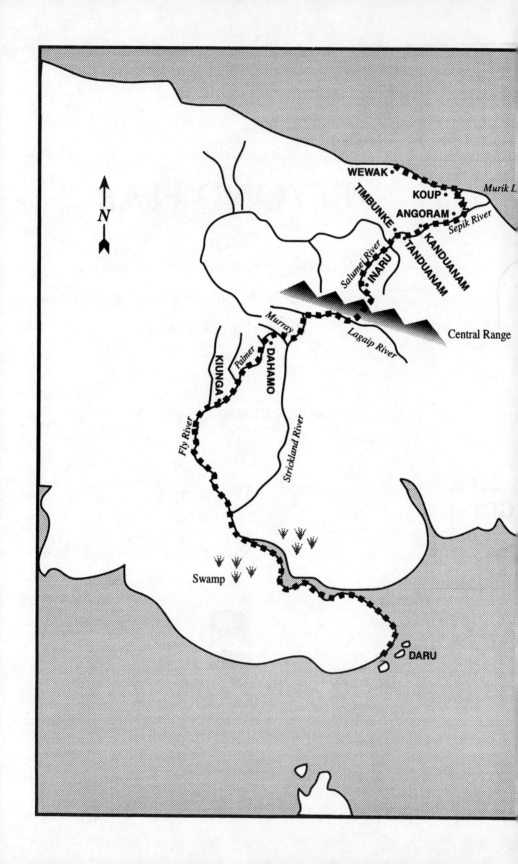

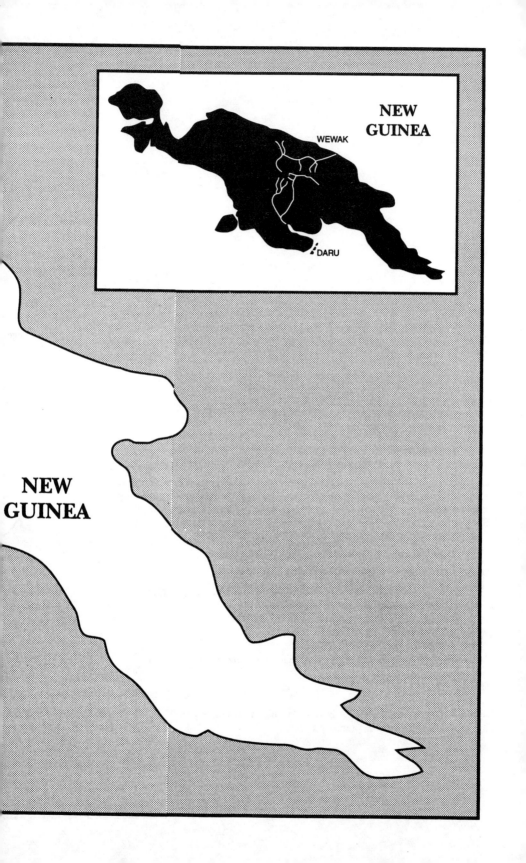

The Lyons Press is an imprint of The Globe Pequot Press.

Printed in Canada

10 9 8 7 6 5 4 3 2 1

Typesetting by Design Type Service

The Library of Congress Cataloging-in-Publication Data is available on file.

ISBN 1-58574-343-7

Originally published by Above & Beyond Publishing Brigham City, Utah.
First Lyons Press edition, September 2001

THIS BOOK IS DEDICATED TO

Jesus Christ

Who is my God

My King

My Savior

My friend

And to His servant, Aaron J. Lippard

Who paddled with me

Every stroke

Who walked with me

Every step

Who was a stranger

My partner

My enemy

But now

He is my brother!

And to the rest of my family

Whose boundaries I cannot fathom

The touch of a thousand fingerprints upon my soul

CONTENTS

FOREWORD

I have written this story as accurately as possible, using both Aaron's and my extensive expedition journals. My journal explores more of what we were feeling, our conversations, and relational conflicts, while Aaron's journal is filled with details, names, and descriptions of terrain and characters. Together, they portray a more complete picture of what we went through. Soon after our return from New Guinea, we also recorded a lengthy discussion, recounting from memory, each of the 102 days of our journey. In addition, the 2,300 color slides taken with our cameras provided helpful visual reminders.

However, even with an exhaustive supply of information, every detail and word spoken cannot be fully remembered or recorded. Therefore, this book records as much as I remember in as accurate a form as possible.

A few of the names used in this book were changed to protect individual privacy. Also, I have taken great liberty with the spelling of the pidgin language spoken by the nationals to help clarify what is being said for those who have never heard pidgin.

Aaron and I conducted extensive research, both before and after our trip which leads us to believe that we are indeed the first to cross the main part of the island of New Guinea without the use of motors. However, such things cannot be known for certain.

*"He is no fool who
gives what he cannot
keep to gain what
he cannot lose."*

– Jim Elliot

CHAPTER 1

Arrival

November 23, 1992: my first glimpse of New Guinea from the window of a small two-engine airplane. An awesome sight! Ragged points of mist-shrouded mountains jab through New Guinea's green skin, a vast ocean of thick jungle. Endless wave-like ridges stretch out as far as I can see. The mysterious scenery creates in me a thirst for adventure. It doesn't matter how long or how hard I stare, nothing is revealed of the struggle for life and death that continually takes place beneath the surface of jungle canopy.

Mysterious stories discovered during the past four months of research race though my mind. Those who know New Guinea call it the "Land of the Unexpected." And for good reason. Its web of rivers and vast swamps are patrolled by man-eating crocodiles and swarms of malarial mosquitoes. The interior highlands host an array of venomous snakes, bird-eating spiders, blood-sucking leeches, bats the size of eagles, and birds the size of men. I discovered healthy rumors of practicing cannibals and headhunters. I have read that the jungle can grow too thick for walking, the mountains too steep for climbing, and the rivers too rough to paddle. The rugged landscape has been carved with an average of 20-30 feet of annual rainfall. All of these adversaries form a conquering army that has successfully warded off exploration well into the twentieth century, protecting its ancient reality from the changing world outside, and making New Guinea one of the most unexplored wildernesses left on earth.

And that is why my partner and I have come: to wrestle with a seemingly invincible adversary, and to attempt to defeat the odds stacked against us. For we not only want to penetrate this forbidding land, we want to cross it without the help of motors! Our goal is to paddle every stroke and walk every step from the island's north shore to its southern coast, something that, to our knowledge, has never been done before.

"What have we gotten ourselves into?" Aaron Lippard's forehead is pressed up against the window; his red hair covers his ears and blends into his beard. His round, gold-rimmed spectacles flash in the tropical sun, momentarily hiding the fear in his light blue eyes.

"Too much, so it seems."

"It's too big!" His voice sounds shaky as he peers back out over the second largest island in the world.

"Bigger than us."

"We just aren't ready." I watch as Aaron's eyes dance between the pinnacles of jagged peaks, then I look back out the window at our adversary.

"We would never be ready." The clouds begin to pinch out our view.

"It's just too big." The cloud cover momentarily takes away the land's intimidation.

"There's only one thing bigger. We have to believe that the God who created that whole big mess down there is able to get us across it," I say.

"Easier said than done."

"We better enjoy *this* crossing of New Guinea, 'cause it looks like our next crossing is going to be a little bit harder." We laugh nervously.

The plane suddenly brushes through a cloud, and I glimpse my own reflection in the window. A young man, twenty-five, glares back at me. His light brown hair is cut short, and there is red stubble covering his chin. His green eyes hold a look of intensity I'd felt there before, but never actually observed.

I think of my family and friends back home in America. They did their best to persuade me not to come to New Guinea. They painted such a horrifying picture of a place they had never seen, gave detailed warnings of obstacles they had never encountered, and feared terrors they had never faced. They called me foolish, and my dream crazy and irresponsible.

The jungle peeks at me through the clouds and my heart races. Maybe they were right. Why <u>am</u> I here? All the legends and stories I have read, the rumors that I have heard of this mysterious island have come together to form an invisible, haunting wall that tries to separate me from my dream. So, I have come to penetrate this wall of fear, to see for myself what exists beyond.

"Did God call you to cross New Guinea?" The question rings in my head. I don't know that God has called me anywhere, specifically. All I do know is that He has been with me and blessed me wherever I have gone. I know that just four months ago I had no money, no equipment, and no partner to pursue my New Guinea dream. Within a month, I got a summer job that paid enough to make the idea a possibility. Then, several companies sponsored all the needed equipment, and, finally, I found Aaron, who was eager to join my quest. My dream was within reach.

So, why am I here? Because I want to be! But I have not come without a deep confidence that God is for me. His blessing is my protection, His grace my hope. I trust that God has come with me to cross New Guinea. If I can't believe that for myself, then I never would have dared to come!

The clouds break up again as the jungle canopy collides with the white foam of rough seas pounding against the shore below us. The plane turns towards the east and follows the north coast toward Wewak, where our expedition will begin. To our right, the clouds begin to catch fire with the setting sun, and the jungle on our left melts into shadows in the waning light.

Aaron made his own choice to follow me, for his own reasons. Right now though, the look of intimidation in his eyes shows me that those reasons don't seem to be enough.

"How are we going to get through all that jungle?" he asks.

Ignoring the question, I claim a vacant seat across the aisle and search the water and land below. The dim jungle breaks suddenly into a snaking river. Its scales twinkle in the last rays of the sun, showing miles of twisting coils.

"Aaron, come here!" He looks over my shoulder.

"Wow! Is that the Sepik?" he asks, amazed.

"That's it! That's our passage to the Central Highlands."

"Too bad it's not straight then, because it looks like an awful lot of paddling."

"And all upriver!" I add.

The golden shimmer of the river causes my stomach to churn. It is out there, waiting, calling. We move to the other window to watch the mighty river wind through the darkness. When the clouds and rainforest extinguish its glowing body, I sit back in my seat, lost in thought. Aaron searches the void below us. I can tell that the edge we are about to leap off is real for him, too. His face reflects that what he sees before him is a bottomless pit.

"There are no lights," he observes so quietly I have to lean in to hear him. "Most places, when you fly over land you can see lights, at least a few. Most places, there are at least watchtowers, lighthouses, ranches, something to let you know there is life below. But there aren't any down there. Not even one."

"Maybe we're completely over the ocean now."

"No. We're not."

"I just wish this plane would hurry up and land or at least start its approach," I complain.

"I could use some more of that mango juice they've been servin'." Aaron finally relaxes for a moment in his chair.

"Every second we are thrust forward by these engines we are going to have to make up the other way by paddling our kayak," I say.

"When you put it like that, I wish we would land too."

I shift in my seat, trying to get comfortable. Aaron slumps in his chair, his knees pressed against the seat in front of him. "Here's a word problem for you, Aaron, for when you make it to college some day."

"If I make it."

After all, Aaron is only nineteen. The reason I chose such a young partner was that I couldn't find anyone my own age "ignorant" enough to go with me. Eventually, I had to start asking the naive and adventurous teenagers. Aaron was the perfect candidate: young, proud, and in good shape.

I go on. "A plane traveling several hundred miles an hour crosses a river and continues for twenty minutes east along the coast. For every minute that it travels east, how long would two expeditioners have to paddle their twenty-foot sea kayak in the opposite direction, at around four miles an hour, through rough seas, to make up one minute of flying east?"

"Too long," Aaron answers without hesitation.

"Ah, a wise answer."

"Okay. Wait. Here's one that concerns me more," Aaron counters. "A river holding several thousand man-eating crocodiles is to be paddled by two foolish men in an inflatable kayak. Their plans are to travel two hundred and fifty miles upriver from its mouth. Each mile hosts an average of ten man-eating crocodiles. In calculating the risk factor and chances of survival, figure out on average, how far they will make it upriver before they are devoured by one of these reptiles of death?"

"Okay." I think a minute and move my fingers as though counting. I turn back to him. "Looks like you won't be making it to college after all." We laugh for a moment, then Aaron stops. He looks at the black night out the window.

"Good answer." He shakes his head. "What have we gotten ourselves into?"

Finally, the hum of the engine gears back, and we begin the descent into Wewak. A thin rim of lights abruptly ends in the dark sea. "Not much of a town," I say.

"At least it has lights." He sounds relieved. We watch in silence as the black void below grows closer. As the plane makes its final plunge, I have a last glimpse of the ocean. Its moonlit waves are lost as we dive down into the black jungle to land. Hundreds of eyes watch us. People press up against a mesh fence just off the runway. We step out into a cloud of humidity.

"Sticky," Aaron comments as we head down the staircase.

"Better get used to it."

We collect our bags from the pile beside the runway and manage to bum a ride from a Catholic priest. We sit in the back of his pickup.

"Wind Jammer Hotel!" The Father shouts out of the window as he screeches to a halt. "Cheapest rates in town."

"Thank you!" we call.

"Enjoy your stay." His truck roars off into the darkness.

Aaron grabs two of our bags and a paddle, and I take the other two. We start for the shadowy building barely visible in the dusk. As I approach, the long building begins to take a menacing shape. The hotel has actually been built to resemble a huge crocodile. In the gaping mouth is a restaurant, and the lobby and rooms make up its massive body.

"Oh, man," I mutter, and readjust my grip on the handles of the bags. I hear a thump behind me. Aaron has dropped both bags and is staring.

"It's just a building," I reassure him.

"Oh . . . yeah, right."

"Come on, let's get checked in."

I push open the lobby door cut into the side of the crocodile. Yellow light seeps out. The wide eyes and twisted mouths of tribal masks line the walls, greeting me from the shadows within. Interspersed are arrangements of intricately decorated bows and sharp-tipped arrows. Painted on the walls in mural form is a story of crocodiles devouring victims. Silent screams are frozen on agonized faces contorted with expressions of terror. I throw my bags in and hold the door open for Aaron. I watch him absorb the first mural, then walk past. The empty eyes of the masks follow us as we cross the lobby to the more brightly lit desk. Immediately, four women in floral print dresses stir from behind the counter. Their squat bodies, flattened features, and wild afros send a chill down my spine, but their voices are warm and friendly.

"Funky masks," Aaron comments as I step up to the counter. His eyes wander around the lobby. He stops a little behind me.

"Welcome to Wewak," says one of the women. "Can I help you?"

"We would like a room for the night, maybe two nights," I reply.

"We only have C-rooms left." She sounds like she's apologizing.

"What do you mean, C-rooms?"

"A-rooms are our nicest with a bathroom, telephone, and air conditioner. B-rooms do not have bathrooms or telephones but still have air-conditioners. C-rooms have two beds and ceiling fans. All we have left are C-rooms." My clothes stick to my body. I had hoped to get out of the humidity, at least for the night. We need a few good nights' sleep before starting the expedition, especially because of jet lag. I turn to Aaron. Beads of sweat roll down his face and drip off his nose.

"Are there any other hotels in town?" He looks desperate.

"How much for the C-rooms?" I ask the lady.

"70 kina per night."

"70 kina? That's 70 American dollars!" Aaron complains.

"How much are your B-rooms?"

"120 kina. But we have only C-rooms. They are the cheapest rooms in town."

"Dang, this island is expensive! What do you think?" I ask Aaron.

"I don't know."

I turn back to the lady. "Give us a C-room, please." She walks over to the register. "Well, Aaron, we're gonna be living in this humidity for God knows how long. Might as well get used to it." He stiffly watches me pay the lady. I bend down to sign the register, feeling the vacant eyes of the masks leering from the lobby walls.

On the way to our C-room, we drift down the hallway escorted by a memorial of carvings. More masks with screaming faces wrenched in pain line the walls. Drums and carved tools hang below them. Along the floor, life-sized carvings of crocodiles squirm in sexually provocative positions with naked women. Wooden Stone Age warriors stand in the corridor holding bows and arrows in one hand and carved heads of human victims in the other. Wild parrot feathers and animal furs decorate the warrior's heads and bodies. Their hardwood eyes watch us from the world we will soon enter. Aaron and I quickly skirt a carving of a man being devoured by a fire-blackened crocodile. We make it to the end of the narrow, haunted-house corridor. Relieved to have survived a look at all our worst nightmares, we step out onto the beach.

"Well, the rooms face the water at least." I rattle the key in the lock. Waves crash on the beach a few hundred feet from us.

Opening the door, I switch on the light. Two beds breathe out a hot, musty greeting.

"Welcome to New Guinea," I say to Aaron.

"Yeah, thanks. Now get that fan going!"

"I guess this is luxury in these parts." I find the switch and flip it on. "This will help matters." A refreshing breeze blows down off the ceiling. I open the screened windows while Aaron locks the door. Then we both decide to try out our beds.

"Joel," Aaron's voice sounds weak, "you think maybe you could go over the maps with me one more time?"

"Are you going to listen this time?"

"I'll listen."

I had tried to show him the maps many times before, but he was too busy goofing around and cracking jokes to pay them much mind. We hardly ever saw the last map unless I got mad and forced it. I always got irritated listening to him talk about his days of surfing and how much fun those big New Guinea waves would be. "God will protect us," was always his answer. And though I believed in God's protection, that was an easy thing to say thousands of miles away from the nearest crocodiles and jungle.

I pull the topographical maps, the topos, out of the duffle bag. "You must have seen something out that plane window today that changed your way of thinking."

"That I did." He looks at the topos spread out over my bed, twelve of them in all.

"All right, here we are in Wewak on the north coast," I point to the spot on the map. "After tomorrow morning's launch, we have about 100 miles of paddling to make it to the mouth of the Sepik River, over here." I run my finger west along the coast to the mile-wide river mouth that we had flown over a few hours before. Aaron is silent. "I think our two major problems along the coast are going to be the waves and possibly mosquitoes."

"Waves are the least of my worries."

"Maybe not to somebody on a surfboard, but for two guys in an inflatable kayak, weighed down with several hundred pounds of gear, they just might be a problem." I'm already getting annoyed.

"All right, all right, go on." I move my finger to two fang-like peninsulas jutting out along the coast between Wewak and the Sepik River.

"If we can make it to these peninsulas and get around their points, the land should break up the waves enough for us to get in and make a camp. The first of these points is only fifteen miles away from Wewak." I tap my finger on the protrusion of land. "We'll camp here in two nights." My finger runs along the coast. "After we make it over here to the mouth of the Sepik, we have 250 miles to paddle against the current before reaching the Korosmeri River."

"Are there crocs on the Korosmeri?" Aaron makes it evident what is most heavy on his mind.

"Afraid so. Anyway, we'll only go up it for a few miles before we branch south on the Salumei River." I glance at him. "And, yes, there are crocs on that river as well." Aaron gives me a testy look before going back to studying the map.

"The Salumei flows right out of the mountains for 150 miles. I can't find much information since it's such a remote river. Hopefully, it won't be too swift to paddle. If you look at the map, it tends to wind an awful lot, a sign that it's moving slow. The mountains seem abrupt, judging from the contour lines. Once the river is out of the mountains, it doesn't cross many contour lines, and when it does, they aren't severe."

"What's a contour line?" Aaron has a puzzled expression. I stare at him in disbelief.

"I guess I truly *am* the navigator of this expedition, aren't I?" I point to the area of the map where the Central Mountain Range begins with a thick mass of brown lines. "These lines show a change in elevation as the land rises up to mountain peaks. The closer together they are, the steeper the terrain."

"Oh, cool."

I point to an area on the map where the contour lines are close together. The thin blue line that marks the Salumei River goes straight through the mass of brown lines.

"This is where we'll probably have to start hiking. I'm afraid this is where our major problems begin." I slap my hand down across the jagged brown and green contour lines of the Central Mountain Range. I lean back against the wall at the head of my bed to rest my back. I watch Aaron's eyes desperately trying to make sense of the confusing scribbles across the map.

"Doesn't look like much fun in there," he finally says.

"Like I've told you before, all the literature on the interior high-lands has been more than depressing."

"That's how it looked out of the plane window today." He looks at me and tries to smile.

"The main ridge we have to top is over 10,000 feet in elevation, and some of the peaks collect snow right next to the equator at over 14,000. No trails. Basically, these mountains are the most unexplored terrain left on earth. These topo maps aren't even complete because the interior is almost constantly cloud-covered, making it difficult to get satellite photos of the area. The Centrals receive around 30 feet of rainfall every year, growing that thick jungle you were staring at from the plane. Some of the early government explorations that I read about were turned back because the jungle got too thick. The water flowing out to the coast erodes the land, leaving extremely steep ridges with deep valleys. All the rain that gets caught in the mountains breeds swarms of flies and mosquitoes, leeches, ants, and all sorts of other insects. It has just about everything we don't want: poisonous snakes, spiders, scorpions, centipedes, and probably other things we've never seen or heard of. Once we're in the jungle, we're in. There's no way to signal planes for rescue, and even if we could, they couldn't see through the canopy to find us."

"Any *good* news?" Aaron asks. He looks like he needs some.

"Well, let's see: it's a bird-watcher's paradise, with parrots and parakeets of all kinds. But not too long ago they discovered the only poisonous bird in the world back in the jungle where we're going. It's got venom on its feathers."

"Great, that's all I need—to be killed by a bird."

"That would definitely be embarrassing," I admit. "Ah, here's some good news." I point to the southern side of the mountains. "See this thin blue line that runs east along the base of the Centrals?" Aaron nods.

"That's the Lagaip River, hopefully our ticket out of the highlands. I have estimated it will take about a month to get there from the Salumei."

"A month!" Aaron raises his voice. "A month?" again, in disbelief.

"Well, we're going to be down to our bare essentials on this leg of the journey. Even then, we might have to take two trips to get it all across."

"So what in the world is the *good* news?" Aaron is growing disgusted.

"Well, the Lagaip runs west to east, so all we have to do is take a southern compass reading and hack our way across the mountains. We can't miss it."

"That's it? That's all the good news you have?" He is obviously disappointed.

"Hey, this isn't the first time I've told you all this, you know. It just happens to be the first time you've listened." I am growing defensive. "All I'm saying is, we have a lot of problems ahead trying to get across the Central Mountains, but at least navigating isn't one of them. These mountains are the very reason why so many of the expeditions before us have failed. So what did you expect? That it would be easy?" He seems to calm down a bit.

"We can't go across there twice. I say we try and get some carriers to help us with our gear," he suggests.

"Believe me, we'll try, but if we can't get help, we'll have to hike in, establish a base camp, then hike back out and bring our gear over in stages."

"That'll take forever." He is growing restless again.

"Which answers your question about why I estimated a month. This means we have to have a month's worth of food when we get to the mountains, where we'll need the military rations. Our food will get lighter as we go."

"Sounds like we're going to get lighter as well." He gives me a weak but goofy grin. "All right. We're on the Lagaip River now." He finds his place on the map again.

"The Lagaip flows into the Strickland River, both of them are right in the heart of the mountains. Most likely they are extreme whitewater rivers. These big white areas here are data-incomplete spaces that unfortunately cover long stretches of the Strickland. It's going to be hairy through here—touch and go—could have waterfalls. It could be impass-able, which means we're hiking again. We'll just have to stay over near the shore and scout any rough water." Aaron shuts his eyes and throws his hands up to his face.

"Too much!" he screams, pulling his fingers back through his hair. "I'm overloading!"

"All right now, don't quit on me. We're almost finished. The Strickland River turns us due south, and once we make it through the whitewater, then we're home free. That is, if a crocodile doesn't eat us." I smile. Not a well-timed joke from Aaron's lifeless response. "It's about 700 miles down the Fly River through swampland and past a few villages to the coast. Then through the Torres Strait, down here, and over five miles to our final destination, the Island of Daru." I conclude with a flourish and a tap of my finger on the little island's place on the map.

"You call 700 miles of river and swamp 'home free'? Where the heck are we gonna sleep out in the swamp? It doesn't even show that there's any land in it. Where are we going to sleep with no land around?" I think he already knows that he won't like my answer.

"In our kayak."

He flops back on the bed. "I don't want to see anymore tonight! I can't see anymore! What on earth have I gotten myself into? I'm croco-dile bait for sure!"

"Mosquito bait, more likely." I am unable to resist. With that, he crawls over to his bed, a heap of exhausted nerves. I shut off the lights to try and get some sleep. Aaron lies silent beside me.

"Joel," he says.

"Yeah?"

"I'm scared."

"I understand. I am too, but that's all part of it." I close my eyes to welcome sleep.

CHAPTER 2

One Leg at a Time

The light blue-green waves sparkling in the morning sun wash away the nightmares of the previous night. We wake up in a paradise of waving palm trees and a white sandy beach. The fresh sea breeze escorts us into the mouth of the giant crocodile building to a buffet-style breakfast. We pass two white men laden with overflowing plates of food, and they motion for us to join them.

"Name's Reggie," says one of the men. He stands to greet us as we put our plates down on their table. "This is Frank." He motions in the direction of another, older man, who pauses in his eating to nod to us.

"Joel," I say. "And this is Aaron." I pull out a chair. "So what brings you all to Wewak?" I hope we will get some useful information.

"Business," replies Reggie. "I'm from Ireland, originally, but live in Cairns, Australia. That's where Frank here is from. We both work for a mining company that is looking to do some mining on an island near here. They sent us to do their dirty work, so to speak." He flicks his hand back through his red hair, smoothing it back into place.

"What's the dirty work?" Aaron asks.

"Oh, it's this Papua government crap that we have to put up with. They make us go through silly routines to make it look like the natives have a say in what goes on. Then they screw 'em!" His eyes glitter. I try to hold his gaze, but he looks away.

"Get me some salt!" He yells to the native behind the serving table. The waiter brings the salt to Reggie without smiling. Reggie says nothing to the man. He doesn't even look at him.

"We'll go out to this island later this afternoon and sit there, and all the natives will come out and stand in front of us. Then their Big Man will approach us and tell us all their complaints. He'll go on about why we shouldn't mine because it will hurt his people in this way or that, yaking on for who knows how long. His people will cheer him on, thinking he's really letting us have it. They'll think he's a brave and powerful leader. We'll just sit there and listen. We only say a few words until he is done. Then, we'll just get into the boat and take off. And that's the end of our dirty work."

"So what happens then?" Aaron looks concerned.

"Happens? Noth'en. We've gone through the necessary routine that this monkey government has set up. It's all a waste of time, see. I guess it helps the government feel like they're for the people if they at least listen to them. But in the end, after we're all done, the government never even asks us what was said. They just ask us if we heard them out. We say 'yes.' They sign the papers, and before you know it, we are out there tearing the island apart." Reggie laughs, and Frank joins in.

"Well, that sucks," Aaron says, cutting their laughter short.

Reggie's eyes fix on Aaron. "It's money, Son. We've got it. They want it, and they'll do anything to get it. Even screw their own people. But, mind you, it's all the better for them natives, anyway. I mean, the mining company treats them like royalty, so they won't complain. We build rain-catchers and trade stores in their villages. Give them work and fair wages, everybody's pockets get full. That's what counts."

Frank sits silent next to him. He nods his head at every word his partner says. His pudgy build only adds to my impression of him as a lump with gray, wavy hair. White chest hair spills out of his unbuttoned shirt. I notice an extensive scar across his chest and up onto his neck.

"So what brings you to paradise?" Reggie asks.

"We are just. . ." I start.

"We're going on an expedition to cross New Guinea," Aaron interrupts. I glance at him with a fierce look to stop him from further discussing our plans with these two sneaky characters.

"And just how do you plan on doing that?" Frank finally speaks up and moves to the front of his chair.

I sip my coffee.

"We have a sea kayak that we're going to paddle down the coast." Then up the Sepik, where we'll carry it over the Central Mountains and down the rivers on the other side, to the island of Daru."

Both men study us in silence.

"I hope you're not serious," Reggie says, leaning over the table, lifting his coffee cup to his mouth.

"He's serious," I confirm. I know what is coming next and am not in the mood to hear it.

Reggie gulps his coffee, and I brace myself. "I should warn you about the Central Mountains. They're the meanest mountains in the world, but you'll never make it that far. Not with all the crocodiles and rascals. Nope, you'll never make it far enough to die in the mountains." Reggie delivers his words with a blow, as if shooting us with a gun.

"The waves are bad enough," he continues. "They aren't so big out in front here because of the reefs. But as you go west, you lose their protection. The waves get monstrous. They'll smash you down. But that ain't nothin' compared to the crocodile problems you're gonna have." Reggie leans back in his chair, crosses his legs, and nods over to Frank. "Show 'em, Frank. Show 'em what they're up against."

On cue, Frank pulls his shirt open. The scar is wider and more gnarled towards his arm pit. Aaron and I are spellbound.

"A croc gave me this. A large croc." He looks down at his war wound.

"Did he bite you?" Aaron's voice is startled.

"He tried. Would have if my mates hadn't pulled me out." He looks up at us. The painful memory creases his face. "See, I was standing on the shore of a river. Wasn't here. It was in Northern Australia. Same crocs though, saltwater crocs. Don't let the name fool you. They live in the freshwater just the same. Anyway, I was standing on the bank and this croc was under the muddy water right in front of me, watching me. I didn't even see the bloody beast. You seldom do. All of a sudden, this huge tail comes up out of the water and slaps me silly, right across the chest here." He runs his hand along his chest. "Amazing power! The slap alone almost killed me. He was trying to get me down in the water so he could devour me. He knocked me right over, but my mates pulled me up the bank before that croc could get hold of me. Saved my life." He buttons his shirt up. "You'll never see them. They'll just attack. One second you'll be paddling along and all will be peaceful. Then in the next instant, churning water and blood—your blood—will be violently splattered all about as he takes you under for the death twirl."

Fear sinks its teeth into Aaron and me. We're on the edge of our chairs, still staring at the visible part of his scar. Of all the warnings we've been given, this one is most real. This man has actually been attacked by a sea crocodile and lived to tell about it. His wound backs up his story and won't allow the denial that has sheltered us.

"What is a death twirl?"

"I don't want to know." Aaron is determined not to hear. Frank leans forward over the table. He feeds on his power to keep our attention.

"The death twirl is the greatest fear of everyone who lives near crocodile-infested water. It is the worst way to die, the very worst. The croc grabs you from the air, clamps down on one of your limbs with his powerful jaws, and pulls you down under. He might get you by your leg or maybe an arm. If you're lucky, it will be your head. You die faster that way. Once he has you solid, he starts spinning around in the blackness. He spins so fast, your body can't possibly keep up, your limb twists right off. He either devours it or leaves it for later. He grabs you by another limb, or maybe by your side and starts twirling again. He takes you apart, piece by bloody piece in that murky water, and somewhere, in all of the spinning confusion and agony, you die! Whether you drown or die from being ripped apart depends on how fast the croc is." Frank leans back in his chair to let his last description soak into our silence.

"What kind of sea kayak do you fellows have?" Reggie asks, trying to throw a lifeline into the pool of fear overwhelming us. It falls short.

"It's an inflatable. . .," Aaron begins, but I cut him off.

"Just a twenty-foot kayak." After all the talk, I don't want to get into the crocodile versus an inflatable kayak issue.

"Well, I think you're crazy if you go through with it, just plain crazy," Reggie insists.

"Suicidal, if you ask me," Frank adds.

"You'll have to watch for rascals all along this coast and up and down the Sepik, too," Reggie warns. "It's like I said before about money. We white skins have it. The natives want it. Them young ones are out to get it from us these days. Don't underestimate them. They'll kill you for it. Two whites in a kayak loaded down with expensive-looking gear? I hate to say it, I really do, but you're a prime target for them, and they're all over the place."

Frank kicks in. "It's true. They're having all sorts of trouble these days with rascals. It's out of hand. They steal everything they can sell or use, that includes the clothes off your back. They'll leave you naked and swimming in the river with them crocs." He laughs.

I take my last bite of breakfast and the doubt that the conversation is feeding Aaron and me. "Well, we're going to have to go see for ourselves." I stand up to go. Aaron stands, too. "We came here to cross this island. Nobody ever said it was possible. But we have come to try, and try we will. So, if you'll excuse us, we have a lot of work to do to get ready for tomorrow." I reach out my hand to shake theirs. Aaron follows my lead.

"What time will you be leaving?" Reggie reaches toward me with a smug look on his face.

"Hopefully, sometime in the early morning. We're launching from right here in front of the hotel."

"Maybe if we are around, not doing our dirty work, we'll see you two expeditioners off. Until then, good day," Reggie offers.

"Good day," says Frank, but all I see is the scar trying to hide under his chest hair.

"Goodbye."

We walk into town. The exercise feels good after the plane rides over the last few days. It is a quiet walk as both of us struggle with the scar we have seen and the words we have heard. Aaron looks exhausted; the conversation has struck him in an already-festering wound of fear.

We arrive in town and wander down the one main street filled with people busy shopping. We enter the largest grocery store we can find. The shelves are lined mostly with canned goods. I grab an old shopping cart and start down the first row. I stop at a stack of tinned mackerel cans. I turn to Aaron who follows me. He seems far away, a bundle of pondering nerves.

"Am I buying food for one, or for two?" I look straight at him.

"For two," he answers with a nervous smile.

"All right, then, for two." I pull several more cans into the basket. We pile in several heavy bags of rice to go along with cans of stew, fish, braised steak and onion, chicken, and spaghetti sauce. I throw in what I think will be two weeks' worth of supplies, enough to get us up the Sepik River to Angoram where we can resupply. Before we make our way back to the Wind Jammer Hotel, Aaron buys some additional medical supplies and a New Guinea calendar to send his parents.

Back in the room, I begin to organize and repack the equipment and food while Aaron writes a letter to his family on the back of the calendar. I know it is a goodbye-forever letter, as the tears stream down his cheeks. I have already written similar letters to my closest friends and family, not so much because I thought for sure I was going to die, but in case I did, I wanted them to know the special way that I loved each one of them. Aaron finishes writing and walks back into town to mail his letter.

Hours later, it begins to get dark, and Aaron has still not returned. I go to the window to see if he is in sight. Where on earth is that boy? Perhaps the rascals have struck even before we can get launched.

I am about to head out to look for him when I hear a knock at the door. I open it to Aaron's pale face, who enters and throws some more bottles of medicine on the bed. He sits down without a word.

"What's wrong with you?" He is slumped on the bed staring at the floor.

"What happened?" I sit down next to him.

"Nothing, really, I guess." He still can't meet my gaze.

"Come on. I don't buy that. Tell me what happened. Did you get robbed?"

"No. No. Of course not." He peeks up at me.

"So what's knocked the wind out of you?" I am getting impatient.

"I don't know." He tries to look at me again, but his eyes only make it to the bedspread. He traces the pattern with his forefinger.

"Well, you better figure it out 'cause I don't want to try to cross this island with somebody who has given up before he even starts." Anger rises up inside me. "I have a lot to do and think through for tomorrow, ya know. I don't have the energy to keep reassuring you back to confidence."

He closes his eyes. "I went in to mail that letter."

"Yeah, I know."

"There were these girls with weird-looking tatoos around their eyes."

"So?"

"And I saw a lot more people with those nasty sores on their legs."

"Is that all?"

He sighs deeply. "Then on the way back I met this American missionary named Joe." Aaron leans back against the wall and props some pillows behind him. Besides his red hair, he blends in with the white sheets.

"Aaron, what did he tell you?" I try to get him to look up, but he continues to trace the pattern on the bedspread.

"Basically, that we will die if we try to cross this island."

"Aaron, what else is new? Everybody tells us that. They all told us that back home, too. We've heard that all along."

"Joel," he says in a quiet voice that stops me. "This guy was different. He knew what he was talking about. He knew of real cases, real people."

"Like what?"

"He knew these people who went rafting on the Sepik. They got caught in a whirlpool. They lost everything, boat, gear, everything. He said that there are these whirlpools all along the river, and they suck you down and drown you." He stares in a trance at his toes sticking out the front of his sandals.

"Did they die?"

"I think so. It sounded like it. I didn't really want to know, so I didn't ask."

"What else?"

"He talked about the crocodiles, like everyone does. Said we will never make it through them without getting eaten. He said that in some places on the river you have to walk through a mile of mud to get to the shore. I don't see how we are going to camp if we have to walk through a mile of mud. He says he's been there on mission outreaches. Says the mud is up to your waist, that you can't really walk through it anyway, even if the bank were closer." His voice drifts off.

"Keep going. Get it all out. I want to hear everything he told you." I lean closer.

"He said the mosquitoes will drive a man insane. He said that from the number of bites we'll get, we're bound to get malaria. This Methloquine that we're taking to prevent it? He says that works most of the time for the average tourist. Of course, they don't get bit all that much, but it's not made for people who are going to try to cross the entire island. He said we are going to get malaria, whether we take this stuff or not."

"Is that all?" I pry at him.

"I wish. He went on and on about malaria. He knew what he was talking about, too. Friends of his have died from it. I tell you, Joel, it doesn't sound good. There are different strains."

"Of course there are. We knew that before we even came."

"Yeah, well, there is one strain that if we get it, we can't treat it because it's resistant to all the known malaria medicines. He called it cerebral malaria. It goes to your brain, makes you crazy. He said if we get it, we'll die within four to six days."

"We have Chloroquine."

"That's what I told him, but he said it won't work." I am silent. I look at my sandals.

Aaron is on a roll. "He told me about elephantiasis and all sorts of gnarly diseases that this island has to offer. It wouldn't really be a risk if we just hung out in places like this and went where the tourists go. But because we're crossing the island, we have a good chance of getting all of them. Joel, I don't want to go home with, elephantiasis, my butt hanging down past my knees." His face is serious.

I catch myself tracing the pattern on the bedspread.

Aaron takes a deep breath and then proceeds with his recital of doom. "He said the Centrals are impassable, especially above the Salumei River. He said that's the most remote country on the island. If any tribes exist back in there, then they are bound to be cannibalistic. He said they still hunt for heads out there where nobody dares go. And that's exactly where we are headed." Aaron raises his eyes to meet mine. "Joel, we should try to hire a guide."

"Is that what he told you?"

"He said don't go at all!"

"But, we're attempting to do something that has never been done before, by anybody. How do we hire a guide for that? Aaron, where were you during all the research? I told you about all of these problems five months ago when we first met. I didn't smooth over the dangers to try and persuade you to come along. I never talked you into coming here! It was your decision! Why didn't you stress out then? You definitely should have known about all the diseases. You're the medical officer of this expedition." I slap the bed in frustration.

"I know, I know. I did know about them, but they were so far away at the time. They didn't scare me. People have at least traveled all the way up the Sepik. We could use a guide until we get the hang of it."

"With what money? We just have to do this. We aren't getting any guide." I can read the edge on his face now. Reality has swept it clear of all emotions but fear.

"Aaron, I told you before, I can't talk you into going. This choice is up to you."

"Wait, Joel. I'm not saying that I'm backing out. I'm going to be in that kayak with you tomorrow. And I do trust you as the leader of this expedition. I'm just scared to death. Each one of these dangers is bad enough by itself, but all of them! If one doesn't get you, then there's ten or twenty more that will. It's just too much, Joel. It just seems like death

is our only way out of this place, and I am just too young to be dying!"
He flops back on his bed. "Tell me I'm not going to die, Joel. Promise
me that. You can't—that's the problem, nobody can."

"Maybe you'll die, maybe I'll die. That's all part of it."

"All part of what?"

"It's all part of expeditions." I roll over in my bed. The room falls
deadly silent for a long time. Aaron doesn't move as his inner battle
rages on.

For at least an hour I lie there wrestling, overwhelmed in a swirl of
thoughts and fears. "I've decided to make a change in the expedition."
Aaron's head pops up from his pillow in the broken silence.

"You are? What kind of change?"

"You're right. This expedition entails too much. Too many dangers, and problems. And, I agree, we can't possibly take them all on at
once. It's enough to crush even the strongest of spirits." I sit up on my
bed. His eyes follow me. "That's a different expedition anyway, too big,
too hard. Tomorrow we start on a new expedition."

"What's the goal then?"

"Do you remember the nook in the shore just fifteen miles down
the shoreline? I showed it to you on the map yesterday."

"The one you said will break up the waves so we can get in and
make a camp?"

"Exactly. Forget about the whole island for now." I move to the
edge of my bed. "Do you think we can make it to that little bay, fifteen
miles down the coast? Do you think we can make it fifteen miles and set
up camp and live through one night?"

"Yeah, I guess we can make that."

"Fine. Then that's our new expedition." I hold out my hand. He
hesitates for a moment before shaking it.

"Then what from there?"

"I don't know. We'll have to figure it out. Are you with me to that
bay?"

"Yes. I'm with you."

"Good. We'll just have to take this expedition one leg at a time." I
lean back on my bed. He settles onto his.

"One more thing."

"What?" His voice sounds small.

"We've both pulled a number of practical jokes over the years.
There will be plenty of opportunities for jokes like that on this island.

We could scare each other to death by pretending we see a crocodile, or snake, or who knows what else. We're in for quite a trip as it is, so we need to know that we can trust each other as partners. What do you say we make a pact not to play any practical jokes? That way if we shout out a warning, we'll know it's true."

"Sounds great to me. No practical jokes." We shake hands again.

"I'm sorry I'm so scared. I know I'm not being a very good partner."

"I understand. Believe me, I do. I wish I could make it all seem better, but I can't. It's your struggle."

"I know."

I watch Aaron curl up at the head of his bed, as if he is hiding from a monster. It is true what I have told him—I do understand. I close my eyes and drift back several months in my memory.

* * *

It is December, 1991. My truck is parked twelve miles behind me, as I trudge in snowshoes against the harness of my equipment sled. Surrounding me are the snowy mountains of the Teton Wilderness in Wyoming. The air is a crisp 30 degrees below zero.

A week before, I had graduated from the University of Arizona, one of the great outpourings of the educated upon the work force. But I went a different way.

I am going to try my hand at being a mountain man, a dream I've had since childhood. Digging through six feet of snow, I set up my tepee and spend the next four months alone, in a world I know nothing about. Raised the son of an oil company worker in the Kingdom of Saudi Arabia and schooled in Arizona, I am truly an alien to the snow drifts that now surround me. I have no idea of the unfolding harsh realities that wait to punish me for my decision to chase my dream. But, if the cold is extreme, the loneliness is worse, much worse. And in the springtime, the hungry, cranky grizzly bears wake from their long winter's sleep, beginning their terrorizing assault on my camp.

* * *

The sticky, New Guinea night brings me back, and I realize it's late. As tired as I am, I can't seem to fall asleep, and apparently neither can Aaron, who gets up and leaves the room around midnight. I get up, turn on the light, and begin to thumb through my journal. I read the first entry I made in the snowy mountains of the Teton Wilderness. I remember being buried in clothing, with my mummy bag wrapped around me, trying to keep my fingers warm by holding them near the stove. My suffering had just begun.

December 27, 1991 entry:

> The world that I have known, I have cut off. The people that I love, I have left. What was comfortable, I have done away with. I have traded warmth for coldness, forsaken what I know to seek what is eternal. I come to meet you, Lord! I come to make the God of truth mine! That I might say my God has delivered me from the pit. It is not enough for me to know men who know you. All my days, You have called to me. The greatest enemy of all, everyday life, smothered my response. I say to you now, "Lord, Here I am!"

And here I am in New Guinea now, facing danger again in the great unknown. Aaron and I both have placed our trust in our King, Jesus Christ. Still, there are no guarantees; Christians die along with everyone else. The wisest of teachers knows better than to take the risk out of a lesson.

I zip through the pages to the last journal entry written after four long months of survival in the Teton Wilderness. I asked God to speak to me about my mountain experience. In silent meditation I wrote down what I felt He said.

*   *   *

April 30, 1992 entry:

> For you were just a babe, when first you came looking for me in the wilderness. And what was it that you came to establish so far from the comforts of home? You came searching for peace but found war. You came seeking wisdom and found foolishness. Wanting love, you were tormented by loneliness day and night. Wishing for courage, you were taught fear. Wanting faith, you were shown perseverance. Asking for compassion, you were made to suffer. Establishing your manhood, I revealed to you the strength of a child. You came exploring the unknown, but found that what you already knew should be put into practice. You yearned for fellowship, but knew only solitude. You begged for mercy, but the hardships of winter

showed you none. You dug for treasure, but unburied frustration, anger, and hate. Yes . . . you came to put the sword down, but you were forced to pick it up for the first time. For you had come hoping for a hill, but I gave you a mountain. Yet I called for you with the passing of winter, and from the mountain top you answered me saying, "Lord, here am I."

And what was the worth of your climb? In the hours of cold, your soul was warmed. In the chill of winter, where so much is laid to die, I brought you to life. In the harshness of winter where day by day, the wild animals grow weaker, you grew from weakness into strength. In the winter cool, where the bears lay sleeping, I awakened you from the darkness of the den. I rescued you from the trap and delivered you from the hands of the trapper.

Reading this takes me back: the cold against my face, the endless days of cutting wood, white clouds pouring from my mouth and nostrils. The trees held stiff in ice; the mountains' majesty before me. I know that I can't return home until my four months are up. I remember how big it seemed, as intimidating then as New Guinea is now. The mountain wilderness taught me so much. I wonder what the jungle wilderness will teach me—if I survive. I read on.

As you set foot in the wilderness, what were you like? You were like a young man asking to join the table of a Great Knight. But He drew his sword on you and fought with you. Your wounds were many and deep, your anguish great. Still, you refused to surrender to what you had begun. So when daybreak came, you were to be found kneeling at his feet. And the Great Knight placed his sword on your shoulders and upon your head, saying, "This day shall you have a place at my table." For the one with skill will take pride in it and fall before his enemies. But the one with courage, he will rise through his learning and overcome his enemies, and they will flee from him. So know that this is why you have been sick in your tent, stranded in the snow, cold without end, lonely and afraid without comfort, suffering. That your courage might be tested! So go from this place and know that I am your friend. And when they ask you how they can know your God, do not

give them an answer, but simply tell them of the setting
and the rising of my Son. And, with challenge and encouragement, point them in the direction of their battlefields.

Yes, go from this wilderness and know that you are no
longer a boy but a man. No longer a babe but a warrior.
But as you leave, turn and look hard at what has been your
home for the past four months. For its cruelty has been
your teacher, its harshness has pastured you, and its quiet-
ness has been its sermon. Without the use of words, it has
taught you to recognize My face, to endure hardships, to
persevere, to explore unfamiliar lands, to climb impossible
mountains, and to find joy in testing. So go and imitate it,
like a man who knows much more than he says.

God answered my prayers then, and I'm sure He'll answer them as
I go again. He is always faithful to the ones who seek Him. I keep reading
the words that I wrote less than a year before. It seems much longer ago.

Go, knowing that, like Moses, I called you into the
wilderness because of your sin. Like Jacob, alone, you
wrestled with God and with man, and overcame. Like
Israel, you struggled in discomfort until you found the
courage to possess the place of promise. Like Abraham,
through faith you set a knife against the things you cher-
ished. Like Daniel, you called upon me to close the mouth
of the bear. I came to you, trembling in your tent, and
taught you to put down the gun in your hand and instead
trust the weapon in your heart, that you might serve Me
with all confidence. And like my son, Jesus, I am calling
you down out of the wilderness to begin your ministry, that
many shall come to know Me. And your ministry shall be
this: To love Me, the Lord your God, with all your heart,
with all your mind, and with all your soul, and with all your
strength. And to love your neighbor as yourself.

I open my journal to a fresh page and start writing.

*   *   *

Journal entry: November 18, 1992.

I sit on a bed, in a small, muggy motel room in
Wewak, Papua New Guinea. The waves crash 200 feet from
the window. Tomorrow is the day! The actual beginning of

the Trans-New Guinea Expedition. Am I afraid? Yes! Is it my master? No!

This little room represents all that I know of this island. But through the screened window out there in the darkness, beyond the sound of the crashing waves, lurks the unknown, all that I must learn, all that I must go through to accomplish my dream. The future looks dark, sounds gloomy, powerful. Yet, through it, there is light and hope. Hope, that whatever happens, it will bring me closer to my God. I must take this step; I must dare to go beyond my fears. I must risk everything that I might gain more.

Crocodiles, snakes, whirlpools, disease, rapids, head-hunters, rascals, and more dangers threaten me with their horrific reputations. But my faith in my God is bigger!

I get off the bed and walk to the window. I stare out at the darkness for a moment, then return and write a prayer. When I finish, I read it aloud.

"Lord Jesus Christ, tomorrow I shall seek You in a new way; all old things will pass away. You know my needs, you are always faithful, your mercy—your grace—is my inheritance. I claim it, I wear it around my neck. Lord, I trust You! Yet more, I love you! Father, I ask for one thing. With boldness I ask, for I have begun to see just what I am asking for. Lord, my God, may I see Your face?"

I close my eyes. The thoughts, the worries are still there, but I feel ready to face the first leg of the expedition. My goodbyes have been said. Everything is done. I am ready, except for one last thing. Feeling a little silly, I pick up my journal again and write:

I would like to say goodbye to myself. Just like a reptile sheds its old skin, so tomorrow I will begin to shed you. Don't get me wrong, I thank God for you. It's just that I'm going somewhere that you cannot follow. So long, old self, I will never see you again!

I close the journal and set it on my bedstand. Tomorrow will be time enough to put together the few details that remain undone. Tomorrow we will begin the impossible with the first leg, the first paddle stroke. I lie back and let the forgetfulness of sleep finally take over.

CHAPTER 3

The Ocean

By the time the morning sun grows hot on my back, the kayak is pumped up hard. Several dozen knots and a hundred feet of rope hold our gear securely in place. Two, two-and-a-half gallon water containers take up the first available space in the rear of the kayak, just in front of the rudder that hangs down onto the sand. These two flexible containers are tied to a large gray bag. Because it is not waterproof, the bag holds the portion of our food rations that can afford to get wet: fifty military-issue rations and several canned goods. Directly in front of the gray bag is our green bag, the largest of our waterproof bags. It contains the mosquito net, camp stove and cooking fuel, machete, film, extra cord, one set of snorkeling gear, fishing gear, pump, repair kit, medical kit, water filter, tarps, cooking and eating utensils, and flare gun. We stand the bag up, and tie it down hard, making a good back-rest for the back-seat passenger. My life jacket serves as a cushion on the back-rest. Whoever has this seat is in charge of working the rudder, by utilizing the adjustable foot pedals located at the end of the limited leg space. Between these pedals are two more two-and-a-half gallon water containers. Just in front of these water containers, about the middle of the kayak, we tie in our two personal waterproof bags. Aaron's is blue, mine yellow. They are side by side, on end, and tied down hard to metal rings located on the inside of the kayak's inflatable wall with Aaron's life jacket tied in place behind them for the front passenger's backrest.

The two bags contain our personal gear, consisting of a blanket, jungle hammock, clothes, rain gear, boots, lighters, journals, and toiletries. Aaron's contains our only comb and Swiss army knife, while mine contains two compasses and a small black Bible.

The legroom for the front seat is crowded with a small waterproof bag containing sunscreen, a Pentax water-resistant camera, the day's lunch, and a bottle of drinking water. Our twelve large topographical maps are safely rolled up in a waterproof envelope and, for easy access, shoved tightly under the spray skirt on the bow of the kayak. They are, of course, connected to the kayak by two pieces of twined parachute cord, which also holds Aaron's skin diving mask by its strap.

All of our possessions lie on the beach: a lump of air, rubber, and bags all held together with a spider web of cord and complicated knots.

A crowd of natives has gathered, drawn by their curiosity to see our packing process. They don't ask any questions; it is enough for them to watch something that they don't understand. Aaron and I grab hold of the kayak and try to slide the brightly colored mass closer to the surf. The kayak hardly budges.

"How much you figure this weighs?" Aaron asks, impressed.

"Well over its limit, I'm afraid." I wipe sweat from my face with the sleeve of my shirt. "I would guess somewhere near 400 pounds."

"If we can ever get it to the water, are you sure it's gonna float?"

"In the water, yes. Over the waves, I'm not so sure." I study the waves—the trip's first obstacles, crashing one after another onto the beach. They are about six-foot waves—six feet too high, I fear. "Even if we absolutely have to lighten the load, I don't have any idea where to begin. Everything we have is essential." I shrug my shoulders.

"Yes, well, I'd say that's obvious by the way we tied it all down." Aaron stares at the confusing net of cords. "Looks like the loser of an amateur knot-tying contest to me."

"Tell us about your expedition!" Comes a booming voice. I turn around to find the lens of a video camera shoved in my face. "What are you planning to accomplish?" comes the voice once again from behind it. It's Reggie. Frank stands by his side with a dumb grin on his face. With his chest sunburned, his scar stands out even more. The crowd eagerly listens for our reply.

"Well. . .," I stutter in the shock of the spotlight. "We are attempting the first-ever crossing of New Guinea without the use of motors, from here in Wewak to the southern island of Daru." I am still somewhat stunned.

"Iiiiiiiiiiieeeeeeeeeeeeeee!" the crowd screeches, startling me for a moment. Reggie quickly turns to catch the crowd's emotion on film.

"You are Americans?" He flips the camera back on us. Aaron, who has been hiding behind me, steps up to my side.

"Yes," he says.

"Are you famous adventurers in America?" Reggie's questions continue. We fidget.

"No," I admit.

"Where did you learn how to sea kayak?" Both of us are dumbfounded.

"Utah," Aaron says weakly, hoping nobody will hear. The camera stops for a moment as Reggie peeks out from behind it.

"Utah? There's no coast in Utah."

"No. It was a lake, a big lake."

"Where on the sea have you kayaked?" comes the next question, this time sounding testy.

"We haven't, actually been on the sea. Well, not in a sea kayak anyway." I feel stupid. The camera drops, revealing Reggie's face, a mixture of horror and disgust.

"Have you ever been in a jungle before?" He asks desperately. Aaron and I look at each other, then down.

"No." The blank stares of Reggie and Frank shame us as the two great expeditioners standing before them are reduced to ordinary people. Ordinary in ability at least, with no more right to take on the impossible than anyone else.

Reggie slowly recovers and raises the video camera back up to his eye. His finger clicks it on. "I am now filming two dead men!" His voice is drowned out by a crashing wave.

I slip my sunglasses onto my lotion-covered face. "Are you ready to start what we came here for?" Aaron nods with a pale sickly look. It is the end of talk, time to venture into that void of uncertainty that separates dreaming from doing. Aaron and I start tugging our load. When the natives see that we aren't getting anywhere, they help us.

"I wish there weren't so many spectators to watch us attempt our first-ever launch off a beach," I whisper to Aaron who squeezes out a smile of agreement. "Front or back?" He simply walks to the back of the kayak and holds on. I grab hold near the bow as we stand alone at the edge of the surf, facing our first foes of the expedition, the next series of waves. The first one crashes in front of us and shoots up past our feet, lifting the weight of our kayak from the sand. The current slows, then hesitates as the momentum of foamy water changes direction. The sand is sucked from underneath my feet.

"Now!" I shout. The crowd cheers as we race along with the

undertow, charging the next wave that quickly forms before us. I lower my shoulder as the wave rolls over me, crashing into its forceful shove. I regain my balance. The water is waist-deep now, making my legs useless.

"Get in!" I scream, jumping into the seat and scrambling for my paddle.

"I'm in!" comes Aaron's voice.

"Iiiiieeeeee!" The crowd warns us of the next wave. It rises above my head, a wall of green. I have time for one stroke before the bow of the kayak buries itself into the face of the wave. With my legs engulfed, a surge of power snaps my head back, thrusting my body against the bags behind me. Violently pinned against my backrest, for a moment I can't move until I finally recoil in the misty air behind the passing wave. New Guinea has thrown its first punch!

"My hat!"

"I have it—paddle!" Aaron shouts. I can hear his paddle desperately pounding the surf. I thrust in with my right, then quickly to my left, and again. We gain speed, popping over a small wave, but the next one has swelled into a mountain of angry sea, the biggest so far. I take a breath, lower my head to protect my neck this time, and clamp my jaw down hard. Once again, I slam against the backrest, but this time the pressure is too much. The bags behind me cave in. My legs shoot up in front of me, reaching for the sky as I leave the kayak, upside down, in the midst of the exploding wave. I break the surface anticipating the next wave. The kayak lies dormant like a log, the only items it lacks are the two that haven't been tied in: Aaron and me. We swim with a paddle in one hand, climb back into the kayak, and once again begin paddling with all the energy left in us, which isn't much. Soon, we find safety beyond the breakers. Laughter from the beach crowd rings in our ears.

"This island sure doesn't waste time getting nasty," I say. Aaron throws my hat to me, trying to ignore the laughter of the crowd behind him. "Thanks, good catch."

"It was the least I could do after you broke up that first wave so nicely for me. Are you all right?"

"I think so . . . looks like we lost your mask though." I notice it missing from the cord in front of me. Aaron springs up and searches the blue water for his prized mask. He soon realizes it's gone forever. The crowd quiets down after the excitement, their many arms waving excitedly in the air. We wave goodbye to them and start paddling west.

The ocean, speckled with whitecaps, stretches out until it bends into the horizon. Deep blue sparkling waves lift and dip us in gentle rhythm. An unbroken wall of palm trees crowds the white sands of shore, like a picture-perfect postcard. The palms' wind-torn leaves flap in the gentle breeze rising off the water. I absorb it with a deep sigh. I raise my paddle above my head, screaming aloud from the excitement of adventure that pulses in my soul. Aaron flinches as my yells of victory take him by surprise.

"Ah, can you feel it, Aaron? The ocean and the second largest island in the world before us. I feel alive! My heart is alert, my soul awake! Like Columbus!"

"I don't much feel like Columbus," Aaron says with a dreary sniffle. He has a bad cold to go along with his fear.

"And where would you rather be, in a classroom or office?" He doesn't answer. "You seemed more excited about crossing Willard Bay than you do now." I am annoyed that there is no one to share my enthusiasm.

"I was."

*   *   *

I think of Willard Bay, the lake in Utah that Reggie had asked about. The scene of our one and only shakedown trip. We had paddled five miles across the lake to the opposite shore, cooked some dinner, threw some rocks at a skunk, made a fire, and fell asleep in mummy bags in the late October chill. Our closest call came the following morning as we paddled back when Aaron was nearly struck by a passing seagull's "white bomb." We had landed next to my truck by noon and loaded everything against a background of majestic snow-covered mountains. And that was our shakedown trip. As ridiculous as it all might sound, Utah just isn't a good training ground for two penniless expeditioners wanting to cross an island more than halfway around the world.

I'm afraid we didn't do much better in the libraries. It's just very hard to prepare for something that has never been done. I remember sitting down with a thick book on reptiles. Reading up on snakes and saltwater crocodiles, I noticed the title of the book that Aaron had chosen for himself.

"*Frogs of the World?*" I had questioned him.

"Hey, there are poisonous frogs."

"Yeah, maybe if you eat them. It's not like they go around biting you with fangs." My comments didn't stop him from looking through the entire book.

*   *   *

The sun is getting hot enough to disturb my thoughts. I glance back at Aaron who remains quiet; his sunglasses hide his panicked eyes. He searches the deep water we glide over. For what? Most likely crocodiles, or maybe sharks, but I seriously doubt that he is looking for frogs.

The long hours drag by as the power of my paddle strokes whimper in the blistering heat. The sunscreen on my face travels in droplets of sweat stinging my eyes. It sure doesn't take long for the glory of expeditions to dissolve into pure misery. The water bottle is empty, and the shoreline in front of us quickly disappears into a mirage of rising heat. I am finding that the coastline looks far different when sitting in a kayak a foot off the water on a hot day, in big swells, than it had on a map. My head throbs as I paddle in silent meditation, lusting for the shady shores that slowly pass us by.

"I saw a crocodile," Aaron says rather calmly. It's a good excuse to stop paddling for a moment.

"What?"

"I saw one."

"When?" I turn to face him. He's serious.

"About forty-five minutes ago, just past the last peninsula."

"Shut up." I turn back around in disgust.

"You can believe me or not, but I saw one." He acts hurt.

"What did it look like?"

"It looked like a crocodile. It was brown and was swimming between us and the beach."

"It was only a piece of driftwood."

"Driftwood doesn't dive underwater, now does it? . . . I'm telling you, it was a. . . ."

"A log," I finish for him.

Some dark-brown huts appear against their green jungle backdrop. In front of them are small, rocky islands taking a severe beating from the high surf.

"What do you think, should we take our chances with rascals and try to stay in the villages or just camp out alone?" I ask.

"I don't know."

"You sure are a help in the decision-making process, let me tell you." I am annoyed. "All right. I guess we won't take any chances. Let's camp in between the villages."

"Well, let's find that camp soon. I can't take this heat much longer."

I turn around to face him. "We can't quit so soon . . . not on our first day," I say this, even though I completely agree with him. He flips off his sunglasses while I'm talking and stares at me in amazement.

"Dude . . . your face."

"What?" I feel self-conscious.

"It's burnt to a crisp. Is mine?"

"Pretty red," I inform him, feeling my face at the same time. "Waterproof, my butt. Where did we get this stinkin' lotion, anyway? All right! We better get into shore and do something about this. It's getting bad."

"No . . . it *is* bad!" It's good just to hear Aaron talk, even if it is about a problem. At least it isn't about crocodiles!

We paddle close to a rocky point, but getting behind it is tricky. Weird currents created by the rocks form a massive sandbar. The shallow water causes the waves to break several hundred yards off shore. They roll across the shallows, intent on the ruin of anything in their path. The waves have doubled their size and power since we left Wewak's protected harbor. It's like paddling through an artillery field. The whitecaps break with thundering violence, sweeping past on both sides. We manage to squeak behind the rocks without taking a direct hit and skid ashore. Soon we find refuge in the shade of the high palms.

An eerie heaviness lingers around us at our first campsite, an overload of the mysterious unknown: a spear stuck in a tree, a washed-up dugout canoe abandoned in a festering tidal pool, strange tracks left behind in the sand. The last tide has marked its spot by leaving a trail of fallen, dark-brown coconuts weaving their way down the coast. In the far distance we make out the tiny huts of a village, but we want to avoid being seen by the people. A towering cliff of shadowy jungle stands in front of us, daring us to explore. The unseen places screech with life and movement, a siren of unfamiliar insect sounds grows louder with the falling darkness. A lagoon between our camp and the rocks of the peninsula reflects the fiery clouds of a brilliant sunset.

After letting some air out of the floor of our kayak, we turn it over and lay out our hammocks on it. We brought no sleeping pads for lack of space, so the bottom of our kayak is the softest place for us to sleep. Our hammocks are different than most, they are jungle hammocks. They're made of a canvass bottom to lay on and a tarp roof, both of which are connected with mosquito netting. It's hard to stretch out when the hammocks are tied between two trees, but by putting them on the kayak we can still get a few feet off the ground. We lift up the hammocks' waterproof ceilings with cords tied around nearby branches. The netting keeps us mosquito- free to sleep.

Darkness falls sharp and deep. It's hard to balance on the pocket of air; the kayak bucks every time one of us moves. We feel surrounded. From one side, waves crash; from the other, the jungle screams. From the lagoon, we fear the crocodile; from the village come eerie drumbeats of Stone Age rhythms. The ground crawls with ants and spiders. It's a wonder that we get any sleep at all.

✳   ✳   ✳

New Guinea has already changed us as we gather our nerves to attempt our second launch. We have a new respect for the incoming waves, especially since they are twice the size of the waves that made fools of us yesterday morning. We're also burnt and blistered, which explains our change in clothing. We've replaced our bathing suits with long-sleeved shirts, pants and socks, for ultimate sun protection. Although we look pretty stupid, we can't afford another second of exposure. Besides, there is no one around to impress.

"Front or back?" I give Aaron the choice again.

"Back." He doesn't appear to have gained much confidence during the night.

"All right then, man your battle station." I pull the kayak out into the calm waters guarded by the peninsula. We paddle along the rocks, staying completely out of the surf as far as we can, then we shoot back out into the incoming waves. With both of us paddling for all we are worth, Aaron weaves through the exploding whitecaps toward the deep water. The waves, which are approaching at an angle, push us down the coast as we slowly make our way out.

"I see the end of the sandbar!" I shout back to him. The pale green shallows meet with a deep blue drop-off, marking our finish line.

"Fifty more feet!" I yell, still straining on my paddle. The sea mounts an attack of waves, growing higher and steeper as they cross the line into the shallower water. The race is on as the first watery wall rises high above our heads. We have to reach it before it grows too steep to climb. The wave is close; I have a sinking feeling in the pit of my stomach as the nose of the kayak reaches for the top of it. All I can see is blue sky as the disintegrating wave grabs the end of the kayak and hurls us around before letting go. To my horror, I see the shore in front of us instead of open sea.

"Turn us! You have to turn us around!" I scream with the next wave swelling behind us.

"I'm trying!" comes Aaron's desperate cry. The wave is on us and with it, an ugly, sick feeling! We grab the sides of the kayak; this time Aaron is the one who shoots up the face of an angry wave. Whitewater boils up, threatening us from all sides. We gain momentum as we slide down in front of the churning foam. At first, I'm relieved that we're riding the wave, that is, until I see a rock cliff coming dead center! And in front of the cliff is a downed tree. The wave rushes us towards them. I decide to jump just as the force of the exploding wave turns us over, right in between the cliff and tree. I hit the sandy bottom hard, the wave slamming the kayak down on top of me. I know at once that I am hurt. I dig my fingers down into the sand as the undertow drags the kayak off my back, then I drift, helpless, into the beached log. Pulling myself up, I gasp for air with what feels like collapsed lungs. They unfold with a forced breath just before another wave hits me. I see Aaron helplessly holding onto our overturned kayak which drags him into the next wave. Trapped between the cliff and the downed tree, we attack the web of cords and knots holding our gear onto the kayak, weighing it down and keeping it trapped. We are mercilessly pounded by the angry surf as we try desperately to untie the knots. A maddening forty-five minutes goes by. It's something like untangling fishing line while getting punched out. There is no time to rest or talk, not with our valuable gear getting battered. Once the kayak is finally empty, we manage to swim it around the tree roots to a nearby beach and escape the torment of the sea. Exhausted, we lie down amidst our strewn gear, our bodies covered in salt and sand, and desperately try to catch our breath.

"What happened?" I gasp.

"That first wave . . . it knocked the rudder into the kayak." Aaron is still struggling to breathe. "I couldn't steer." He sits up looking at the kayak, empty except for the ropes that spill out across the sand. "I'm not so sure I like this island."

"I thought you said big waves are fun?"

"They are, if you take away the cliff, and the tree, and maybe 400 pounds of the load we're carrying."

"Oh, no! My sunglasses are gone." My eyes are squinting in the bright light. A major loss beneath an intense tropical sun, but there's nothing I can do about it. "Day's a wastin'. We better get it all packed up and try again. What would this be now . . . the third ocean launch for us? Heck, we're zero for two so far." I pull myself up.

"What do you say we tie a few less knots this time in case we end up at zero for three?" Aaron says, trying to brush the sand off his wet pants.

This launch is successful. We make it across the blue line into the safety zone, but not without a half-day's worth of time and effort.

We battle the day's intense heat by taking refreshing dips into the cool saltwater. Without my sunglasses, I get a severe headache that grows worse as the afternoon wears on. The throbbing pain makes it so I hardly notice the hum of a distant motor interrupting the tempo of our paddling. Suddenly, a canoe with pontoons bursts through the heat waves in front of us. It changes direction almost immediately, heading straight for us. Its engine cuts off, causing it to glide silently across the crystal water. One of the many men aboard stretches himself out across the water reaching for the front of our kayak. Aaron and I instinctively back-paddle to avoid contact. I glimpse their old, ratty, western clothes and become certain they are out to rob us.

"Come here!" one of the men calls to us.

"Why?" I ask, keeping my distance. I search their faces for smiles. There are none. My tension grows.

"Where you go?" one questions us. There is nothing friendly about his tone of voice.

"Sepik River." I wonder if I should have told him.

"Youpella can't go Sepik," he announces like he is pronouncing our doom. "Bigpella waves." He points out to sea and then towards the beach. The shoreline rumbles with a low growl. They try hooking the rope onto our bow with a long pole, but we dodge their attempts. The puzzled men give a uniform shrug, and the man at the rudder fires up the engine, setting his course in the opposite direction. Soon our nightmare melts into the horizon.

We begin a long recovery from our first encounter with rascals. I feel vulnerable: too colorful to hide, too slow to run, too outnumbered to fight. The experience leaves me feeling uneasy as we paddle on into the unbearable heat.

Late in the afternoon, the shoreline turns sharply north, and the wind picks up behind us, pushing us across the wide-open bay. Although hugging the coastline seems safer, I choose to let the wind blow us across the vast mouth of the bay. The clouds block out the heat from the sun, and the wind breaks up the humidity. We move effortlessly, climbing the watery mountains peaked with foam, and descending into the valleys between each swell. The shiny green back of a sea turtle sinks like a boulder, disappearing in the depths beneath our kayak. Driftwood, loaded down with silky-white sea birds like refugees from the sky, slowly passes us by. I lie across my seat, feeling the warm water on my toes with each dip of the bow. Beneath my hat, I pull the cool, white cloth of an extra pair of boxer shorts down around my head to protect my sun-poisoned face.

"Now this helps," I say out loud.

"Uh . . . Joel!" Aaron's voice is strained. "I think we have a problem."

"What now?"

"Behind us," comes his faint answer. I roll over on my seat and pull my boxers down to see. My body goes limp. A solid curtain of dark rain is sweeping inland, engulfing the swirling shadows of ocean behind us.

"Our kayak is twenty-feet, isn't it?" Aaron asks as we crest the top of a wave. I look to shore.

"Yes."

"Then these swells are bigger than twenty-feet," he calculates as we slide down the back side. The wind, blowing moisture off the wave's crown, whips into my face.

"Shore's still a good couple of miles off . . . we could make a run for it," I suggest.

"Yeah, like we can paddle faster than the storm."

"Maybe this is what he meant. Maybe these are bigpella waves." Butterflies dance in my stomach as we tighten straps. "Land of the Unexpected," I smile. "What an appropriate name." I untie the life jacket from my backrest and put it on. The wind whips up, driving ripples across the angered sea.

"I think we should pray." Aaron suggests.

"God help us!"

"Amen!" The waves curl and grow steeper; the kayak buckles beneath us. The shore grows steadily closer as Aaron keeps us straight. Our backs act as sails in the driving wind. The water sprays across the skirt, causing the rain to soak us, sending goose bumps down my sunburn. The thunder rolls, and the shore roars in pounding surf, warning us of danger. We approach the very place we do not want to go. To our right, high rocky cliffs come into view, clouds of white spray reaching their highest ledges. And above them are the huts of a village, with two men waving a white cloth frantically in the air. We ignore them. Soon a string of people of all sizes and shapes sprint down from the village and across the beach. Men, women and children, all of them running as fast as they can. Rascals? Maybe . . . whoever they are, one thing is certain, the storm is delivering us into their hands.

We cross into the shallows. The kayak picks up speed as a wave catches us from behind. I feel the angle of attack sharpen until my feet slide to a stop underneath the spray skirt. I stand up, my back flat against the upended kayak. White foam engulfs me, the kayak folds as the wave crashes down on top of it. All direction lost in the spinning turmoil, my arms and legs helplessly slap against the sea floor. My life jacket guides me to the surface, and my lungs gasp at moist air. Then the undertow drags me under the next wave. I shoot up the beach, choking on saltwater, dig in, and struggle towards the dry sand. The undertow is alive with natives prancing through the currents. I crawl free and roll onto my back. Young, naked boys fish some of the strewn gear from the shallows. Two men dare to go deeper, dragging the kayak out of the surf. Aaron is picking himself up just beyond me, once again covered in gritty sand. The villagers gather around us. I look down at my sunburnt feet, one bare, a sock hanging halfway off the other. Drenched and half-drowned, we stand before the villagers. I loosen my boxers which have been wrung tight around my neck. The men and women stare at the boxers. The little children hold giggles in their eyes, as their faces speak amazement at the power of a wave that could knock a man's boxers clear up to his neck!

"Oh, no." I pull them over my head and then down again. "I was wearing them up here, not down. . . ." I hesitate in my explanation.

"They won't understand any better why you are wearing underwear on your head," Aaron points out. I shake with laughter. They explode into hysteria after politely waiting for my permission.

Like a string of ants, everyone pitches in to help carry our gear up to the village. They calm our sea-battered nerves with friendly talk and a refreshing bath in a nearby creek. The name of the village is Koup, which turns out to be a boarding school of sorts, where children from the nearby villages are learning English. The two men who befriended us, Gabriel and Alex, speak English well because they are the teachers.

It is wonderfully relaxing to find a safe place in the midst of danger and a cool place after a blistering day. The pouring rain outside makes me thankful for the dry shelter of Alex's hut. It's built high up on rocky cliffs, far above the ocean that has beaten on us all day. We have been rescued from what otherwise would have been a beach-side camp of wet and misery. Alex's hut is raised up on stilts above the muddy ground, its roof and walls are made of palm leaves, split wood, and bamboo. Sea bass and oysters are roasting on a fire pit in the middle of the hut. Pots of rice boiling in fresh coconut juice hang above the fire that lights up friendly faces. Bewildered children carefully study our every move. Dinner is splendid! Aaron and I waste no time swallowing the flavors of our new home. Behind us, our blankets are laid out under a mosquito net that awaits our exhausted muscles and frazzled nerves as soon as our meal is over.

During dinner we tell our friends about the adventures of the last two days and our plans to cross their island. They let out gentle cries of sympathy as they try to comprehend such a mighty task. After we finish our explanation, the hut is quiet, except for hands slapping mosquitoes against bare skin.

"Do you think it is possible?" Aaron asks the men.

"Did you see the white flags we waved at you from down on the rocks?" Gabriel asks in response. Aaron and I look at each other, uncomfortable with the question.

"Yes, we saw," I admit.

"Why did you not come?" he asks with concern. Neither of us know what to say. "We have a harbor below the cliffs. Big rocks protect from waves. You would have been safe." I feel foolish.

"A small boy spotted you in the storm. He knew you were not one of our people. Our people would not be out in a storm," Alex adds. I just can't bring myself to tell them that we thought they were rascals.

"Next time we will listen," I murmur.

"Is it possible?" Gabriel repeats the question, Aaron has asked earlier. "Tomorrow we will take you to see the Old Man of Koup. He will answer this question you ask."

"Why this man?" I am curious.

Alex watches me, his face seeming to dance in the firelight. "Only a few men grow old on this island," is all he says.

We thank our friends many times for their hospitality because we are truly grateful, then we climb under the mosquito netting for some sleep. We have another good laugh about the day's events when Aaron tells me how the kayak flung him out like a sling shot after it folded and sucked me under.

"You know those rascals today?" I ask him. "They weren't rascals at all. I mean, think about it. They knew there was a storm coming. That's why they were talking about bigpella waves. They weren't trying to rob us, they were trying to rescue us." We laugh ourselves to sleep.

In the morning, the women cook sago cakes out of a white starchy powder that they make from the stalk of a sago palm. It is relatively tasteless. We spend the day resting and doctoring our sun-poisoning. Late in the afternoon, Alex leads us down a path away from the school, weaving for a few miles through the jungle to the main village of Koup. The Old Man of Koup climbs down from the dark entrance of his hut and fiercely glares at me. Alex serves as our translator, explaining to the old man our desire to cross New Guinea. The Old Man of Koup steps forward to study us more carefully. Blocking the last rays of sun from his face with his hand, he searches me with eyes of wisdom. As he reads me, I see in him the scars from the world we have come to cross. His feet are flat and swollen, his toes gnarled by a lifetime in the jungle. His body, once powerful, has wasted away into folds of wrinkles and tufts of gray hair. In this man lives the memory of his people.

"He speaks no English," Alex informs us. "He knows only the old ways. He has collected many heads and eaten from the flesh of our enemies. He has traveled further, killed more game, fought more wars than anyone else in the village."

Alex again speaks to the old man. "I have asked him if your crossing is possible," he tells us. The old man ends his silent staring by shaking his head and clicking his tongue several times. He lets out a long wail, lonely and sad, a song of suffering that he has learned from a true teacher, the land itself.

He speaks to me. "He wants to know if you see his eyes?" Alex translates.

"Yes." I nod.

"They know what you do not."

"Yes."

"The old man says you must look for such eyes along your way," Alex says, still listening. "When you find them, you must listen."

"We will!" Aaron agrees. The old man shakes our hands before climbing back up his ladder. Just before he disappears into the darkness of his hut, he speaks again. Then he is gone.

"He says it is possible," Alex announces with a rejoicing smile. I feel strange. For the first time, somebody has believed in us. I don't know what he saw in us, but somehow I know that in this unfamiliar world, we have been blessed by an unknown father.

"Do you know the land between here and the Sepik?" I ask Alex as we make our way back to the school.

"Yes, I am from a village on the Murik Lakes."

"How far to where the Sepik meets the sea?" I slap a fly on the back of my neck.

"You no go that way. Waves are too big and there are strange currents that will drown you. If you go that way you will die." After hearing the old man's wisdom and remembering yesterday's near drowning, I believe him.

"There is another way." His voice is confident.

"What other way is this?" Aaron sounds interested in the prospect of avoiding big waves.

"It is a shortcut, a canal that connects the Murik Lakes with the Sepik River."

"Can you tell us how to find this canal?" I ask.

"No. My father knows this place. I will send a note with youtwos and he will help you."

Next morning, we immediately start taking the advice of the Old Man of Koup and the wise suggestions of Gabriel and Alex to launch from the rocky harbor below the school. It pays off. We make it out beyond the breakers without any trouble at all. Soon our heads throb behind our squinting eyes as the sun glares from the ocean's surface. We are both without sunglasses now. One of the young boys sat on Aaron's pair last night, breaking them.

Saying goodbye to our friends who have transformed our original perceptions of them as rascals and headhunters is sad. They send us off with two written notes, the first for Gabriel's brother, Raphael, who lives in the next village down the coast. He is to lead us to Alex's home village, where we will stay the night with Kabasa, his father. He too is a very old and wise man. The second note is for us to give Kubasa, asking directions to the canal.

The day's plan works just as Gabriel and Alex have foretold. After several hours of potential heatstroke and paddling, just beyond a rocky point, we see a shoreline speckled with huts on stilts. We wait in front of the shallows as a crowd of several hundred gather to watch us over the incoming swells. As predicted, canoes come out to greet us, three men balancing in dugouts sloshing water out the front with their paddles. The youngest of the three volunteers to take our note in and try to find **Raphael**. We wait.

"Joel," Aaron gets my attention. I turn to face him.

"I think I'm okay now." He smiles.

"Good. I knew you'd come around." I had noticed the difference in Aaron this morning after he woke up. His eyes seemed calmer, his actions more relaxed, and his words less anxious. There is no doubt about it, our time in Koup has done both of us a lot of good.

A large motor canoe, with long pontoons on each side, comes toward us, crashing through the pounding waves. The several men that fill its hull shout greetings to us as it approaches.

"Hello, is one of you Raphael?" I ask, as they draw close.

"Raphael, Raphael," comes a chorus of cheerful voices as the men push him to the front. He points to himself with a white-toothed grin.

"Raphael," he says and sticks his chest out proudly.

"Raphael, Raphael," again comes the chorus from behind him. He holds up the note which we have sent in to him. His importance grows. The other men become silent. Raphael loses his smile.

"Alex?" he asks.

"Yes." I answer him.

"Alex father's house?" he points beyond his village.

"Yes,"

"Wepella go," he announces. His men cheer.

"Good," I agree. They take our bags and equipment into the canoe. Without the extra weight, we easily catch a wave and put on a show for the crowd as we smoothly glide up onto the beach. The crowd swarms, hands everywhere shaking Aaron's and mine. Several men throw our kayak up onto their heads and march between the huts. Raphael lands just down the beach, shouting orders to the people who surround our gear, fighting for the honor of carrying it for us.

The village is built on a narrow strip of beach, sandwiched between the roaring coast and the quiet waters of the Murik Lakes, which are a blend of salt and fresh water. The swamp's muddy shores are hemmed in tight with solid rows of stubby mangroves whose intricate root system, revealed by a low tide, serves as a shelter for small crabs that scurry about among the shadows. The water appears muddy and lifeless, though its man-eating legends swirl about in my mind. In minutes, our kayak is tossed upon the swampy surface, and our gear, brought forth piece by piece, is offered to us like farewell gifts. The handshaking tapers off enough for us to get the gear tied back into place. Raphael and his faithful followers board another motor canoe, this time without pontoons, and throw us a tow rope.

"Oh, no, we have to paddle," I insist. The men look confused. We try to explain our goal of crossing the island without the aid of motors, but they show no signs of understanding. Finally, they seem to accept the fact that we prefer to paddle.

In the end, Raphael shoots us a big grin. "Not very far," he says. The man in the back of his canoe revs up the engine and steers out into the maze of mangroves. We follow in its V-shaped wake which ripples gently in rolls across the glassy water. The rhythmic roar of pounding waves, like a conquered enemy, dissolves behind us into silence.

CHAPTER 4

The Sepik

The night is dark, like being in an unfamiliar room with the lights out. The kayak tremors from Aaron's frequent mosquito-slapping frenzies, and my heart skips beats as I imagine the beginnings of a horrifying crocodile attack. We paddle hard into the misty darkness of the swamp, not so much because we know where we're going, but because we dare not stop to pose as crocodile bait.

❊   ❊   ❊

Raphael's canoe had left us and started back to Murik a half hour before sundown. They had tempted us with a tow several times, but compromise was not in our hearts. We knew if we cheated, even in the least way, it would torture us for the rest of the trip. Raphael's men had given up and motored ahead to let Kabasa know we were coming.

Forty-five minutes have passed since they rumbled by us, waving and shouting their goodbyes. Raphael had been on the bow, looking as proud as ever that he had been the one chosen to help us.

"Not very far!" he had shouted and waved as he went by. He'd been saying this all day, and as the hours of paddling had melted away into night, we realized that he had no idea what the saying truly meant. Once in the swamp, their canoe had weaved us through an intricate maze of turns and canals, well-guarded by webs of vines hanging down like long snakes from the canopy above. The way was so confusing that many times I felt as though we were going in circles.

❊   ❊   ❊

We've been paddling for nine hours now, the last four without a good break, but the fear of being left behind and lost forever keeps us moving, along with our fear of what lurks under the dark surface.

I can't get Frank's words at the restaurant in Wewak out of my mind. "One second you'll be paddling along and all will be peaceful, then in an instant, churning water and blood will be violently splattered all about as he takes you down for the death twirl." I shudder.

"Did you hear that?" I whisper loudly. "Shhh! Stop slapping for a second."

"What?" Aaron's voice is tense. I can tell it is taking all his willpower to stop slapping at the cloud of mosquitoes feeding on him.

"There," I point out a voice that cracks the night. It is searching, hopefully for us. The presence of another human on the black waters of these hunting grounds is comforting.

"Hello!" yells Aaron.

"Happy nun," comes the voice again.

"Hello! Hello!" Aaron and I take turns shouting, hoping that the voice will locate us.

Then, not far away, emerges the indistinct form of a man. The ghostly image, only slightly lighter than the surrounding night, hovers over the water until I make out the dark wood of his canoe. The man stands in his canoe, testing our friendliness with more cries of "Happy nun" as he paddles cautiously towards us.

Drawing near, he sits down and reveals a wide smile. While gliding alongside us, he reaches out his hand and rests it on the side of our kayak. For a moment I think it is the Old Man of Koup. His hand squeezes at the rubber of our kayak, which seems to puzzle him.

"Kabasa," he lightly taps his chest.

"Yes. Alex's father?" Aaron points to him. The old man's smile grows wider.

"Aaron. Joel." we say simultaneously, pointing at each other.

He agrees with a nod. His native tongue sounds wild and full of sparks. He excitedly motions for us to move on. He waves out across the eerie expanse of water and yells "Puk puk!" Then he motions for us to follow as his finely carved craft glides smoothly out into the night. We struggle to keep up. His barely visible form threatens to disappear as quickly as he has appeared. The old man keeps signaling for us to hurry, chanting "Puk puk. Puk puk."

"Man, what's this guy's hurry? I'm too tired to keep this pace," Aaron whines.

"Do you know what a 'puk puk' is?" I ask, feeling the fatigue myself.

We are well past the point of being weary. We are plain exhausted.

"No."

"Then keep paddling."

We feel like we're going to pass out when forty-five minutes later, hut fires appear on the horizon ahead of us. We skid to a stop in front of several huts built on tall stilts. Fires built within them are glowing. Kabasa starts calling out commands, and more ghostly forms climb down ladders from the huts to approach the water's edge.

Soon our gear is safely piled next to our mosquito net and bedding in Kabasa's hut. We are much too tired to cook, so we eat a nasty can of corned beef with some crackers. A young man, named Toby befriends us, practicing the English that he learned as a boy in Wewak. He reads the letter from Alex and translates it to Kabasa, who cheerfully agrees to lead us to the secret canal tomorrow morning. We thank the old man several times before saying goodnight.

"Toby!" I stop him as he walks out the door to retire for the night. His head pops back into the fire-lit room. "What is a 'puk puk'?"

"Crocodile," Toby says just before disappearing into the framed darkness of the door.

* * *

I am a mass of reddened lumps when I wake up. The annoying high-pitched whine of mosquitoes had rung in my ears all last night like an alarm clock that couldn't be turned off. They had blanketed our net, each one busily searching for a way in. Unfortunately for me, many of them were successful. Aaron simply rolled up in his blanket for protection, leaving me as the main course for their feasting little snouts. I tried to follow his lead, but the night was much too hot and sticky to be rolled up in a polar fleece blanket.

I climb down the ladder, still drowsy after breakfast, and look back in the direction of the previous night's paddling. During the night, the low tide of the sea has sucked the water out of the Murik swamp. The mangrove trees crouch on their many legs like stranded spiders. A plain of mud stretches out between where our kayak is tied and the deeper water. Small birds, with long beaks and large feet, chase crabs into puddles trapped on the mud flats.

Aaron helps me pull our kayak across the slick mud, sinking in past our knees with every step. The old man, true to his promise to guide us, also drags his canoe behind him with the help of an old woman, who seems to be his wife. Minnows frenzy in front of us as we reach shallow water; terns dive in and out of the chaos, snatching up wiggling fish in their beaks. Soon we are off with the sun beating down on us full force. Because of the low tide, the shallow water depth separates us from the shade of the mangroves. We sweat out our water as fast as we can drink it, our heads throb in the heat, our eyes sting from the sweat that pours out from under our hats. We long for the protective black skin of the man and woman we follow.

Around high noon, just before a long point of tall trees that might provide some much-needed shade, Kabasa stops to fish. He attempts to explain things to us in sign language. From what we can gather, if we round the point and follow the far shore, we will soon come to the canal. We shake Kabasa's hand and thank him before making a run for shade, where we eat some tinned fish and crackers. Soon, however, attacking mosquitoes drive us back out into the sun. This becomes a routine. The sun gets to be too much, so we find shade until the mosquitoes seem worse than the waiting heat. Back and forth between these two miseries, we make our way down the left shore of mangroves. The black silhouette of a smoldering volcano stands on the distant horizon, reminding us of the ancient world into which we are paddling. A dinosaur feeding on the leaves of the mangroves would not look out of place at all.

Much to our surprise, a small island, covered in grass, drifts slowly past us.

"What in the heck is that?" Aaron asks.

"We must be close to the canal. I've read about floating islands on the Sepik."

The squatty mangroves are suddenly swallowed up by thick rain forest. The trees tower into the sky, a welcome block from the sun's intensity. The jungle is webbed together by a mesh of vines making its dark pathways impenetrable, even by sight. Then slowly, as we paddle steadily along, a tall but slender crack reveals itself in the thick green foliage. It is a passage, a dare to come even deeper into the grips of a hidden world where the land has not changed over the ages. The muddy currents of the canal, maybe fifty feet across, spit clumps of moss out into the salty swamp. The high walls on either side of the narrow canal rise, forming a narrow slit of blue sky above that separates the tree tops like a long, deep scar cut into the jungle canopy. A narrow gorge of vegetation is formed by the flowing canal that slices its way through the thick undergrowth. We hesitate in awe, peering down the dark throat of our next adversary.

"I wonder what time it gets dark in there?" Aaron wrestles with the thought of entering.

"Looks to me like it's always dark in there, except maybe at high noon." I raise my paddle above my head and then draw it down like a sword, pointing it towards the opening of the secret canal. "Onward!" I shout out loud. "Onward to Daru!"

The jungle screams with life and movement as we enter, the gorge gives us a glimpse of jungle life. Birds of all different sizes and songs fly back and forth across the gap. Parrots dance like rainbows on fluttering wings. Hordes of parakeets fly in brightly colored clouds up and down the crack of air. Cockatoos, violently squawking, hover like angelic ghosts suspended on blurred white wings. And butterflies, hundreds of them, float on the light breeze, disappearing for a moment into the dark shadows of the jungle, only to flush back out into the sunlight. All of them are different, no two the same, unless they are together; some are as small as my little fingernail, others as large as my open hand. But all perform their dance of life for the two strangers who paddle through their midst.

The jungle walls crowd our narrow path. We strain against the swift currents for several hours, dodging large clumps of floating lilies. The afternoon is growing late, though under the dark canopy it seems much later then it actually is.

Suddenly, within the jungle noise, I hear a faint sound, like the beating of drums. I become motionless. "What in the heck is that?"

"I hear it!" Aaron turns around in his seat, searching in the undergrowth for the unknown source of rhythm. It echoes through the trees and across the water, growing louder with every passing second.

"What is it!" Aaron screams in a panic. It is on us now, a violent noise, like the footsteps of a hundred warriors. I hold my paddle out in front of me, still desperately searching all about. I am almost lying on the floor of the kayak when I realize the throbbing noise that has tortured our bewildered ears is fading away as quickly as it came. My hands shake, white knuckles still clamped onto my paddle, eyes wide open with surprise. Cautiously, I sit up.

"Was it people?" Aaron's voice is shaky. If it weren't for his look of shock, I would be wondering if it had all just taken place in my head.

"We would have seen them, wouldn't we? It was close, whatever it was. I just can't figure why we couldn't see it." I am trying to relax.

"Maybe it was some kind of spirit," Aaron suggests with a shrug.

"Spirit? What? You mean like jungle spirits?" I begin to realize that we are drifting backwards.

"I'm not too sure about anything around here," he says disgustedly, starting up his paddling again. I certainly can't argue with that.

Just as we are beginning to feel claustrophobic, a bright light shines in front of us, ending the darkness of the jungle trench. My eyes squint from the sun's reflection off the wide-open waters of the mighty Sepik River. The tall rainforest shrinks in size behind us as we paddle out into the middle of the river. Eagles fill the skies, soaring and calling in clouds of swirling majesty. Great white herons line the shore, fishing with their spear-like beaks. An assortment of other long-legged shore birds hunt the shallows, much too busy in the process of survival to pay us much mind. A flock of black ducks flies overhead and lands upriver, diving beneath the muddy surface to search for food. The half-mile-wide river pushes the jungle far apart, muffling its deafening siren of insects. The river water, so pigmented with mud, looks more like soil with endless clumps of green lilies planted across its surface, a garden blooming with violet flowers. Rolling hills of grass also disperse themselves across the muddy surface. These floating islands, move with the lilies, gentle and constant, like a silent parade of greens and purples. We know where they are headed. The coast can't be far. But where have they all come from? That we don't know.

Suddenly, the air is filled with the strange noise again, rising in tempo as it draws closer. I search the water, then the sky. Four large birds with hooked bills travel slowly across the skyline near the edge of rainforest, their nearly black wings beating the air as they lumber into the horizon.

"There're your spirits." I point towards the birds.

"I seem to recall them scaring the piss out of you as well," Aaron defends himself. "What do you think they are?"

"Looks like they're vultures or something. I can't believe they make all that racket with just their wings."

"They're awful big, whatever they are. Maybe if we had spent a little more time reading up on such things, we wouldn't get freaked out over everything."

"You can't read about everything. But if that's true, then you shouldn't get frightened by any frogs along the way, now should you?" I smile. He gives me an unappreciative glare.

"Congratulations on a job well done!" I try to calm him down, reaching out my hand. "We made it to the Sepik. The first major leg of our expedition is complete."

"Something tells me the ocean and the swamp were the easiest . . . and they weren't very easy." He shakes my hand.

"No doubt the worst is yet to come. . . . It's getting late. Should we try and make it to a village or make camp?"

"I don't know," comes his usual reply.

"I sure am glad I brought you along to help with the decision-making process." I turn to face him. He continues to paddle.

"I trust your judgment," he tells me, avoiding eye contact.

"You trust my judgment. And just why would you trust that?"

"Because you're more experienced." He looks past me up the river.

"Hey, I hate to tell you, but you've been on this island as long as I have." He still won't look at me.

"More experience in tight spots is what I mean," he explains. I look to the far bank. Swamp grass creeps up from the water's edge and disappears into the steamy jungle.

"Yeah, well, just keep in mind, this is a whole lot different than the mountains back home."

"Is it?" he asks, finally looking at me.

I check the sun. "It's getting late. We better make camp."

We quickly fight our way through the deep moss bunched up against the shore, eager to get out of the potential crocodile attack zone. After we empty the kayak, we pull it over the steep-lipped bank. The jungle towers above us, warning us with the buzz of a million little creatures not to enter.

"What's your plan?" Aaron voice is behind me.

"For you to think for yourself," I snap, still uneasy with my decision to camp. "Where is the machete?"

"I don't know."

"Figures. All right. Let's go in, flip the kayak, and set our jungle hammocks up on the bottom of it with parachute cord." I wade into the shadows, dragging the kayak behind. Wet leaves slap me in the face as I weave my way between large tree trunks. I can't find my own feet, much less a place to make camp. The constricting vines bring me to a complete stop.

"What is it?" Aaron asks.

"I need the machete. I can't move." I wrestle with a thick vine across my chest. I drop the kayak and pull on it, rustling down droplets of water from the leaves above. I manage to duck underneath but then trip on something else and end up sitting down in thick mud. I Pull the kayak up to me before feeling around above my head, I get a hold on two vines. I feel little needle pricks of pain shoot up my leg. I pull myself quickly back up on my feet, slapping frantically at the bites. At first I am relieved when I discover that the enemy is a group of ants, that is, until I realize just how many there are. I feel a sting on the back of my neck. Aaron shoves into me from behind, going "ballistic" in a mad frenzy, ripping down the surrounding leaves covered with ants. The ground becomes a mass of tiny legs and jaws swooping in on our feet.

"This will do!" I shout in the chaos. We flip the kayak and immediately jump up on top of it, still slapping at the surrounding leaves and branches.

"These little suckers hurt!" Aaron yells, looking up at me. Two mosquitoes are sucking blood out of his cheek, unnoticed with the more excruciating pain of the ant stings. I slap him a good one across the face.

"What's *your* problem?" He feels his cheek before pulling away a blood-covered hand. His shock fades just long enough to throw me an angry glance.

"Mosquitoes. . . .." I try to explain, but something is biting my back, so I slam it up against a tree, only to get several more ants in my hair. Aaron keeps moving, shaking his body as he digs for the hammocks. We can never be still, not even for a second without getting tortured by sharp jaws. The ants are the biggest I've ever seen, and seems to be many different kinds. The biggest ones are black and red, and their bites seem to hurt the worst. There's something about ants. When they decide to do anything, including bite people, they always seem to give it one hundred percent effort. So, we dance around like madmen tying up our hammocks. Our feet jitter beneath us as we loop the cord over a branch, then slap and brush several times with both hands to clear our bodies of the pests before concentrating on tying a knot. In the middle of this dance a fly the size of my thumbnail takes a bite out of my arm. I swing at him and miss. The fly swoops out towards the river past two native men who stand completely still, staring at our bizarre ritual. The shock of seeing them sends me hurling backwards onto the overturned kayak.

"Hello," I say, baffled. Aaron looks at me as if I've gone crazy.

"Happy nun," one of the men says. Aaron spins around to see the men, his body flinching with surprise.

"You twopela sleepem Singoren village belong we twopela," the other man invites us. "Bigpella rain come. Village no lobis mosquito." Though we only understand a portion of what he says, it is all we need to hear to abandon our first attempt at making a jungle camp.

Within the hour we sit in a large, men's hut in Singoren. It is built high on stilts with no walls. Only the men are allowed in this hut.

"Hut belong men, no belong women, no belong boy," one of the men who rescued us had explained. His promise of no mosquitoes in his village is simply not true. Our slapping continues, though there are many more bodies for the mosquitoes to choose from. A tree trunk with carved footholds leans up against the side of the hut for a ladder. Men from the surrounding huts climb up and sit, staring at our every movement. The river people are quiet individuals. I guess they don't have much to say in their world. I imagine they would ask us several questions if they knew English better, or if we knew pidgin. But it is an ordeal to communicate anything.

As frustrating as it is to us, they seem quite content to observe us, which might explain why I feel the need to entertain. I reach for our finest piece of modern equipment, the gas stove. This will do the trick, I think to myself. Two birds with one stone: I can cook dinner and entertain at the same time.

I pump more pressure into the stove than is needed as suspense builds in the eyes of the men. Maybe it is the excitement of having the full attention of so many men, or maybe it is my hungry stomach. Whatever it is, it blinds me to the fact that the stove has leaked gas all over itself, the fuel bottle, and my hands. By the time I light the match, I am just plain showing off, having no idea of just how much exciting entertainment I am about to provide. The stove immediately bursts into flames. The men flinch and, in the next moment, flames engulf my hands and swish down onto the gas on the hut floor.

"Iiiiiiieeeeeeeee," the men screech as many of them spring to their feet in an attempt to save themselves. I, in turn, have dropped the stove and am trying desperately to slap out my flaming hands on my pants, and at the same time stomp out the flames that are quickly spreading across the floor of the hut. By the time I get all the fires put out and everything is back under control, I have the undivided attention of every man, woman and child in the entire village, not to mention an extremely red face. If we were to whip out a bunch of gas cooking stoves to sell right now, I doubt anyone would buy one! It isn't until we have finished cooking and shut off the stove that the men are able to relax enough to chatter in excitement about the ordeal that they have just witnessed.

After we finish eating, a young man emerges from the jungle with a guitar strapped onto his back. He climbs up into the men's hut and quietly sits down.

"Where you get guitar?" I ask him.

"Catholic Father."

"Ah, what's your name?" I am eyeing his instrument.

"Name belong Joel," he answers with a smile.

"*My* name is Joel!" After thinking about it for a moment, I give Aaron a weird look.

"May I play?" I point to the guitar. The crowd murmurs with anticipation. I try a few songs, but with one of my hands working the chords and the other strumming the strings I can't slap at the mosquitoes that are tapping into my bloodstream.

"Me no play . . . too many mosquitoes," I complain. The crowd is disappointed. One of the men shouts down commands to some children who quickly build a fire underneath our hut with wet leaves. Soon a cloud of smoke rises up through the matted floor. It filters up, filling the hut, which drives away the flying pests. So now, with two free hands, I am able to play the guitar. However, attempting to sing in the midst of a cloud of smoke so thick that I can hardly make out the black forms of my audience is a task in itself. Aaron and I cough and sputter our way through several slow songs learned around campfires long ago. But it isn't until I break into the fast-paced "Battle of New Orleans" that the crowd goes wild. The men clap, women dance around the fringes of the hut, below the floor children giggle. Though they can't understand a word I'm singing, they enjoy the enthusiasm of the quick tempo.

I hand the guitar back over to Joel, while I choke on the smoke that flows in and out of my lungs with every breath. He sits still and silent for a moment before starting in on a simple chord progression. Slow and easy, his fingers dance across the strings, changing the mood of the night with every peaceful stroke. The dark forms of the men sway ever so slightly in the smoke, their eyes closed as they feel out the melody and begin to sing. Deep and strong, brave but gentle, their voices soothe the chaos of the jungle. The sweet song from the hearts of the children rises up from below with the seeping smoke, filling the hut with small voices of innocence. On the fringes, the women join in, ever so softly, as their surrounding circle tightens around the hut, their voices woven through in simple harmonies. It is a swirl of different voices, all flowing together like the creeks and streams that form a river. It is not a song sung for us, nor for the jungle, it is sung to something bigger. Only one word do we recognize; it appears again and again throughout their praise. It is the name of our King, the name of Jesus.

This is a song of peace in the midst of turmoil, a song of survival under the onslaught of so many enemies. No voice is expendable; each one adds to the strength of the whole. Each one is honored and valued, no matter the gender or the age. Each gift is an absolute necessity to the bigger picture: the song of a tribe, one voice made from many; the voice of the hunter and the warrior; the voice of knowledge and of learning; a song of gathering and nurturing, compassion and violence; the dying voice of the old falling down with all its wisdom upon the young below, so full of energy and life; a song of teaching and learning, dying and being born—in praise of the Creator. I can hear no competition, no struggle for equality, just a security of individual parts, each with something valuable yet different to give, each knowing that they sing because they belong, and because they are able to stand together, fight together, live and die together, rejoice and mourn together. If their song should perish, then they will perish with it.

The powerful unity of their voices wraps comfort around us as we listen to its simple beauty. Inside of me, I feel hope rising that we really *will* make the southern coast. I turn to Aaron who is soaking it all in, and I know. I know, that if our merciful God allows us to make it across this merciless island, then He wants us to make it together. For the greatest of teachers knows better than to give the treasure without the lesson. My prayer is that God will reveal to Aaron and me the gifts and talents He has given to each of us, so that we can better use them and honor Him. Somewhere along the way, I know that we will learn what these people already know. We will come to understand how to serve one another, so that we can sing our praises together.

The night drifts from the peaceful melodies of the Singoren villagers to the harsh realities of the land, the continual torment that has written their songs. Days and nights pass us by, leaving a mark of misery on our weary bodies, heat-exhausted minds, and smashed spirits. New Guinea begins to sing its own song to us, with a rhythm of suffering and lyrics of warning, saying the same thing in so many different ways: "You're going the wrong way!"

The river winds through an unchanging landscape of swamp that separates it from a distant jungle; towering trees are much too far beyond reeds and grasses and clumps of sugarcane to cast any cool shadows of relief across our path. The sun beats on us from above, and the current resists our every stroke as we painfully watch the shore slowly pass by, one agonizing foot after another. We retreat to the still waters amongst the reeds, hosting a variety of spiders which, much to our disgust, crawl across our faces to the high perches of our hair. Breaking up the tempo of our paddling, we try to rid our sweaty skin of the movement of their tiny little legs. They drive us back out into the current until our muscles ache, forcing us through another cycle.

Storm clouds roll in and relieve us of the heat, dumping rain until our bodies tremble uncontrollably with cold chills. But the storm blows over us, and the sun warms us until the heat overpowers us and we long once again for the rain. We spend the days being traded between extremes of miseries.

The nights are better because we don't have to paddle and can sleep in the villages along the river, but with no cushion, the hard, rounded logs that form the floor of the huts makes even sleeping a difficult task. The mosquitoes come with sunset, covering our protective netting like hair on a dog. And though I search and search, I can never discover how they are getting in. When I sleep, I sometimes roll up against the net, succumbing to dreams of torment as mosquitoes by the hundreds feast through the netting. Several times I try to roll up in my blanket like Aaron does, but I just can't do it in the intense humidity. The pigs beneath the floor of the huts dig with their snouts, and dogs and chickens fight one another all night long. Night after night, I listen to the noises, slap at the bugs, and try to ignore the heat and the high-pitched whine of a million mosquitoes. And even with the ache of a full bladder, I dare not go outside to relieve it. That is a mistake a man makes only once! I try desperately to gain the sleep that I need, but what do I have to really look forward to? Just another endless day of paddling. I curse this dream of mine.

Back out on the water I sing. My head throbing in pain with every stroke of my paddle.

> "*When I was a young man and never been kissed, I started thinkin' it over and how much I missed,*"

> "*So I grabbed me a girl and I kissed her and then again. Oh, Lordy, well, I kissed her again.*"

I go on with my therapeutic rhymes as we run aground on a clump of lilies. "Sorry, can't see with all the sweat in my eyes." I make an excuse, breaking up the entangled moss with my paddle. Aaron says nothing.

"Because she had kisses sweeter than wine,
she had, mm, mm, kisses sweeter than wine."

Our muscles ache after four long days, three villages, and over sixty miles of upriver paddling since the night of singing at Singoren. In the village of Angoram a few days ago, we picked up some more rice and canned foods and invested in a bigger mosquito net.

"Well, I asked her to marry and to be my sweet wife
I told her we'd be so happy for the rest of our life
So I begged and I pleaded like a natural man
And then whoops, oh, Lordy, well, she gave me her hand."

Singing is the only thing that seems to help keep my mind distracted from the misery that surrounds me. The little relief singing gives is worth it, even if it does make my head hurt worse.

"Because she had kisses sweeter than wine
Mm, mm, kisses sweeter than wine."

"Would you shut up!" Aaron's annoyed voice rings out from behind me. I unscrew the lid from my water bottle; my chapped lips find the edge as I let the hot water drain down my dry throat. I wipe my mouth with my sleeve, watching the dead skin from my lips stick to it. My eyes sting.

"No girl would want to kiss these lips anyway," I say, wiping my forehead and pulling my drenched hair back under my hat. I begin to stare at the water, lusting for its cool refreshment. "I'm going to take a swim."

"If the crocs don't get you, then the amoebas will," Aaron insists. The fear of dysentery, funky skin diseases and man-eating reptiles keeps us from the cool refreshing swims that we had enjoyed along the coast.

We have seen the effect of the crocodile on the culture much more than that we have seen the actual crocodile itself. The deep, magical fear of the Indo-Pacific crocodile has cast its spell on every village where we have stayed. The people refer to the most powerful of their foes as the "Great Water Spirit." It casts its shape in their carvings, and its teeth adorn their ritual symbols. The dugout canoes are carved with the head of a crocodile at each stern, complete with a mouthful of nasty wooden teeth, a symbol of protection while out on the river, so the natives fear for us when we paddle up in our headless inflatable kayak. Even the people themselves begin to resemble their most-feared enemy. Boys undergo ritual attacks as initiation knives cut deep wounds into their backs. If they survive the infection, they are said to have possessed the power of the crocodile, the link into manhood. The permanent scars covering their backs resemble the backs of a crocodile, a reminder of the journey they have taken. Before the missionaries arrived, the people believed that they themselves had evolved from the Great Water Spirit who had created the world. Even now, under the Sepik's strong Catholic influence, the people of this culture still cling to the old god, for it is easier to change religion, than it is to change fears.

At first, we thought it foolish to give godhood to a mere reptile. However, the deeper we paddle into his domain, the more we see his reflection of horror: rumors of recent attacks on villagers, descriptions and warnings of particular crocs who torment villages. What do you call something that you watch for all day across the muddy surface of water? What do you call something that haunts your thoughts and dreams? Does a simple reptile have the power to alter the way you live your life? For us, it is a constant struggle to trust in God, and not to be controlled by the Sepik god, not to bow down and worship him with our fear.

Our battle is much more in the realm of fear than in actual sightings. We have seen a few smaller crocodiles slide from the river banks into the water. One came within a couple feet of our kayak before we spotted it, but it was more like twenty-five inches in length rather than twenty-five feet, and it quickly disappeared in the murk of the water.

It is late afternoon when we finally make it to the village of Kanduanam. We've heard from the natives that a Catholic priest lives here named Father Don. Aaron goes to search for him, and to ask for a place to sleep tonight. I stay with the gear. The villagers swarm around me as I begin the usual routine of shaking all their hands. Suddenly, there comes an angry cry from somewhere beyond the crowd, disrupting the friendly atmosphere. The crowd in front of me clears as a young man steps into my view. His pupils roll back until all I can see are the whites of his eyes. He leans back, hopping towards me on both legs, crying out in long, agonizing wails. I stand up, desperately searching for an explanation; but the villagers, to my surprise, aren't even looking at the crazy man. Instead, they are staring at me. The man screeches at me as I jump backwards. His arms flail wildly over his head before he drops to his knees; his body contorts in bizarre, jerking motions.

"Man sick?" I ask the crowd, but no one speaks. The man now places his forehead on the muddy ground and begins to moan, a moan that starts from the pit of his stomach and grows deeper and louder as he raises his head. The whites of his eyes now roll forward, revealing an evil stare. I back away from his insane, shaking body. His moan grows louder than ever. He thrusts his fist out towards me.

"Sangoman!" he yells, rising to his feet. I flinch with the crowd's panic. Women scream as they rush their small children into the cover of a large hut. The circle of men around me swells with fear as they back away.

"What? What I do?" I plead with them, but they don't dare speak. The crazy man runs off through the village screaming warnings, waving his hands wildly above his head. Distressed voices come from the huts trying to calm children crying out of control. I stand alone, shattered and confused.

"What's wrong with you?"

I spin around. It's Aaron.

"Let's get the heck out of here!"

"What? Father Don says we can stay with him in his house," he pleads. I glance at the black men with Aaron. They seem calm.

"House, did you say house?"

"What's wrong with you? You look like you just saw a ghost."

"Me? It's them, the whole village just flipped out on me." I notice my hands shaking. Aaron looks puzzled. "Some wild man was screaming and moaning like he was insane."

"Well, maybe he *was* insane." Aaron starts to blow it off.

"He called me a Sangoman."

"What's that?"

"As if I know."

"Well, Father Don will know. He sent these men to help carry our stuff. His house is mosquito-proof."

I try to forget about the strange occurrence as we hike up to the house. A mud trail leads us for a quarter of a mile until a wood house comes into view, finally, drawing my attention away from my turmoil.

A tall, white man with dark-brown hair steps off the porch; his lonely eyes look genuinely glad to see us. He wears a button-down, collared shirt that is somewhat clean. Along with navy blue shorts, his long, white legs stand out in contrast to the black legs of the other men. His feet are bare and swollen, not exactly what I expected of a Catholic priest.

"Welcome! Welcome! Won't you come in?" He greets us in a friendly Australian accent. After Aaron properly introduces us, I follow him into the house, through two mosquito-proof doors. It is the first bit of comfort we have experienced in some time. Both of us take real showers with soap and shampoo. While Father Don boils noodles over the stove for dinner, we explain our expedition plans to him. We add a can of braised steak and onions to the menu as he tells what living in Kanduanam for nearly thirty years has been like. With the excitement of having on clean clothes over the top of my clean skin and no mosquitoes biting me, I forget all about my earlier ordeal in the village, until we sit down to enjoy our meal and new company.

"What is a 'sangoman'?" I finally ask. Father Don freezes in the middle of taking a bite, his eyes dart towards me.

"Why do you ask such a question?" He lowers his fork onto his plate, and listens intently to my story of the encounter with the crazy man. He looks sad after I finish and gently pushes his plate away.

"Yes, well, I'm afraid . . . . ," he starts to say before Aaron slaps his leg with a loud smack. Father Don struggles to gather back his thoughts. "I'm afraid it all has something to do with the incident last night." He glances over at Aaron who is now whacking the back of his neck, checking his hand after each slap.

"What happened last night?" Aaron asks, showing that he is still listening.

"Murder." He speaks quietly, looking down at the table.

"Murder?" A cold lump rises up from the pit of my stomach. Aaron's wide eyes stare at the priest, while he scratches his arm.

"Yes, last night, I'm afraid," he pauses. "Last night they found Binsin, the strongest man of the village floating dead in the river, underneath the logs where they tie their canoes." He changes position in his chair, looking uncomfortable. "He was a good man." His eyes are sad.

"How do you know he didn't just drown?" I ask curiously, trying not to be insensitive.

"I have been over it and over it in my mind, and I have to agree with my people. It just doesn't make sense. He was last seen after nightfall when he left his friend's hut to go back to his own. Nobody goes swimming at nighttime on the river, nobody!" He looks up at us. "I hope you know that."

"We don't even swim during the day," Aaron assures him, then bends over and starts brushing his ankles with his hands. Father Don gives him a queer look before going on with his story.

"Besides, Binsin was one of the best swimmers in the village. There was nothing off that dock that could have drowned him, except a crocodile, of course. But I looked his body over thoroughly, and there were no teeth marks. It had to be murder, had to be."

He sighs. "Besides, he led a revenge party a couple weeks ago to a neighboring tribe. No one was hurt, but they ended up burning some huts and killing some pigs."

"Why?"

"Revenge." He looks down again at the table. "All of the villages have deep scars of hatred. Most of it started back when they used to engage in tribal warfare, when they practiced cannibalism and headhunting. They still practice such things in the more remote parts of the highlands. . . ." Aaron and I give each other a nervous glance. "Now, it's more of a spiritual revenge. They put curses on each other, a practice my colleagues and I have been struggling against for decades." He looks tired. Aaron begins slapping himself again.

"Are you finding mosquitoes in here?" Father Don asks in a distracted tone. Aaron freezes in the middle of a slap. He searches for the little devils, looking under the table at his legs and ankles, then back to us. We stare at him as if he has gone mad.

"Um . . . no . . . I guess not," he says with a shrug and a sheepish grin, his face flushing brilliant red.

"It's skeeters of the brain!" I laugh out loud. "You'll have to excuse my partner; he's been in the bush too long." We all get a good laugh out of it. Father Don seems to be in need of laughter even more than we are.

"I understand," he tells Aaron politely, who has gone back to eating his dinner.

"So, what is a 'sangoman'?" I ask again. Aaron and I both wait patiently for the answer. Father Don turns slowly in his chair, looking out the window into the night.

"'Sangomen'. . . the people of New Guinea have always believed in them. They are said to be spirit beings. . .," he glances at me, "Demons, I would imagine. Violent demons of murder. The people call upon them to possess certain men in their village, for purposes of revenge. The demons bring the men supernatural powers as well as a thirst for bloodshed."

"So how do they do it ?" Aaron is intrigued. Father Don stares back out the window at the dark.

"They are said to have an enticing whistle. More beautiful and lovelier than the song from the Bird of Paradise. When you hear it, it captivates you and draws you into the jungle where you are ambushed by the 'sangomen.'" He sighs heavily.

"You don't believe in them do you?" I need to know. He thinks a moment, then leans across the table with a very serious look on his face.

"After thirty years on this island all I can tell you is this . . . there are things that take place in these jungles that I just can't explain."

My scalp begins to itch with a sudden hot flash. I can see Aaron's pale face out of the corner of my eye. "All I know is, I have a naked, dead man without a mark on his body, and I have a village that is scared to death. They all sleep in one hut, and go to the bathroom in groups of twenty." He shakes his head and flops back in his chair. "I know that this morning they took two men from the village and prayed for them to be possessed by a spirit that would enable them to see the 'sangomen' who are invisible to everyone else. I also know that those two men have been acting like lunatics ever since. One of them, it seems, has now made your acquaintance, Joel. You were accused of being a 'sangoman' because you are different, and you showed up unexpected at an uneasy time. Please don't take the accusation hard though, they meant no harm. They are afraid." He stands to his feet. "And now I will have to go and try to explain to them about the power and grace of God once again, and try to convince them that my two visitors are not 'sangomen', but rather crazy explorers." He starts picking up dishes.

"Well, we will be sure not to do any whistling tonight then," I tell him. It takes a while, but he finally cracks a smile and then shows us to our room which feels dark and spooky after the night's talk. Two beds, complete with sheets and blankets, against opposite walls, welcome us to a night's sleep.

"A mattress and no mosquitoes, what more could a person ask for?" Aaron sounds relieved.

A huge, hairy spider, the size of my open hand, scurries across the floor under one of the beds. Both Aaron and I jump back, giving it lots of room. Father Don calmly watches it run past his bare foot, as if they are friends.

"That's your bed," I say to Aaron.

"I don't think so," he argues.

"Don't worry about him, he's harmless." Father Don assures us about the spider and then leaves, wishing us a good night's sleep.

"I don't know about you, but I can't sleep with a spider large enough to palm my face crawling around my bed somewhere," I complain. Aaron pulls off one of his sandals and raises it over his head. I grab the bed, wait for his nod, then pull it quickly away from the wall. The spider darts for the opposite bed. Aaron retreats a safe distance and throws his sandal, but it falls well short of a kill. We play the game several times, trying to get a kill shot in between the two beds, but the spider is too fast. Finally, it figures it has had enough and comes charging, full speed, out from under the bed, straight for Aaron. In shock, he swings and pins the spider to the floor, instantly killing it.

"What on earth are you two doing?" Father Don calls through the wall. We thought he was gone to the village.

"Nothing, we're going to sleep now," I assure him. Turning off the light, I nestle into the comfort of my mattress. The room is hot, making it hard to sleep. I can't get the image of "sangomen" out of my mind. Every time we hear a bird sing outside, Aaron and I sit up and listen. Until today, I was beginning to trust the kind hearts of the people. But tonight feels evil. My trust for them has been wounded. The Old Man of Koup was right; their wisdom can help us. But their evil may rob us, or kill us. I feel cautious. There is nothing left for me to trust completely, but my God.

"As if we don't have enough to worry about in that darn jungle without a bunch of murderin' spirit beings," Aaron whispers before I finally fall asleep.

CHAPTER 5

The Salumei

With each stroke, more and more water trickles off my paddle onto my lap. The muscles in my arms and shoulders feel like they are on fire after six long hours of paddling from Kanduanam. We set off this morning after having replenished our freshwater supply and being blessed by Father Don.

"I will pray that the hand of God protect you on your journey," he had promised, bidding us farewell.

"Thank you . . . for your hospitality and your prayers," we said gratefully. He shook our hands firmly before we climbed into the kayak and pushed away from the bank. We watched him stand silently on the shore, his eyes once again growing lonely.

"You do not understand where you are going," he had told us looking up river. "If things get too rough, don't be too proud to turn around." He had looked straight at me. "Pride is never worth dying for."

All day, I keep hearing his words echoing in my head, which once again throbs in the heat. I close my eyes against the fierce sun. Am I leading a nineteen-year-old boy to the slaughter? I am feeling an incredible weight of responsibility.

"Joel, it's time to switch," Aaron says from behind me. I drop my paddle with a sigh and climb past Aaron to the back, being careful not to knock him or myself into the infested river. The back of the kayak is the more painful place to be, because you have to keep your eyes open nearly all the time in order to steer.

"Why did you come on this expedition?" I ask Aaron, fitting my feet onto the rudder pedals.

"I've been asking myself that question," he says, loosening the cloth around his head and face to sip from his water bottle.

"Did I talk you into it?" I want to know.

"No," he answers after thinking a moment. "You told me from the beginning about all the risk. In fact, if you'll remember, you told me that chances are I would die." He tightens the cloth back around his face and pulls his hat down tight. "I spent two nights out under the stars praying for direction."

"So what did you hear?"

"I'm here, aren't I?" We start paddling again to stop from drifting backwards.

"What if we don't make it? I mean, God forbid . . . but say you should die . . . then who would you blame?"

Aaron becomes still. He carefully balances his paddle on the front of the kayak and turns around. "Not you," he says, looking straight at me and then beyond. "Canoe," he announces, changing the subject. I turn around to see a carved, wooden crocodile head, blackened by fire gliding smoothly above the water, a demon of terror guiding its inhabitants along the reeds. A man sits just behind the jagged teeth of the prow, his powerful upper body useless without a paddle. Behind him, a little naked boy pounds the man's back, trying desperately to get his attention. The boy is the only one who has become aware of our presence. A bare-breasted woman labors with her paddle against the oncoming current. She is paddling her entire family upriver while nursing a baby and smoking a huge cigar, all at the same time.

"Now, there's a woman for you!" Aaron says, under his breath. I smile at him. They all see us now, the woman steers the dugout next to the reeds, grabbing a wad of them in her hand to keep from drifting backwards.

"Happy nun," we greet them, pulling up beside her. She gives us a silent nod. The cigar, wrapped in a dried, green leaf, protrudes from her mouth. A puff of smoke rises up from her lips, seeping into her tight afro before rising into the air.

"Happy nun," the man interrupts, pulling our kayak up to him and shaking our hands. Two young girls lie curled up on the bottom of the canoe along with several catfish whose gills are slightly moving. "Where you go?" the man insists.

"Timbunke," I tell him.

"Too far, too far," he chants. "Where you twopella come?

I notice that the girls look strange, as if they are cold. They lie shaking out of control, with their shocked eyes slightly open.

"Wewak," Aaron speaks up.

"Iiiiiiieeeeeee Wewak," he repeats to his wife.

"Iiiiiiiiiieeeeeee," she wails.

"What name, village, belong you twopella," Aaron tries out his pidgin.

"Tanduanam," the man proudly answers. One of the girls begins to cry, distracting me again. They look as though death has them by the necks. The man watches Aaron and me staring at his suffering children. "Malaria," he says, his eyes are scared. The dread disease that we have heard so much about is now doing its killing right in front of us. "You twopella come village, sleepem night, hut belong me," he invites. "Close too."

The woman glances down with worry at her sick daughters, taking another puff from her cigar. She picks up her paddle and begins to pull her family upriver. We follow her.

"Well, we have a decision to make, and don't you dare try to get out of it by telling me that you don't know," I tell Aaron, as we fall in behind the canoe. "You're the medical officer of this expedition, so what will it take to save those girls?"

"Two full cycles of chloroquine, a cycle for each of them," His voice is strained. "We only have six cycles with us."

"So, if we give them our medicine, we can only afford to get malaria twice each?"

"Yes."

"Why did we end up bringing only six cycles?" I ask, disgusted.

"They were expensive, we couldn't afford anymore." His voice sounds defensive.

"What if we get it and we're out of medicine?"

"The nationals have a natural resistance to malaria, sometimes it kills them, sometimes it doesn't. But, if we get it, it's more serious," he explains. "We'll die without the medicine."

"So what do you think we should do? Those girls look pretty bad." Their dying little faces haunt me.

"I don't see that we have much of a choice, not unless you want to live the rest of your life with the thought of them dying on your conscience."

"Lord God, have mercy," I pray with a sigh. "You better dig up that medical kit."

Aaron pours two cycles worth of pills, twenty pills in all, into a zip-lock bag as we strain our weary muscles to catch up with the woman who is still doing all the work. Her face lights up with hope as we hand the chloroquine pills over to her husband.

"Youpella come village, sleepem night!" he says with new enthusiasm. He treats the pills like precious diamonds as he takes some from the bag. The woman fills a leaf with water and props up the heads of her daughters. They look too delirious to understand what they are swallowing. The woman smiles with joy in our direction.

"Congratulations," I say, as we begin to follow the canoe upriver again. "You helped to make a decision." But Aaron doesn't say anything, not a word, for the next two hours.

The huts of Tanduanam are monstrous, built on a foundation of fifteen-foot-high logs cut from the biggest trees that the jungle has to offer. They are completely enclosed with high, arching roofs making their interior a vast, windowless room of darkness. The villages we have previously slept in were made up of several small family huts, each one constructed with long slender poles. Tanduanam has only a few huts; but their thick, heavy, log structures are so massive, they can easily house several families. Even our twenty-foot kayak sits insignificantly in the corner of the hut where we sleep tonight. Aaron and I sit in the pitch-black expanse of the inner room waiting patiently for our eyes to adjust. Some thick beams above our heads come into focus. They are all we need to tie up our mosquito net. After throwing our blankets underneath the net, we sit back down to enjoy a fruit roll from a can. We are much too tired to cook. Fire-pits filled with hot coals illuminate, in dull orange, the forms of women and children sitting around them.

A storm sweeps in on the village just after nightfall. Its violent, thrashing wind and rain beat against the thick walls and roof surrounding us. Aaron places his hand on my arm and squeezes.

"Look," he whispers, staring up at the ceiling. My muscles tense. Five evil faces loom down at us, suspended in the over-hanging darkness. Carved, wooden demon masks, as large as shields, hang in a row on the main ceiling beam directly above our bedding. Cold, hollow eyes sunk into the white paint of each face reveal the black night beyond. Contorted mouths of sharply carved teeth stained with blood are frozen in the praise of cannibalism. From the tops of their heads dangle a mass of vines, winding like snakes across their cruel expressions.

"'Sangomen'," comes a booming voice. We jump forward, scrambling to our feet to find the man from the river stunned by our panic.

"You twopella buy?" he asks, pointing towards the masks. "Mepella carve 'sangomen'," he tells us, proudly.

"No!" Aaron says, rather quickly. "I mean, no thank you." The man looks quite disappointed. "Umm. . .no room," Aaron finds an excuse, pointing to our kayak. It is then that we notice another medium-sized man sitting among our bags on the side of our kayak.

"This man guard, all night," he assures us.

"Why?" Aaron looks worried.

"Rascals."

"Ah, tank u tru." Aaron thanks him in pidgin, not really knowing what else to say. We crawl under the mosquito netting, to rest on the hard floor, our muscles sore from the ten-hour day of hard paddling. According to the map, it is our best mileage upriver so far. We have covered nearly twenty-five miles today.

"A lot of sleep I'll be getting tonight," I mumble in sarcasm, "with rascals about and all these demon masks staring at us." I shut my eyes and try to ignore them, checking now and again to make sure they haven't moved.

"Annoying little devils, aren't they?" Aaron speaks up, after an hour of tossing and turning. It is good to know that he can't sleep either.

"I wish they were real—then we could just call upon the name of Jesus and cast them out," I say, rolling onto my side. "Looks like our all-night guard went for a piss or something." There is nobody at the guard post. As I'm looking, a ghostly image steps into the outline of the door. At first I am not alarmed, thinking it to be our returning guard. But the harder I stare, the more I begin to realize that he is a much bigger man than the one who has been sitting with our gear. My heart races in horror when I see the moonlight reflect off a long machete he holds in his hand. I realize what the man is doing. He is waiting for his eyes to adjust to the darkness inside of the hut. I tap Aaron several times with my foot.

"I see him," he whispers in my ear. The man looks our way as every muscle in my body freezes solid. And then, like a terrible nightmare, the form steps out of the moonlit door frame and approaches us.

I roll onto my back, everything inside of me panicking though I pretend to be asleep. I keep my eyes pinched slightly open. The dark form raises the knife above his head, blocking out the stare from the sangomen masks. I prepare to dodge the thrust of the blade. My emotions begin to protect themselves as I drift into shock, questioning the reality of the horror that threatens me. The moment seems to last forever before the man finally steps back from our net. I dare not breathe. Then slowly, he lowers the knife and walks away. For a brief moment his shirtless body appears in the moonlight, before he disappears outside. We exhale!

"I thought he was going to kill us," I speak as quietly as I can, sitting up with my eyes still glued to the door frame.

"That *does* it, I mean, that really *does* it!" Aaron says out loud.

"Shhh, keep your voice down."

"Do you want the first watch or the second?"

"Like you can stay awake for five minutes," I reply.

"I'll stay awake all night after that." He checks his watch. "You sleep, and I'll wake you in two hours."

"It'll take me two hours to fall asleep," I complain. "If he comes back, you better wake me."

"I will," he agrees, and then sighs deeply. "It's going to be a long night!"

"You know how you said today that I didn't talk you into this expedition, how you made up your own mind to come?" I ask. He gives me a nod. "Well, now you see why?" I lie back down. "So that at times like this, you would realize that it's your own dumb fault you're here."

There are few things in life that can make a person stronger than drowsiness. Eventually, everyone gets tired enough that all they care about is sleep. I'm not sure how long it took to conquer Aaron, but it was less than two hours, because I don't hear from him until the next morning. It makes us angry that the man, who we gave our precious medicine to for his daughters, charges us ten kina for sleeping the night. We are happy to leave Tanduanam and get out on the river.

We paddle the morning away, watching a twisting funnel of rising air reach to the clouds. Its invisible, swirling currents are outlined with hundreds of white-headed eagles effortlessly soaring high above the swamp and river. It takes six hours on Day 12 of our expedition to reach the Catholic Mission of Timbunke. The three local priests allow us to rest our weary bodies for two days in a rundown shack next to the mission airstrip. Fortunately, the airstrip supplies a trade store which will be our last chance to resupply until well on the other side of the Central Mountains.

Over the past twelve days, with only two days of rest, we have paddled over two hundred and fifty miles from Wewak. We have consumed twenty-four cups of rice, ten cans of stew, fourteen cans of fish, and twenty-eight small packages of crackers. Our next stretch of river will bring us to the base of the Central Mountains, measured on the map to be about the same distance we have already traveled. I figure it will take three weeks to cover our next two hundred and fifty miles because the current will be stronger. I stick to my original plan to save our fifty military ration meals, which are lighter and more compact, for our mountain crossing. We need an additional three weeks' worth of rice to go along with them. Much to the delight of the store owner, we buy six-weeks' worth of rice, along with three weeks' worth of canned foods and crackers.

To make room, I go through our gear carefully, leaving behind for the mission's use everything that is not absolutely essential: a snorkel, three large duffel bags, a how-to book on wildlife photography, several plastic fasteners, and a handful of clothes that are already wearing out.

We leave Timbunke on December 8th, Day 14 of the expedition. Our kayak sinks deep into the water with the extra weight of food and water. At least we don't have any ocean waves to battle, just a forceful current which seems to grow stronger with every passing mile. At high noon we bid the mighty Sepik River goodbye as we turn south on one of her tributaries, the Kawari River.

The next week moves as slowly as the banks along the rivers. After two days, we leave the Kawari, having reached the Korosmeri River; and then three days later, we join up with our final river before the mountains, the Salumei. There is little to do but paddle and sweat away the long hot days. Lunchtime becomes the most enjoyable part of the day. We tie off on stranded trees caught in the middle of the river. The sun keeps the mosquitoes away, and the massive army of ants, as persistent as they are, can't walk across fast-moving water. Our lunches mostly consist of a can of the nastiest tasting corned beef that either of us has ever eaten and a package of two salty, beef-flavored crackers. I swallow the corned beef as quickly as possible and do my best to wash the disgusting flavor out of my mouth with water, so as not to ruin the delicious tasting crackers which follow. I lie back on the bags, eating one little bite at a time, savoring every nibble, dreading the depression that always follows the last crumb. It will be another, relentless, twenty-four hours in New Guinea before I can begin my lunch ritual again.

Each night as the land grows dark, we search for shelter in a village. The fading blue of the sky fills with the gloomy forms of fur and skin, as giant bats, by the thousands, drift down from the southern highlands, their five-foot wing spans blowing down an eerie wind as they pass over our heads.

"Evil spirits," an old man had told us one night about the bats called flying foxes.

Each village welcomes us and leads us to their men's hut to rest and sleep. The walls of the huts are always riddled with ritualistic tools and masks, each one intricately decorated with teeth, bones, and brilliantly colored feathers. The huts are often guarded by towering demon statues, four times the size of a man.

When the night grows dark, a fire is built and a story teller is chosen to spin a tale of his struggle with the powerful spirits of the surrounding jungle. Though Aaron and I don't understand a word from the story tellers, their facial expressions and body language speak loudly to us. The farther we paddle, the more lost we become to the outside world, and as we go, the stories grow richer, springing to life amid flickering flames.

One night, the men of Mumeri village choose us to be the story tellers. "Oh, no, you wouldn't understand," I object. They wait for me to begin, not even comprehending my complaint. So Aaron and I, feeling quite stupid, start to tell of our home in America. Seeing their blank faces, we form an airplane with our hands. We fly it across the hut to show how long it took us to fly to their island. Puzzled looks cross their faces. Soon, we start shouting, "Wewak!", showing with our arms the waves crashing on her shores. Aaron sits on the back of a log bench and I on the front pretending to paddle out to sea. We wipe our foreheads in the hot sun. And then, there we are, back in the fierce seas of the north coast, fighting against the waves of that storm with the same energy, only this time before a crowd of "tisking" men. Their faces show us that, at least for the moment, they are in our kayak with us. Our faces speak horror when we see that big wave coming at us once again, striking us with such force that it throws us from the bench, spinning us in circles across the hut floor.

"Iiiiiieeeeeeeee," the men wail in unison.

We struggle for the log bench, but the waves pound our every effort, washing us to the far side of the hut where we can finally stand. The men sigh with the relief that comes with escape. They beg for more. We relive our trip over again that night, the fears, the mosquitoes, the long, laborious hours of paddling deeper into the trials and tribulations of the jungle. And the men understand! They have lived it every day of their lives! They understand our story better than our family and friends will—if we ever make it back home to tell it. Although we don't speak the same language as our new friends, we are at least beginning to share a familiar story of life in New Guinea.

Each morning we eat a half cup of rice with tinned fish and bid our village friends farewell. As we work our way up the forbidding waters of the Salumei River, the jungle walls creep closer together forming a winding trench that grows darker and lonelier every day. We are traveling back in time, with every passing village, the ragged clothes the people wear are being replaced with grass skirts. The few recognizable, broken English words of the pidgin trade language begin to fade into native talk. Languages completely change with each new village. The people have not yet experienced the influences of missionaries and are still wrapped in the ancient beliefs of their ancestors.

The sharp, swift bends of the Salumei grow closer together, the villages farther apart. Three-foot long lizards drop from the tree tops, disappearing in a splash beneath the river's surface.

Hundreds of cockatoos dart between the jungle cover, squawking continual warnings to us, reminding us that we do not belong. We slowly push flocks of ducks and other water fowl upriver. Giant black parrots with red heads rustle in the canopy. Rainbows of parakeets float up and down the river, while the butterflies continue to dance for us on wings of beauty. Crocodiles slide from the banks igniting our fears. The current steadily grows stronger, teaching us to work together. It takes one of us paddling at full strength to keep stabilized in the rushing water, while the other painstakingly pulls us upriver, one stroke at a time.

It is now nearing the end of Day 20 of our expedition, and the land begins to grow dark. We continue our nightly routine of searching for a hut to sleep in and have managed to find abandoned huts along the river bank, but it has been three days since we have come across a village or even another human being. However, the gardens surrounding these abandoned huts always seem to be picked clean of their fruits and vegetables. The vacant river reeks of mystery with all the signs of inhabitants but not a soul to be seen. We just hope they won't return in the middle of the night to find two strangers asleep on their floor. The setting sun reveals a garden on the high bank, but we can't see a hut.

"There has to be one nearby." Aaron urges me to keep on into the night.

"All right, we'll keep going, but we better camp if we don't see one in the next few minutes," I say. The night begins to cast its spell across the sky, speckled with the silent flight of bats. The jungle screams above eight-foot-high mud cliffs that hem us in on either side, running the entire length of both shores. These cliffs have been formed by endless erosion as small handfuls of dirt continuously slide into the water rushing by. Soon it is completely dark, robbing us of sight. Searching the blackness for the fire lights of a village, we paddle on into nothingness. In a panic we dig into our bags for flashlights, fastening their straps around our heads. Beams of light slash into a cloud of blood-thirsty mosquitoes that engulf us. Our small lights are little help in the overpowering darkness.

"Watch for crocodiles!" Aaron shouts from behind.

"Yeah, right," I respond in a helpless voice. We can't see if we are in the middle or towards the side of the river, nor which way the river bends. The battle rages in the thrusting current, our strokes interrupted with bloody slaps against feasting mosquitoes. Are we making any progress or losing serious ground? Then it begins to rain.

"Get to shore!" I scream in surrender.

"I'm trying!" comes Aaron's miserable voice, overshadowed by the intensifying jungle noises ringing like a loud siren. We come to a sudden stop, my flashlight picking up a mud wall that separates us from the jungle above. We quickly untie the bags, throwing them up and over the cliff as sheets of water fall down its face and under our slipping sandals as it flows into the river. I wedge my foot into a crevice in the dirt ledge that gushes draining water and pull myself up with the help of a tree root. Aaron pushes the nose of the kayak on end until I get hold of it and pull it over the lip. My feet go out from under me as I come crashing down in the thick mud. I roll over to find Aaron's white face appear over the edge of the river bank. I scramble onto my knees to help pull him up. Soon ants join the mosquitoes, sinking their little jaws into our skin. We dance about, stomping down the underbrush so we can get the kayak flipped over. We tie a long rope between two trees and pull our blue tarp over the top of the rope to escape the drenching rain. We get our hammocks up in record time, driven by swarming insects, and soon lie down in the hammocks, killing off the intruders that have managed to slip in with us. A package of crackers will have to suffice for dinner. We eat them, bouncing each other up and down on our inflated kayak bed with every little move. We are too exhausted to even talk. Soon Aaron is asleep.

I try to sleep, but a deep suspicion that something is watching me keeps me awake. On edge, I shine my flashlight against the leaves right beside my hammock. The biggest, ugliest spider I have ever seen sits with his glowing eyes fixed on me. Beneath his eyes hang large, nasty fangs. The spider's thick, hairy legs are tightly crouched, ready to pounce on any part of my body that leans against the netting that separates us. "Aaron! I see a bird-eating spider, like we read about." But, he is sound asleep. I move toward the opposite side of my hammock after flicking a centipede onto the ground, and try to forget about my creepy foe.

Several hours later, a herd of wild pigs wakes us as they noisily make their way into our camp. Their squeals dart in all directions once they become aware of us.

"I sure am glad we took that shakedown trip across Willard Bay back in Utah to prepare us for all of this," I say. We laugh ourselves back to sleep. Like two aliens, we are lost in time, hidden in a little section of jungle beneath an endless green canopy. Beside us, the Salumei River funnels the interior rains out to the roaring coast. We lie within a cocoon of protective netting, covered with a multitude of creepy-crawly explorers searching for a way in. And as we sleep, the black New Guinea sky pours forth its drink upon the land, beating against the tarp above, sometimes dripping onto our sweaty, exhausted bodies. Above the drench, we hear the echoing roar of the jungle, and as the hours pass, the river rises higher.

By morning, the river has flooded its mud-cliff banks, spilling out across the jungle floor. It comes within a few feet of washing away our equipment and food bags. The fact that it didn't happen is just one more of the many reasons we have for giving thanks to God.

We continue our upriver battle early in the morning. The currents of the higher flood waters whip around a long bend just ahead of us. Moving too fast for us, we paddle across its main stream to take the shorter, inside corner of the bend. To avoid the whitewater, we are forced to put down our paddles, strip down to our boxers, and step out into the water on the shore to pull the kayak.

As Aaron rolls over the edge of the kayak, splashing into the knee-deep water, the front of his leg reveals a festering sore that spits out black pus. He grabs the front tie line and begins limping along the shallows, dragging the heavy kayak behind him. I shove the end of my paddle beneath the green bag, pushing the load from behind. He hesitates for a moment to splash water onto his oozing sore.

It had started just a few days before as an innocent-looking in-grown hair. He popped it without a moment's thought, forgetting that infection runs rampant in the humid tropics. Now, just two days later, the sore has become a hole deep enough to engulf a Q-tip soaked with iodine. We had read so much about the horrors of tropical infection that we decided to leave our razors at home and grow beards on the trip. Microscopic creatures drift about the jungle atmosphere feeding on the slightest cuts.

We pull past the bend, jump back in and paddle up to the next bend in the river.

The lonely day of solitude begins bonding us together. To help pass the long hours, we tell stories of better times gone by, times of childhood and irresponsibility, when life was carefree and simple, when being a kid was just having fun. There was always food on the table and friends knocking on the door to see if we could come out to play. We talk about our boarding schools and we laugh at all the pranks when we made fools out of our teachers and friends. We remember romance, the thrill of teenage love, and the pretty girls who had brightened our past. We laugh, remembering all the wonders of being a child. But it all seems so long ago now, and our laughter falls away into the silent meditation that comes from endless paddling. Soon, Aaron puts down his paddle and turns around to face me. He stares deep into my eyes and thoughts.

"I didn't realize until now, all that I have left behind," he says sadly. He is looking past me now, down the winding river. "I'm not going back, am I?"

"No," I gently confirm what has already been revealed in his heart. I understand. When I left the mountains and my tepee, buried beneath the drifting snows of last winter, I was different! I couldn't tell you exactly when I changed, or even how, only that I had. God will allow us to choose our classroom—for Aaron and me an island wilderness—but the lesson is His to teach! We must be willing to let go of old treasures in order to find new ones. In my journal, I had written myself a goodbye note the night before we launched from the shores of Wewak. Today, Aaron has realized that God is making him into a new creature. The old things are passing away; new things are coming.

He glances down river one last time before turning back around in silence. He reaches down to pick up his paddle and begin again. Then, to a slow and steady rhythm, he begins to sing.

"Lord, you are my God,
and I will ever praise You.
Lord, you are my God,
and I will ever praise You.
I will seek You in the morning,
and I will learn to walk in Your ways,
And step by step You'll lead me,
and I will follow You all of my days.
Step by step You'll lead me,
and I will follow You all of my days!"

The longer he sings, the harder he pulls his paddle through the water and the louder his voice grows. "Onward!" he shouts, his voice full of confidence. "Onward to Daru!"

CHAPTER 6

Inaru

I stare in shock across a kitchen table at Aaron who is busily loading his mouth with food. His fork, moving in and out of his mouth in a blur leaves a little from each bite behind on his beard. I look down at the plate in front of me: roasted chicken, a heap of mashed potatoes and turkey dressing smothered in rich, creamy gravy. American voices fill the mosquito-free room. Women are busy cleaning in the kitchen amidst the sound of playing children. The pleasant faces of several men around the table watch Aaron's long shaggy hair bounce with every move of his crazed feeding. Charlie Minter, Jay, Rudy, George, Wayne, and Mike. I grip my fork, my fingers aching with the pain that has come after five hundred miles of paddling. I take a bite, savoring the wondrous flavors in my mouth. It tastes incredible! I think to myself how our expedition has taken such a glorious and unbelievable change for the better.

It was enough for us that we had come across a village so high on the lonely Salumei River. It had been so long since we had seen or talked to anyone, that even the foreign tongues of the nationals brought us human comfort. But God has been faithful once again to meet our needs above and beyond anything we could possibly dream or imagine. An old man led us into his village to introduce us to three New Tribe missionary families who had been adopted by his people, the people of the Inaru tribe. And, as if that wasn't enough, other missionary families had flown into the village's airstrip from neighboring tribes to celebrate Christmas ten days before the actual holiday. December 15th was the only time they could all get together, as one big family, to celebrate the birth of our King.

To top it all off, they were just sitting down to their Christmas dinner when Aaron and I came along. After they recovered from the wildness of our looks and the surprise of our visit, they gave us a bar of soap and towels to wash with before inviting us in. Then they unloaded their hospitality on us.

It is taking me some time to recover from this enjoyable surprise. One moment we are living on rice and canned meat, wondering how we will ever get across the intimidating mountains which loom before us. Then, in one bend of the river, everything changes. Now we are dining with friendly souls celebrating the true spirit of Christmas. We meet Santa with a large bag loaded with gifts. He has some for Aaron and me to open: a can of peaches, a jar of peanuts, a bottle of mosquito repellant and itching cream, Christmas gifts they say we will need on our journey.

We spend that night and the next day visiting and laughing with all our new friends, and trying to adjust to our radical change of diet. We tell about the countless miles paddling and our hopes of crossing the Central Mountains. They, in turn, provide us with warnings and advice but are careful not to rob us of our hope. They understand what it means to chase after things that don't make a lot of sense to other people. After all, they have given up their lives in America to come and live with primitive tribes, to learn their languages and understand their customs so that they can prepare an accurate translation of the Bible.

The following day at lunch, Wayne shows us where he had his nose pierced by an old man with the sharp sticker found on sago palms. Wayne stuck a tooth pick, much to the disgust of his wife, through the pierced hole that penetrated the cartilage separating his nostrils.

"Will this old man pierce my nose?" Aaron asks.

"You're not getting your nose pierced," I quickly respond.

"I will if I want to."

"Oh no you won't." My face grows angry. "You will not put this expedition in jeopardy or use our valuable antibiotics just so you can have a party trick when you get home." Aaron decides not to push the issue and finishes eating. After lunch, a plane lands on the airstrip to take the three visiting families back to their villages.

George calls us on the radio after he arrives back at Bosorio, his village located fifteen miles southwest of Inaru. He informs Aaron and me that four of his men are interested in helping us carry our gear over the mountains for six kina a day. He arranges for us to meet them three days upriver from Inaru where a konda- vine bridge stretches across the Salumei. It will take his men two days to hike there from their village of Bosorio.

When Rudy and Jay hear these plans over the radio, they decide to take some of the Inaru men and go with us in dugout canoes up to the bridge. They can introduce us to our carriers and serve as translators between us. It seems like things just get brighter and brighter! The only bad news is we will have to leave Inaru the next morning in order to meet the men on time. Inaru has been too wonderful a place, a refuge that will be hard to leave.

That night at dinner, we hear a knock at the door. A young village man asks to talk to Rudy, who follows him out into the darkness. When Rudy returns through the door, he has lost his smile. "You two better come with me," he tells us. We get up and follow him back out into the mosquito-filled darkness.

"Sorry to cut your meal short, but a problem has come up that you should learn about if you're going to attempt to cross the mountains." Aaron and I give each other a nervous look as we follow him down the trail.

"What problem?" Aaron questions him.

"Have you guys come across any leeches yet?"

"No."

"There aren't too many in the lowlands; the mosquitoes are the problem there. In the mountains, the leeches will become your new misery." He stops and turns around in the moonlight showing us the skin of his arm. "They twirl around in circles on the ground and vegetation, searching for something warm and alive to cling to when it walks by." His finger twirls in imitation and then finds his arm. "Once they get on you, they stick a hook down through your skin and inject your bloodstream with serum."

"Sick," Aaron murmurs.

"That serum thins out your blood so they can suck it easier." He explains this when a low, mournful wail comes from the hut at the end of the trail. Three men are waiting for us on the porch of Rudy's hut, one of them sitting hunched over with both hands on his face. He rocks slowly back and forth, in pain. Rudy kneels down and gently puts his hand on the man's shoulder, helping him up and into the light of the hut. He speaks softly to him in the man's language as he sits him down in a chair. He cocks the man's head back. Rudy carefully pries the man's eyelids apart with his fingers. Aaron and I step back in horror! A two-inch, black leech clings to the center of the man's eyeball! The long, slimy body of the leech convulses as it takes its drink of blood through the surface of the man's eye. The man wails to the rhythm of its sucking motions.

"Lord, have mercy!" Aaron prays, looking away from the gruesome sight.

"I'll try to get it out with tweezers." Rudy starts briskly searching nearby drawers for the instrument. "If this doesn't work," he says, holding the tweezers up, "then we'll have to smoke it out." Rudy tries to calm the man by speaking gently to him. He holds the man's bloodshot eye open once again and pinches down on the leech, but its slimy body quickly wiggles free. It begins twirling in a circle to avoid the tweezers as Rudy patiently tries several more times to get it. Finally he gets a good grip on the end of its body. He pulls!

"Iiiiiiiiieeeeeeee," the man cries out. His friends join in with cries of sympathy. The man's eyeball pulls forward as the tweezers stretch the leech out long and thin. Then suddenly, like a rubber band, the leech snaps free of Rudy's grip back into the man's eyeball! His eyelids fly shut from the impact, and he grabs his eye once again.

"Missed," mutters Rudy, cocking the man's head back again. When he pulls the man's eyelids open, no leech is found.

"Did he come out? See if you can find it on the floor," he tells us. We get down on our hands and knees and begin a careful search.

"I see him," Rudy says, disappointed. "He's crawled up into the corner of his eye." I stand up and look for the leech which is barely visible now, hiding deep in the man's tear duct. Rudy speaks to the man's friends for a long time.

"They are going to build a fire and smoke it out," he tells us in defeat. "I'm afraid there is nothing else we can do for him."

"Every minute," Aaron says.

Rudy gives him a strange look, "What's that?"

"When we're hiking in the mountains, we're going to be checking our face for leeches every minute," Aaron explains.

"They're even harder to get out of your ears," Rudy adds with a grin.

"Like I said, every minute."

That night Aaron and I sleep in the Minter's hut on a large cushion. It is so comfortable that I don't even want to fall asleep, knowing that the morning will come too soon. I have no idea when our next chance to sleep in such comfort will come again.

I was right. The morning comes too soon. "Thank you very much for the breakfast, Carol," I tell her. She smiles at me. "Aaron, I'm afraid we have some work to do," I announce, standing up from the table. Aaron quickly grabs another piece of toast to eat on his way out. Charlie walks over and unlocks his office hut where our equipment is stored.

"Thanks, Charlie," I say. "If you don't mind, there are a few things I would like to talk over with Aaron before we tackle the Central Mountains." Aaron looks rather uncomfortable with my comment, but Charlie shows that he understands and makes his way back to his hut. Aaron sits down on one of the bags looking very much like he would rather be somewhere else.

"What is it?" His voice sounds worried as he finishes his last bite of toast.

"My hands hurt," I start. He gives me a blank look. "Every morning I have to go through a painful stretching process just to open them and half-way use them."

"Sorry." He gives me an unsure shrug.

"I'm not after your sympathy. I simply want to know why my hands hurt so bad, and yours don't."

"I don't know." He is looking down.

"I didn't either, not until a few days ago on the river." He looks up at me with a blank face. "I always wondered why you liked the back of the kayak so much. I let you sit there because I didn't like hassling with the steering all the time. A few days ago, though, I figured out what you were up to." He starts fidgeting. "You can see me from the back of the kayak, but I can't see you from the front. So I think to myself, maybe he isn't paddling very hard back there, taking little vacations behind my back!" Aaron won't look at me. "A few days ago I decided to test my theory by checking up on you. Several times, if you'll recall, I swung around without warning to look at you. I'm afraid you didn't pass my little test . . . ."

"I paddled!" Aaron defends himself. I stare at the top of his head as he continues looking at the floor.

"Did you paddle as hard as I did?" I hold him in my stare. He doesn't answer me. "I busted you several times not paddling at all, and when I did catch you paddling, it wasn't very hard, not very hard at all." I walk to the other side of the hut. "I used to feel the pain in my hands and fingers and wonder if there was something wrong with them, maybe arthritis or something." I walk back over to him. "But now I feel the pain, and I get angry, downright mad. I get mad at you! Because now I know that I've been pulling more than just my share of the weight, and with the Central Mountains of New Guinea as our next obstacle, I'm here to tell you, Aaron, I'm not going to do that anymore!"

"I'm sorry," he whispers, peeking up at me.

"I don't want your sympathy or your apologies."

"Then what do you want?"

"I want change! I want you to learn to think for yourself, Aaron. You just stand around and do nothing until I tell you what to do. If you'd just figure out by yourself what needs to be done and then do it, I wouldn't need to be so bossy all the time."

"Well, I thought you were the expedition leader," he says.

"I am. But, I'm not your mother." The room fills with silence. "Aaron, we have come a long way. We have paddled five hundred miles. I led and you followed. I told you what to do and you did it. But we were never a team. We were never two minds, two hearts, two different sets of talents and gifts working together for the common goal." I place my hand on his shoulder. He feels tense. "Do you see what's in front of us now? Do you understand what it means to try to cross the world's most rugged and unexplored jungle terrain? You can't rely on me to get you across, because I just can't do it. Life is about to get rough, rougher than either of us have ever experienced before, and I don't want to take these mountains on with a follower behind me. I don't want to try to cross them with the help of a boy. I need you to be an individual. I want a man by my side when things get ugly and turn against us."

"I know."

"It's going to take everything I have and everything you've got to make it, everything! What you don't know how to do, you're going to have to let me teach you. . . ."

"You're going to have to be willing to teach me," he interrupts, looking at me. "If I have to learn to take responsibility, then you have to learn to give it. And if you want me to speak and help make the decisions, then you have to learn to listen and respect what I have to say." He is pleading. I think for a moment.

"You're right. I haven't been trusting you, and I guess that's the same as me treating you like a child." I pause. "For that, I apologize. Who and what you are isn't my business anyway, that's between you and God. So from now on, I'll start treating you like a man."

"What exactly does that mean?" Aaron doesn't look too comfortable with my new commitment.

"It just means that if it's your turn to cook, then I won't do it for you, even if you don't know how. I will teach you though, if you ask me to. If not, I guess we go hungry. It means when we stop to make camp, I won't tell you what you have to do. I'll let you figure it out for yourself. I guess what it means is that I'm now willing to let you fail, so that you can learn. And I will listen to you because I know that the same God who lives inside of me also lives inside of you, which gives us both the same potential—to be used by Him on our journey. So I'll try and give more responsibility and you try and take more. Does that sound like a deal?" I reach out my hand. We shake hands and then embrace each other. "We'll make it across . . . We'll make it with our God," I pull away, making him look at me. "We'll do it *together*. But to do that, we have to be honest with each other."

"Yes," he agrees, shutting his eyes. "Lord, our God, we ask that You show us mercy! Show us how to love You by teaching us how to love each other."

"And grant us the courage and the strength to drink from this cup that you have set before us. Amen," I say. And then I leave him alone.

It isn't long before Rudy and Jay start yelling from the river that they are ready to go. I meet Aaron on his way to the river with about three times the weight of a normal load.

"Don't go killing yourself now," I say, smiling. He looks right at me as I take some bags from him.

"I'm ready," he tells me.

"Onward to Daru then."

∗　　∗　　∗

Goodbyes are always quick when you don't want to say them. Leaving the hospitality of Inaru for the hostility of the jungle doesn't make much sense. Charlie trots along the bank with his video camera in one hand and waves goodbye to us with the other.

"Be sure and radio us from Daru," his fading voice calls to us. Soon all the comforts of Inaru vanish like a dream, dissolving in the miseries of the battling current. Rudy and Jay have mastered upriver travel. They each brought their own thirty-foot dugout, fully equipped with two highly-skilled village men, one for the front and one for the back of their canoes. It is evident from the muscular frames of their paddling teams that Rudy and Jay have carefully chosen the strongest men that the Inaru tribe has to offer. The men have wooden paddles with thick, dagger-like teeth carved into the ends of them which dig deep into the gravel floor of the river. The paddles are also long enough so that the men, while standing in the canoes, can push off the bottom, giving them excellent leverage as they force their way quickly upriver. This makes perfect sense to Aaron and me. When the powerful currents of a river are trying to force you backwards, then the part of the river that isn't moving, namely the bottom, is the best place to push off for leverage. Unfortunately, it takes us several painful falls before we discover that this technique doesn't work so well in a narrow, inflatable sea kayak with rounded paddles. Our paddle strokes get robbed of power by the current swiftly moving in the opposite direction.

Both canoes wait for us around several bends before Jay informs us that the men want to hunt tree kangaroos. I recognize one of the men as the one who had the leech in his eye. Rudy told us that they had successfully smoked it out, and he looks fine now. We all agree that the best plan is for them to push upriver until three in the afternoon when they will stop and wait for us to catch up. The men can hunt while Rudy and Jay set up camp for the night.

The day falls into an agonizing routine that wears our patience thin. The Salumei begins to roar, deep and steady, as its whitewater pounds its way through a maze of boulders and log jams. Its winding path sharply bows back and forth, forcing us to wade along the shore, pulling our kayak around these frequent bends. The slick moss-covered stones hiding beneath the rushing surface make our going treacherous. Our feet take such a beating that we eventually dig our hiking boots out of the gear bags.

It is a frustrating several hundred yards of exhausting work before we can finally reach the swift arching currents as the river turns away from us and around a point. The outside edge of the turn proves to be the longer and harder way around as the currents constantly swing our kayak onto shore. The only answer to this problem is to paddle across to the opposite shore to take on the swifter, but shorter, inside corner. Paddling with all our might across the main stream of the river is always depressing as we watch a hard-earned fifty yards of shoreline fall away. After making up the lost ground, we have to wade deep into the swirling currents spinning around the tip of the protruding point. The lead rope digs into my shoulders as I lean into the incoming whitewater, searching desperately for foot and handholds, anything to help me move a little farther around the rocky point. By the time we have the battle won, all we can do is crawl ashore on hands and knees, trying to catch our breaths. Somehow we must find the energy to start the process all over again by pulling up to the next straightaway which leads to the next bend. We repeat the exhausting routine over and over again, all day long.

The sun sinks below the tree line as giant bats, "evil spirits," drift overhead on dark wings, vanishing into the coming night. Again my foot slips out from under me, taking the other one with it. I crash face-first into the shallow water, striking my already sore knee against the rocks below. The cool water rushes up to meet my over-heated face as I drift backwards for a moment before finding my footing again.

"Iiiieee," I moan, massaging my swollen knee. "Wait up!" I yell, but Aaron continues pulling from the front, slapping at the cloud of horse flies swarming around his head. He stumbles, and that is all I need to catch up. The walls of vegetation, holding us in their shadowy grip, spring into noisy life. The orange water of the river, our adversary, slowly turns blood red and then black night approaches.

"Rest," I shout, pulling the end of the kayak up onto the gravel shore. Aaron collapses on a flat, moss-covered boulder. "You worked hard today," I tell him. He groans in agreement. "I'm proud of you." He rolls over on his side and attempts a smile.

"How much farther do you figure they went?" he asks.

"Too far, I'm sure." I dig the flashlights out of the green bag. Aaron rolls over onto his back.

"I feel weak all over," he moans.

"Well, you've been pushing and pulling like a madman all day," I say, looking at him.

"I need food." Aaron curls up on the moss carpet.

"I'm impressed with your response to our little talk this morning. So don't get me wrong, but you're going to kill yourself working like you did today." I pause, slapping a horse fly biting the back of my neck. "You don't owe me anything you know." He looks at me. "I mean, don't feel like you have to prove anything or make up for anything from the past. All we need worry about now is what's ahead of us. I'll take my share of it, and all I'm asking is that you take yours . . . no less, but no more either." I toss him his flashlight.

"All right," he agrees, with a whimpering grin as he pulls his weary body from its perch and harnesses the lead rope around his shoulders. It cuts into his skin as he leans forward, helping me pull the stranded load back out into the water. "I hope this water is too swift for crocodiles," he comments before pulling upriver.

The troubles of traveling by day worsen by night. The tormenting mosquitoes come to replace the flies. The flashlights don't help prevent our constant falling down. Every stone beneath our boots is slippery, whether we can see them or not. Each time I fall and strike the rocks with my sore body, my frustration swells, along with my bruises. It takes all my concentration to hold my tongue, to get back up and carry on. Several times, I come close to losing my temper, but realize it takes too much energy. The hours pass as we stumble our way slowly upstream, pushing our bodies and souls far beyond their limits.

The only good thing about the pitch black of night is that it prevents us from seeing the weary slowness of our progress. Aaron slips and falls hard. My flashlight picks up the water that sprays from his splash. He quickly drifts underneath the kayak, struggling to free himself before he makes it up onto his knees.

"I can't take this!" he screams, violently slapping the water with his hands. He looks at me, his long, drained face illuminated in the night by the flashlight strapped across his forehead. "I can't make it much further, Joel . . . I just can't." I look behind us to the flowing water quickly disappearing beyond the scope of my flashlight beam. A strip of brilliant stars outlines the gap in the canopy overhead. The jungle screams at us from both sides.

"What other choice do we have?" I ask him. He swings around with a jerk on the rope and starts heaving back into the current. His anger burning his last remaining energy.

My mind becomes dull, protecting itself from the miserable reality at hand. I move through the night, forgetting where I am, ignoring the mosquitoes that drink my blood, falling and getting back up again without hardly noticing. My body tingles with exhaustion. Like birds, my thoughts fly from treetop to treetop but never choose a place to land. My hands shake as they thrust the kayak forward. A light appears in front of us, flickering in the late night. It grows closer before my mind is able to comprehend that it is the welcoming firelight that marks the end of twelve hours of agony.

My ears ring in my head as Rudy and Jay come to help us. In my exhausted stupor, I can't really make out all that they are saying. They must have done most of the unloading as well as the cooking. I only remember sitting next to the fire, trying to recover.

Hot rice with tinned fish helps me to regain some energy, enough to set up my hammock and bedding on the bottom of the kayak.

Rain hits the tarp overhead as I wipe away as many ants as possible before climbing into my hammock. Aaron moves on the other half of the inflated tubes. The coolness that comes from the rain allows me to roll up in my blanket, and soon I sleep.

Moments later, my eyes shoot open. I feel stings of pain all over. I grab my flashlight and find my blanket covered with ants and the inner netting full of mosquitoes. I kill them all and shut off my light. If I turn my light back on and there are more, then I know I have a hole somewhere in the net. I flash my beam back on, see a centipede and quickly flick it off my arm. I aim the light toward the end of my hammock where, to my utter horror, I find my feet sticking out through ripped netting into the open night. I freeze! My protective shell is useless as an army of New Guinea's little scavengers scurry up my blanket to feed on me. I stare, motionless, my mind racing. Pity fills me—I feel helpless and victimized, sorry that I have come to cross this miserable island. The thought of giving up comes to me, then the ants start to bite again, snapping me into a rage.

"It's too much! Too much!" I scream with all my strength! I feel Aaron's response, a sudden flinch that rushes through the kayak.

"What is it?" His voice sounds afraid. I explode!

"I warn you, Aaron, not a word! Don't you say a word, or I'll kill you! I'll kill everything that lives!" I scream, as I roll out of my hammock.

"What happened?" I rush his hammock, my face against its netting.

"I said not a word!" My violence quiets him. I rip my blanket out of the hole in my hammock, shaking it off in a violent storm of cursing, and then shove it back in. "I'm coming back to this island with a bomb, I'm going to blow up the whole damn thing . . . everything will die." I start to laugh maniacally as I untie a piece of parachute cord from the tarp overhead and tie the torn end of my hammock down tight. I crawl back in, my face tingling from the intense release of madness. I begin to taunt my little enemies.

"Oh, come on in. All of you, come in . . . if you want to die!" I zip up the hammock, trapping several ants and mosquitoes. I feel crazy! I crush the abdomen of a large ant. "How does that feel? Does that feel good?" I wound some more, enjoying their dying squirms. "What goes around, comes around! What goes around, comes around! What goes around, comes around!" I chant, slapping mosquitoes. An ant bites my leg. I close my eyes to the pain, then open them. "You bite me. I'll bite you back!" Reaching down with my finger, I crush its head against my leg. "There now, you're all dead!" I whisper in anger to the little bodies of dead insects covering my blanket. With my foot space now reduced, I curl up into a claustrophobic ball to try to find sleep in my insanity.

Everyone grows quiet as I approach the fire the next morning. It's embarrassing to have to apologize to everyone for my extreme, late-night outburst. They all assure me that they understand. I sit down and breathe in the smell of the boiling rice on the fire. Aaron sits next to me, his eyes watching me to make sure I have recovered. He still hasn't said anything. So, I give him a wink, and he seems to relax a little more. Having made my amends, I sit and watch the village men, loaded down with spears, hunt for crocodiles in a deep canal just across the river.

"Why don't you guys go ahead of us today and let the men finish their hunt?" Jay suggests.

"You catching up with us sounds easier than the other way around," I agree. Rudy smiles.

"Sorry you had to paddle so far into the night. I guess we kind of underestimated how long it would take you," he apologizes.

"It's not your fault, but it sounds like a good idea to let us go first," I say, finishing my rice. Aaron takes down camp without me having to tell him to, while I tie down the gear. We are back out on the river within ten minutes.

By noon, Aaron and I have pulled over onto a sand bar to rest after four hours of fighting the mounting currents. We are sprawled out, searching for energy and sipping water when the two canoes pull up.

"They killed him!" Rudy shouts, holding up the tail of a crocodile. It is enough to get us on our feet again. We walk over to find a nine-foot croc, lying belly-up, in the bottom of one of the dugouts, its dagger teeth protruding from all sides of its clamped-shut mouth.

"Which one killed it?" Aaron asks. Jay translates. One of the men proudly steps forward. The tip of the spear that he holds in his hand is dramatically bent to one side. Then, his face turns serious as he begins to act out the story. He imagines that the "Great Water Spirit" is alive once more. He raises his spear slowly above his head then thrusts it deep into the sandy-colored head of the croc. He holds on with all his might to the end of the spear, as the croc thrashes in all directions. His companions cheer him on. They race into the scene, each character with his own important part to play. Spears jab, bush knives slash until, with the stillness of the crocodile's death, they break forth into a victory dance.

After telling us about the hunt, the canoes, along with Rudy and Jay, leave us behind once again. They are looking for a camp where they can cook the croc meat before it spoils. They promise they won't go too far.

Our pace slows as the day wears on. We are just too exhausted with the frequent rapids sapping our energy. We take another short rest before attempting to pass through the longest and swiftest rapids we have yet encountered. I study the swift current before beginning the steady pull. The rope digs into my shoulders. I feel completely exhausted as I near the end of the rapid, only ten feet in front of me. I stop and try to rest, something I should never do. A wave knocks me off balance, and I lose my footing. I search for something beneath the surface to hang on to, but the current sweeps me away. Everything is too smooth and slick. Aaron pauses at the back of the kayak, his eyes filling with hate as I helplessly drift past him. He knows that he can't hold the kayak by himself in the powerful flow of the river. When the water sucks me under, I instinctively hold onto the rope, which quickly tightens, yanking the front of the kayak around. And so we lose all the hard-fought ground we have just pulled through. I am in the lead, helpless, with the rope towing the kayak, which in turn drags Aaron across the rocks all the way to the calmer waters at the base of the whitewater. Aaron, who is too angry to speak, takes the rope from me, not impressed at all with my performance. His anger is quite ironic when the whole process repeats once again, only this time with Aaron dragging us away. Eventually, we manage our way through the rapids, only to find that our idiotic routine has been witnessed by several spectators. Atop a large boulder, just up from the end of the rapid, sits an audience of ten men. The closer we get to the boulder, the louder their laughter rings out over the roar of the river. We don't care. This boulder is the meeting place for the mountain carriers that George has sent from his village, and marking the golden end to the upriver leg of our expedition. The feeling of accomplishment balances out the humility of our recent performance. We tie our kayak off and climb the boulder to meet our carriers.

"Joel, Aaron, this is Stew." Rudy introduces a man whose large brows cast shadows across his deep-set eyes. His jaw muscles protrude from the sides of his face which is covered in black sideburns. He tilts his head slightly as he extends his muscular arm to shake my hand. His bright, turquoise-colored shirt is missing most of its buttons, something he doesn't seem to mind.

"Happy nun," we greet him.

"This is Mowga," Rudy says. Mowga is younger than Stew, with a large round head and puffy cheeks, giving him a boyish appearance. He looks a bit out of shape with his belly hanging down over the front of his shorts and his skin covered in ringworm. But his face peels open in a huge, friendly grin as we shake his hand and greet him.

"Aguy," Rudy says, of the next man in line. Aguy is taller than the others and skinnier; he wears a highlander's cap on his head made from the twined fibers of tree bark and several brilliantly colored parrot feathers. Below his hat, his large, very wide nose with big nostrils, stands out from his otherwise ordinary-looking face. He seems a bit shy when shaking our hands because he looks away, down the river.

"Happy nun," we say, greeting him.

"And this is Sogamoi." Rudy finishes his introductions.

Sogamoi is the kindest-looking soul I have ever seen, and I immediately like him. His face holds a certain humility. A smaller man than the others, Sogamoi looks as though he is built to endure just about anything. His eyes dance with joy as his face reveals a balance between the compassion of a child and the strength of a man. "Happy nun," he says, shaking our hands firmly.

"Happy nun, nice to meet you all," Aaron and I say together.

From the boulder, we move upriver a few hundred yards where another smaller river flows into the Salumei, forming a strip of land where the men have made camp. Just a few hundred feet farther up the Salumei, we see the konda bridge: a web of thick, long vines falling from the top of a tall tree towards the water for some distance before stretching across the rapids to rise steeply into the high branches of a tree on the opposite shore. The vine bridge seems so ancient and lost, a symbol of how far we have come and how far we are going. The vines are like a passage, a gateway to a place untouched by the changing world around it. It invites us deeper into our quest, to lead us into places that men such as ourselves should probably never go.

"Once we cross that bridge," I whisper to Aaron, "we will be past the point of no return."

The sky turns black and begins to pour down rain as we hurry to set up our tarp. It becomes a shelter for all of us as we soon realize the storm isn't going to blow over. In the rain the men can't cook any of the crocodile meat.

"Ask our carriers if they know where the Lagaip River is. It flows west to east somewhere on the other side of these mountains," I say to Jay, who in turn speaks to the men.

"They don't know of this river. They have never been where you are going," Jay announces. "The names of these rivers on your maps will do you no good. They are the English names given by Australians. These men call the Salumei River the Celum. You will have to describe the river to the people that you meet along the way, just as the men described their crocodile hunt to you today," he explains.

"All right," I agree. "How long do they think it will take us to cross the mountains?" Rudy talks to the men. "They say seven days."

"Sweet," Aaron quickly adds.

"There is something you need to know about New Guinea people," Rudy looks a little uncomfortable. "They um, how should I say . . . lie."

"It's not that they are purposely trying to deceive you. They just tell you what they think you want to hear," Jay adds.

"Take the crocodile they killed this morning, for instance," Rudy jumps back in. "They will tell you it's huge, if they think you are excited about the hunt. They'll tell you it's small, if you seem afraid. If you don't look like you want to hike for a long time, they will tell you how close your destination is. It all depends on how they perceive your desires. It really doesn't matter how big the actual crocodile is, or how far your destination truly is."

"We ran into that on the Sepik," Aaron speaks up.

"So how long do *you* think it will take us to cross the mountains?" I ask.

"My rule is, take what they tell you and double it," Rudy says.

"Two weeks is probably more realistic," Jay agrees with him.

The crocodile hunters sit watching the mountain people strip down, wrap their clothes and cover themselves with large leaves they have plucked from the surrounding bushes.

"They are going to sleep in a hut up on the side of this ridge," Rudy explains.

"Why don't your men go sleep in the hut with them?" Aaron is curious.

"They are afraid."

"Of what?"

"You must remember that these two tribes have quite a long history of turmoil. Some of their fathers have eaten each other," Jay says with a sigh. "You can't expect age-old scars to heal overnight."

The mountain men say their goodbyes and then vanish into the pouring rain. After dinner, when the other men go to their tents, I sit in the falling darkness. Below me is a small river, a tributary of the Salumei. It's barely bigger than a stream, only a couple of feet deep, but our kayak only needs six inches in order to float.

"Well, God has conquered the ocean and the upriver legs, I guess, tomorrow it's time for the mountains," Aaron says after climbing into his hammock.

"See that stream down there, Aaron?" He leans up against his netting and stares down at the water below.

"That's all we need . . . just got to find something that big on the other side of the Centrals. If we can just find a stream that big, it will take us to the Lagaip." I close my eyes, memorizing the sound of its gushing water.

"That's all we need."

CHAPTER 7

The Mountains

The carriers have arrived with some new faces. We are introduced to Stew's wife, Agomi, who is toting a large belum full of sago. Belum bags, which all the natives have, are made from the fibers of tree bark. The fiber is rolled into strong, thin strings that are tied together to form large net bags. There's another thinner but tougher-looking woman who, except for her breasts, looks more like a man. She seems quite a bit older than Agomi. Both women wear grass skirts and rotting, dirt-stained t-shirts. A long, black loop, made from the stalk of a Cassowary feather, hangs from the older woman's right earlobe, and a dirty, cloth hat covers most of her short afro. Her face shows little emotion as she gives us a slight nod when introduced. She then proceeds to light a large cigar wrapped up in dried leaves. A boy in his early teens stands by her side; his name is Eabay. He wears a grass skirt, and is armed with a hardwood bow, strung up with a vine. He waves his greetings with his other hand holding several sharp-tipped bamboo arrows and his bush knife.

"The men have brought these three along to help carry and gather their food along the way. You do not need to pay them," Rudy informs us.

We divide our equipment between the four carriers. Sogamoi volunteers to carry the heavy kayak, now deflated, rolled up, and tied to a backpack frame. We give Mowga the green bag loaded down with the military rations, rice, and crackers. The rest of the gear we divide and load into two belum bags. Stew and Aguy heave their loaded belums up onto their backs, securing the long ends over their shoulders as they tie the load in place just below their necks. Our long kayak paddles are designed to break down into two pieces; we take half of a paddle, leaving the other hand free to use our bush knives.

Seeing that we are ready, the older woman blows out a big puff of smoke which rises slowly in the humid air. She pulls her belum filled with potatoes up onto her shoulders, slipping the knot that holds it together over her forehead. This frees her hands, allowing her to take a few more puffs from her cigar before pulling her bush knife from its place in the trunk of a tree; it has no handle. She turns around in a cloud of smoke and begins hacking her way into the dense brush. The men follow her lead.

"I guess this is goodbye . . .," I say sadly to Rudy and Jay.

"Goodbye . . . to a lot of things," Aaron adds, putting on his pack.

"Thank you for your valuable help." I shake their hands with sincere appreciation.

"Don't forget to radio us when you make it to Daru," Rudy reminds us, shaking Aaron's hand. Aaron turns to stare into the distant jungle.

"Will we make Daru?" he asks, turning back toward us. Rudy and Jay look rather uncomfortable.

"We will be praying for you," says Jay, slapping the back of his neck.

"Please do," I say, raising my hand to wave goodbye. The cheers and shouts of encouragement from our two missionary friends and the crocodile men quickly fade into the jungle buzz.

We follow the sound of our carriers' hacking bush knives, along a trail of freshly cut vines, bushes, and tree limbs. My eyes search the ground for poisonous snakes as we jump logs in a mad attempt to catch up. The fear of being left behind moves us along quickly. We catch a glimpse of our kayak as it drifts silently up the side of a steep ridge tied to Sogamoi's back. Aaron bounds up the web of exposed tree roots just ahead of me, pulling himself up the steep bank and holding onto long green vines dangling from the high branches of the thick canopy above us. I follow behind him with no time to spare, as Sogamoi has nearly disappeared again.

"No!" I look up to see Aaron, legs flailing, sliding swiftly towards me, wailing as his body slams across tree roots. I launch myself across the ledge just as he crashes through my legs, his momentum flips me onto my back, knocking the air out of my lungs. I gasp for breath. Then, the canopy becomes a blur above me as I slide headfirst down the ridge. My hands desperately grab at vines rushing by. The roots beat my head and shoulders. I cry out in pain as my body picks up speed. Somehow, I manage to grasp one of the vines. I hold on with all my might, the world spins, until the vine suddenly snaps tight, bringing me to a jerking halt.

The high branches send down a storm of water from the impact. Parrots jump from the swaying limbs, squawking as they fly off in search of a safer perch. My body throbs from the beating. I catch my breath and sit up.

"Me sorry!" comes a shout. I look up to find Sogamoi staring down at us. Aaron squirms in the mud at the bottom of the hill just below me.

"Are you all right?" I call.

"No," he moans. "Iiiieee!" "Iiiieee!" Suddenly, he jumps to his feet and rips off his shirt, slapping ferociously at several ants clamped onto his skin.

"Well, at least nothing seems to be broken," I say to him. He gives me a fierce look. "Hey, keep in mind that you're the one who almost killed me." I look back up the trail. Sogamoi has gone.

"Let's go!" I shout, starting to climb.

"I can't. I'm hurt!"

"We can hurt tonight," I say, looking back at him. He puts his shirt back on, noticing for the first time the broken vine that he still clutches in his hand. He stares blankly at it for a moment before throwing it down.

I try to steady my out-of-control breathing from the stiff climb, by raising my hands above my head as I top the ridge. I take my hat off to slap at the swarming horse flies and to wipe the sweat from my eyes. Then, I begin searching for fresh signs of bush knife cuts in the thick foliage surrounding me.

"Which way?" I ask frantically, just as Aaron's pale face pops up over the lip of the ridge. He bends over, sucking for air. I slap at the horse flies landing on his back.

"Thanks," he says, between deep breaths.

"Here. Hurry up!" I shout behind me, as I storm down the trail, now a series of downed trees that are lying across a mosquito-infested swamp. The hard soles of my boots don't grip well on the slender, moss-covered logs. Soon I slip off to one side, up to my thighs in water and muck, engulfed by a cloud of mosquitoes rising up from the swamp grass. Ants tear into my hands when I grab the log in an attempt to pull myself out. I try standing on the narrow pole, but end up sinking my arms into the ooze on the other side. I hear a loud thud. Aaron's boots are sticking up over the log a short distance away from me. He crawls up onto it, his back dripping with the smelly mud. We pull ourselves across the stagnant surface, wading and crawling whenever possible, until we make it to the other side of the sago swamp. I kick as much of the heavy mud off my boots as I can; my socks are soaked. "Have to find the carriers," I tell myself, picking up the trail again. We rush along through cut vines, tripping on roots and rocks, climbing steep ridges on all fours, just to come straight down the other side, hoping, around every bend, that we will see one of our carriers. But we never do. I fall over a rock as the thick underbrush attempts to swallow me up. By the time I crawl free, Aaron is ahead of me. I brush the ants off my clothing and fall in behind him.

"Iiieee!" he yells. He dances in front of me, pulling his shirt up to reveal a long, black leech hooked onto his stomach. Blood squirts across his white skin when he pulls the leech off. He stomps it to death on the jungle floor and lifts his shirt again to look at the wound. His sweat dilutes the blood trickling down into his shorts. He looks up at me, his eyes wide with horror.

"Do I have any on my head?" he asks, yanking off his hat.

"No, just horse flies . . . What about me?" He shakes his head, after inspecting me.

"You can't stand still for one minute!" he complains, shaking ants from his legs. "Let's go!"

The cut trail follows along the top of a narrow finger ridge. It rises higher and thicker until it ends on the summit of a high knoll. I am feeling dizzy as I stumble up onto it. Sharp ledges drop off all around us, falling into deep, forgotten places.

"I have to rest." Aaron collapses onto a small boulder.

"We have to catch . . . "

"We're not catching up with anybody . . . look at your hands," he interrupts me, pointing. My hands are trembling.

"I just need some food."

"And a good rest. So sit down and try to relax," he snaps at me, before taking off his hat to wage war on the growing swarm of horse flies. I search for where the trail leads off the crest of the hill.

"How can we expect to keep up with men who have lived in this place their whole lives?" Aaron asks.

"That is the very reason we have to keep up."

"We've been sitting on our butts, paddling for the last three weeks. Our legs are completely out of shape," he points out.

I kill a horse fly on the back of my neck before giving up and sitting down on a rock across from him.

"All right, let's eat some crackers." I dig into my bag.

"If we just stay on the trail, eventually, we'll find their camp," he says to encourage me over the whine of mosquitoes growing thicker by the moment.

"And it will be just like with Rudy and Jay, only, instead of paddling up a river, we'll get stuck wandering for hours through this jungle at night. At least you can't lose your way on a river. I mean, how are we going to follow this trail when it gets dark? It's hard enough in the daytime with . . . Iiiee!" I screech, slapping a large black ant biting my leg. I kill another one before throwing Aaron his crackers. He doesn't catch them because he's busy battling three enemies at the same time: the ants from the ground and the horse flies and mosquitoes from the air. I pull at the back of my shirt as the flies bite right through it. A leech attaches to my arm. By the time I get it off, I have several more ants biting my legs.

"Let's get *out* of here!" Aaron shouts, throwing his crackers back at me and jumping to his feet. He dances about while slapping his hat madly against his body. "Where does the trail lead?" His voice is desperate.

"Straight down!" I seal my bag and throw it up and onto my fly-covered back. "This way!" I shout, slipping and sliding my way down. The trees and bushes stick out below, their leaning trunks and stalks serving as foot and handholds. The canopy tilts down in front of me. I feel hooks dig into my thigh and look down to find two large leeches attached to my upper leg. Their nasty blood-sucking is enough to make me forget my whereabouts for the moment. In an attempt to pull them off, I let go the vines. Instantly I forget my leech problem when wet leaves start slapping me across the face as I shoot past them. Soon I am smashing through bushes, rolling over roots and bouncing off trees, my momentum clearing a new trail down the mountainside. I grab something along the way which might stop my forward progress, but quickly let go when I realize it is covered with thorns. I enter a thicket, the many branches slowing me down, just before I burst out the other side, landing with a thud on smooth stones lining a creek. I shut my eyes, waiting for the pain and shock to subside enough to allow me to think again. The bushes on the ledge above me move, and Aaron's red hair breaks through, tilting up to reveal his concerned face.

"Are you hurt?" he asks, as his legs drop down, swinging underneath him. "Are you hurt?" he asks again, sliding onto the rocks.

"I don't know," I whimper. It is the truth; I can't tell.

"Ooooh, dude!" he says, kneeling down.

"What? What is it?" I struggle to sit up. "Did I break something?" I search my ribs and arms, feel my legs, afraid of finding a bone jutting out.

"Leeches," Aaron reminds me. Two large, black balls hang from my upper leg. They didn't stop sucking during my fall.

"Get them off!" I scream, grabbing hold of one. My fingers sink into its oozy body, as I clamp down hard so I won't lose my grip on it. As it begins to come loose, blood shoots from its mouth onto my leg. Aaron rips off the other one and throws it against a rock where it bursts like a water balloon, spraying the creek bed in red. Aaron helps me up. My body shakes in revulsion. I try not to think about what has just happened.

"Nothing seems broken," I announce in relief.

"What would we do if something was?" Aaron asks, slowly looking around.

"You would have to pick out a creek rock and kill me with it." Neither of us laugh. Truth is, we don't know if I am joking or not.

We search for several minutes, trying to locate the trail before we start yelling for help. Eventually, Eabay pops out of the dense undergrowth. He hangs back and lets us follow him at our own pace, saying, "Me sorry," every time one of us falls down.

The sky grows dark as thunder rolls across the canopy. I remember looking down on it from the airplane that flew us to Wewak. I remember that endless ocean of green which so effectively hid from our naive eyes the cruelty that exists beneath its leafy surface. The rain splashes against my face, bringing me back to the present. I limp along, taking pressure off my swollen knee which was injured during the fall. It begins to rain so hard I lose sight of Aaron hiking in front of me.

One more step, Joel, now another, I encourage myself. The thought of two solid weeks of this misery hits me. Don't think about it, one step at a time. These weeks will pass, just don't think about it. I try to chase away the panic in my heart. An image of myself as a shaggy-haired madman flashes across my mind. One step at a time, you can do it. I try to chase the madman vision away. What if I lose it? I ask myself. For the first time in my life, it seems possible. Although it's only been one day in the mountains, insanity seems close at hand. I see myself again forty years from now with a dirt-stained face and a crazed expression, gray-headed, still wandering the jungle, trapped forever in my insanity. "Shut up!" I yell.

"What?" comes Aaron's voice from somewhere, lost in the rain. "Nothing!" I yell through the downpour. "Dang you, Joel! How do you always get yourself into these situations?" I interrogate myself aloud. "You never learn, do you? What were you doing just four months ago? Freezing your butt off in minus-forty degrees, all alone, in a tepee buried in snow! You thought the tropics would be better, didn't you? You just couldn't wait to suffer again, could you? Five years you spent in college? You could be sitting behind a desk in a comfortable chair with a mug of coffee, making lots of money to support a beautiful wife. But no!" I shout at myself. "You had to come here, didn't you? You have to be an expeditioner rotting in the jungle . . . ."

"Are you all right, Joel?" I hear a voice. I stop in the rain. Aaron stands beside the trail with a concerned look on his face.

"Huh? . . . oh, yeah, fine," I am shocked at his sudden appearance. "What are you doing here?"

"I heard you yelling, so I waited." He seems unsure of my behavior. "You sure you're okay?"

"Yeah, yeah, I'm sure. Let's go before we get a leech."

*　　*　　*

The rain races down the slope in front of me as I wearily climb one miserable step at a time. I am alone; even Aaron is too far ahead of me to see. I can hardly walk; my exhausted body hobbles along on a wounded knee. It is almost dark now. I place my steps in Aaron's bootprints in the rain-loosened soil. How long since he made them, I don't know. One more step, just one more, I tell myself. But I know I'm not going to make it much further. I finally top the ridge. Aaron is waiting for me. Like a dream, he tells me the men have stopped for the night in a hut just down the hill. With this new hope I limp down to the camp. They have already set up our blue tarp, extending the shelter of their hut. It isn't really a hut, just a thatched roof built over a flat mound of dirt. The men call it a "bush camp" in pidgin. Aaron cooks some rice and a military ration (MRE) for us to eat. Eating gives me enough energy to set up the netting. I shed my drenched clothes and put on some dry ones before crawling under the net for the night. The ground is hard and bumpy beneath my blanket. Several tree roots cause my back to hurt, but I am too tired to notice.

A loud buzz wakes me. I sit up blinking in the sunlight, to find the bush camp swarming with bees. The carriers are cooking potatoes over a fire.

"Happy nun," they chant, noticing that I am awake. I look beside me. Aaron is gone, and a large pool of water fills the place where he had been. The tarp hangs loose above the water, vines dangling from the metal rings that line its edge. I look under the thatched roof to find Aaron wrapped in his blue blanket, lying in the dirt. A rip opens as he begins to hatch from his cocoon, and a tuft of red hair emerges, revealing Aaron's weary face.

"Bees," he grunts, in a harsh, phlegmy voice.

"What are you doing out there?"

He looks at me. "It rained all night and filled the tarp until it got too heavy for the vines to hold; then it dumped a bathtub full of water on me," he explains, letting his blanket drop from around him. "Scared me half to death. I was asleep when it happened. Aguy helped me dry my blanket over the fire, but it was too wet to get back under the net, so I just rolled up in my blanket here and went to sleep."

Our dishes from last night's dinner are hidden beneath a mound of solid ants. I kick our cooking pot across the ground, then pick it up and shake off the rest of the ants. The ants acted like a dishwasher throughout the night, picking the pot, bowls, and forks perfectly clean. Our wet hiking clothes are also buried beneath a thousand bees. After breakfast, Sogamoi carefully reaches his hand in through the mass of angry stingers and lifts the "hive" up off the ground. He begins shaking it slowly. As bees fly everywhere, I can see the "hive" is my shirt. He shakes the last remaining bees off it and throws it over to me. Aaron and I repeat the ritual with the other mounds, having fun guessing what piece of clothing it is and letting the retreating bees reveal the answer. We put the clothes back on, but the smell of mildew in them attracts the bees to us. We put on pants rather than shorts, having experienced enough yesterday of the hardships on bare legs. I get stung only once when I step on one of the bees. I put my boot on quickly before my foot finishes swelling.

Eabay hangs back from the others to make sure we don't lose the trail again. The canopy overhead casts its dark shadows on the earth below, shadows filled with tormenting flies, ants, and leeches. Spider webs cling to my hair; their sticky strands snap across my face as I move through the thick brush. A storm rolls in and pours down on us; the water trapped temporarily on the leaves and branches above trickles down vines until it falls in giant drops on the jungle floor. We climb steep ridges only to descend straight down the other side and lose all the elevation that we have fought so hard to gain. We wade across large creeks and streams flowing with rain water before starting to climb again. Once we top a ridge, the top of the next one stands just in front of us. It seems close enough to jump to. But, instead, we are forced back down, deep between the steep ridge faces until we reach the lonely shadows at the bottom. Once again we cross the gushing currents of the creeks that splash their way down to the Salumei.

"We're losing him," I say of Eabay, whose black body is disappearing up ahead.

Aaron wades into a creek in front of me. He pauses for a moment. His whole body flinches just as I catch up with him. "Wasps!" he screams. In that ugly moment, I see the gray nest and the black, evil-looking wasps swarming out of it in full attack. The knee-deep creek water splashes up in front of us, slowing our attempt to retreat. The wasps' tiny poison daggers sink into my neck and shoulders. Pain jolts me forward. I crowd Aaron. Both of us scream in agony with each new sting. We rush down the trail, desperately trying to outrun each other. We are running side by side, arms flailing in the air, when Eabay comes into view. His eyes fly open wide at the onslaught of our violent charge. Terrified, he leaves the trail and sprints off into the jungle. And, instinctively, we follow. The cloud of angry wasps motor us over logs, and we snap through vines as we tunnel our way through thick jungle. Eabay lets out a bewildered cry for help when we close in on him. I fall, still scrambling across rocks. Then, I'm up again, running through a creek, chasing the water which sprays up behind Aaron's feet. Finally, we dive for cover over the top of a log in a heap of heavy breathing. The stinging ceases. I carefully poke my head up above our hiding place.

"We lost 'em," I say, trying to relax.

Aaron sits up and stares into the empty jungle. Eabay is nowhere to be seen. "That's not all we lost," Aaron adds. As I lift my shirt to study my red, puffy stings, he asks, "How many?" My body throbs from the trauma.

"They got me twice on my shoulders. How many are on my back?" "One, two . . . three . . . four . . . five, six." Between the two of us we have fourteen stings.

We have no idea where the trail is once we crawl out from behind the log, so we start shouting for Eabay. After a long time, he peeks around a tree. Aaron and I go into an elaborate display of sign language, attempting to explain the wasps. He watches from a safe distance as we try to convey to him that we meant him no harm. Eventually, he leads us back to the trail, but we have lost his trust, and he stays well ahead of us the rest of the day.

By late afternoon, we drop back down to the upper reaches of the Salumei, slowly working our way across its boulder-choked shoreline. Its current has grown white as it quickly drops through long, winding rapids. A strange coldness sinks deep in my bones, shooting chills throughout my body. I look at the sun blazing down, its heat rising off the boulders that I am crawling up and jumping across. The chills hit me again a few minutes later. Goose bumps cover my arm. They become more frequent and powerful as each grueling mile falls away. Aaron gives me a strange look when I stop to put on my rain jacket.

"I'm cold," I say.

"It's ninety degrees and humid." He looks confused. Sweat pours down his face. "You must have a fever." A look of horror comes over his face. "You must have . . . ."

"I know," I cut him off. "We'll deal with it when we make it to the next bush camp."

The carriers head up a steep ridge, and we climb for an hour before finally reaching a garden at the top. A hut is built upon several rows of stilts. Each row has been cut to different lengths matching the angle of the slope on which the hut is built. The men quickly build an extension with the blue tarp on the roof of the hut, and Aaron sets up our net and bedding. After getting out the malaria medicine, he gives me my first cycle of chloroquine pills. I slide under the net. My cold flashes grow more intense and frequent. My head pounds with pain; my mouth dries out. A sensation of nausea settles in my stomach; my face feels cold and clammy. I can't believe that I have malaria.

Aaron's concern switches from my malaria to his feet once he slips his boots off. They are a gruesome sight! He has been complaining about his feet itching and being sore nearly all day. Now it is easy to see why. Large blotches of red, oozing sores cover both feet.

"What on earth? My feet! They're melting or something," he whimpers.

"Athlete's foot! Worst I've ever seen," I say. He turns to look at me.

"If they're this bad after just two days, what are they going to look like after two whole weeks?" I don't have an answer for him. Aaron slips off his rain pants. He has three new sores on the front of his leg, the worst of them a gaping wound. He cries out as he squeezes it from both sides. A large ball of black puss rises to the top of the crater in his leg and spills out onto his blanket. Cold chills chase each other through my body as I watch him squeeze his other two sores. Blood gushes out with the white puss as he finishes draining them. He pulls out some Q-tips and a bottle of iodine from the medical kit. He holds one end of the Q-tip down in the bottle and then raises it slowly over his leg and shuts his eyes to prepare himself. Once he finds the courage, he brings the Q-tip down like a dagger, sinking it deep into his largest wound. His eyes clamp shut and his body trembles as he lets out a cry of intense pain. He twists and turns the Q-tip, pushing it in and out of his sore, wincing with every movement. The iodine stings and the pain becomes too much; he flops back onto his blanket waiting for the sting to subside. Once it does, he forces himself to repeat the process until each sore is saturated with iodine.

Then he hands the bottle over to me. I decide to go the fast route. I grab the Q-tip and soak both ends, then thrust it into my leg. The burning pain rises through my shaking body. I quickly pull the Q-tip from my first wound and stab the other end deep into my other sore. Screaming, I lie down on my blanket; my headache becomes a wild fury. Next, Aaron puts drying powder on his feet, and I put it on a rash that has developed where my legs have rubbed together while hiking.

After our commotion ceases, our carriers climb into the hut. The jungle shadows overtake our bush camp with the coming night. The men have lit a fire from which dull, orange light begins pouring out through the cracks in the thatched walls, giving the hut a glowing appearance. Soon, the mountain people begin to sing. It starts faintly, buried deep in the background of all the jungle noises. As more voices join in with harmony, the song gains strength. The jungle seems to hush and listen. It is a song of hardship, a calling out of gentle voices searching for the mercies of God.

"Joel." Aaron's voice comes quietly as the singing dies down. "I honestly don't know how much more of this I can take." I roll over to look at him. I look at him but the dark night hides his expression. "These have been the hardest two days of my life . . . I mean, do you really think we can make it? Just look at us after only two days." My face burns with fever; my body flashes between hot and cold.

"It's even worse than I imagined," I admit. "Do you want to give it up?" He lies in the dark night listening to the screeching jungle. "How are your wasp stings?" I ask him. I can make out the white teeth of his smile. Then we both start to laugh.

"We're sure a sight to see, aren't we?" He is laughing harder.

"I wonder...." I try to gain enough composure to speak. "I wonder what Eabay thought when we came tearing down the trail after him?" I burst out laughing; rolling over, I grab my side. Soon both of us are out of control. Tears stream down my face, my stomach aches, my head throbs, but I can't stop laughing. The carriers listen to us in silence, like the sane listening to the insane.

We laugh because there is nothing left to do. We have reached our breaking point—the jungle has dished out too much for us to handle in a normal way. Here we are, under our netting, me burning with feverish malaria, my legs in a rash, Aaron with "leprous" feet, all our legs speckled with nasty sores, our bodies covered with ant, mosquito and leech bites, and swollen areas where wasp stingers are still embedded. The bottom of my foot is still swollen from the morning's bee sting. In addition to all of that, we are a collection of bruises and knots from having fallen down the side of steep ridges, and my knee is wrapped in an ace bandage. Just when we start to gain control of our laughter, one of us says something like, "It's only been two days," or mentions the name "Eabay," and we lose it again, roaring with laughter. I guess Aaron and I have to lose it before we can gain it back: our wits, our humor, our faith, our hope. The laughter dies down after a long while.

I begin to feel drowsy again. "No," Aaron whispers. "I don't want to quit."

*   *   *

I wake to alarming squeals outside. As I'm trying to figure out what the disturbance is, I realize that I am feeling better, even though fever kept me up much of the night. I'm sitting up on my blanket when Eabay rushes into the hut. He is holding captive in his belum bag, a squirming, wild pig, its broken leg dangling out through the bag's woven strings. In one motion Eabay drops the boar from his back onto the ground, and, with the flat side of his bush knife, delivers several damaging blows to the animal's head. High-pitched squeals ring through the camp as I stare in disbelief at the merciless scene before me. Again and again, he strikes until the blade drips with thick, dark blood. Finally, the squeals of agony quiet down, and the belum bag lies in a heap of twitching, mangled nerves. Eabay walks a few feet away and calmly wipes the blade across the grass. He catches my eye, his face breaking out into a friendly smile.

"Happy nun, trapem pig." He thinks nothing of the incident.

"Its still alive," comes a disturbed voice from beside me. I turn to find Aaron awake, his face flushed with horror. "You must kill pig!" He demands. He signs to Eabay to cut the animal's throat. Eabay refuses and points to the morning sun hanging low in the sky. Aaron turns his frustration to me.

"Why won't he put it out of its misery?"

I feel uncomfortable. "There are no refrigerators out here."

"So?"

"We need the meat for dinner. The meat'll go bad within a few hours in this humidity and with all these flies." Aaron glares at me. "I'm not saying I like it. Just that it makes sense. As long as that poor pig's heart keeps beating, then the meat will stay fresh."

"That's sick!" Aaron says turning around, trying to ignore the situation. He picks up his little black Bible and begins to read.

"The Lord is my shepherd; I shall not want. He makes me lie down in green pastures; He leads me beside quiet waters. He restores my soul; He guides me in paths of righteousness for His name's sake."

He stops for a moment and looks at the pig, its body sucking tiny breaths of air. The painful squeals start up again. Aaron reads louder:

"Though I walk through the valley of the shadow of death, I fear no evil, for Thou art with me; Thy rod and Thy staff, they comfort me."

He wipes a tear from his eye before continuing:

"Thou dost prepare a table before me in the presence of my enemies; Thou hast anointed my head with oil; my cup overflows. Surely goodness and lovingkindness will follow me all the days of my life, and I will dwell in the house of the Lord forever."

He slowly closes the book and sets it down gently beside him.

"Psalm 23 . . . Are you feeling better?"

"I think so," I respond. He doesn't look at me. "This isn't much of a place for peace freaks is it?" I ask him.

"No." He doesn't smile.

"Is something else bothering you?"

"Just a hard night."

"Bad dream?" I ask.

"I wish." He looks very uncomfortable, staring down at his feet. The sores on them have dried up and scabbed over during the night.

I notice a large bloodstain soaked into the side of the mosquito net hanging next to his feet. "What happened?"

"My feet itched all night, but I didn't scratch them. I knew it would only make it worse." He pulls the bottle of chloroquine pills out of the medical kit. "There was one place that hurt especially bad, right between my toes." His eyes are sad as he passes me a cycle of pills and the water bottle. "I was going nuts for a long time. Finally, it got so bad I just couldn't take it anymore. So, I turned on my flashlight to see why it was hurting so much . . . ," he hesitates, looking extremely depressed.

I swallow the pills, their sour taste filling my mouth.

"It was awful, Joel." I wait. "When I flashed the light on my foot, I found a giant black leech hanging right in between my toes." His body quivers with the memory. "I felt him sucking my blood that whole time, and thought it was just my athlete's foot. He was full of blood by the time I discovered him. I tried to pull him off, but he was so mushy and slimy it was hard to get a good hold on him . . . I ah . . . ripped him open trying to pull him off and . . . blood went everywhere . . . as if my feet don't have enough problems without some leech sucking all the blood out of them."

I look at the stain on the net, then back to Aaron who looks depressed and angry. I have nothing to offer—no words, no comfort.

CHAPTER 8

Bushy Man

The table in front of me is crowded with my favorite foods. My mouth waters, as my mother comes in from the kitchen with a basket of warm rolls, straight from the oven. Her face lights up with joy at finally having her only son home again. My father leans back in his chair at the other end of the table, relaxing. Heather, my older sister, leans in, listening to my wild stories of New Guinea.

"Please pass the turkey," I say. Mom hands the glazed, gravy-smothered heap of delicious-looking meat over to me with her gentle smile.

"So what are your plans now?" Dad asks. I'm so intent on the food, I hardly even hear the question.

"I must return to New Guinea." Even I am uncomfortable with my answer. Mom's smile vanishes and is replaced by a worried expression.

Dad re-positions himself in his chair. "Do you know how hard this expedition has been on your mother?" I can see that it's been hard on him as well. "I'm sorry, but, I must go back and finish what I've started."

All three of them stare at me as if I have just gone mad. I search the room for a mirror. It has been so long since I've seen myself.

I desperately try to grab some of the food that is disappearing— Then, the table is gone. The familiar room in my parent's house vanishes; all that is left are the fading, bewildered faces of my beloved family.

*   *   *

In the black New Guinea night, I hardly notice that my eyes are now open. My right shoulder aches from the roots and rocks beneath me as I roll over onto my back. Millions of tiny voices from the surrounding jungle scream, waking me to the reality of where I am. The dreams of escaping these jungles and returning home to friends and family have now become a nightly ritual for both Aaron and me. Dreams are a way of dealing with the mental anguish of our island burdens, a short vacation from the turmoil surrounding us. But waking up is always the hardest part. It takes hours to get over the loss. Our minds try to trick us and convince us that our anguish is over, that we are safe and sound.

I watch the pale moonlight reflect off the mosquito net, which is dancing around me in the humid breeze. With roots cutting into my back, I roll over onto my left shoulder. I review the days since leaving Stew's hut.

*   *   *

The pig had finally been given the pleasure of dying and was roasted for several hours over a pile of hot rocks. It was difficult to eat him after watching him suffer so intensely all day long. The carriers offered us some of his guts and brains, but Aaron and I passed.

The next morning, I had recovered enough from my malaria to hike. We made our way down a steep slope, where even further below us, we could see the Salumei River. Our only way to cross was a konda vine bridge tied high between two tree tops. It was well over 100 feet long, with the middle sagging dangerously toward the raging whitewater thirty feet below it. The ends of the bridge were tied to support beams wedged into the upper branches of towering trees on each side of the river. To get up the trees, we climbed a ladder made from branches and vine.

The bridge itself consisted of three large vines making up the walkway and two large vines on either side, higher up, acting as hand-rails. These vines were held together with other small vines which had been split down the middle, tied to the handrail on one side, run underneath the floor vines and attached back up to the hand rail on the other side.

The old woman, Stew, Aguy, and Eabay who carried a dog, each made it across, followed by Aaron. After watching Aaron make it safely to the other side, I started down the bridge. Everything seemed steady until I reached the bottom of the sag. There, in the middle, the bridge suddenly came alive. With my every step, the konda bridge buckled. Suddenly, my feet shot up causing the heavy weight on my back to pull me down. For a moment, I hung across the mesh of thin vines, parallel with the raging water below. My heart raced as I struggled in the tangled vines while the bridge whipped about like a convulsing snake. Somehow, I managed to get back on my feet to begin again the long climb toward Aaron who was waiting for me on a branch, on the other side.

A commotion broke out. The old woman, Stew, Aguy, and Eabay ran about, shouting loudly at one another before disappearing into the jungle. Aaron's face paled with fear.

"What's wrong?" I asked him.

"Just keep climbing!" He was serious. And then I discovered why. The support beam of the bridge had snapped when the bridge tilted me over on my side. A few thinly stretched vines were the only things holding the entire bridge up. Unable to resist looking down, I froze. To my dismay, I was no longer swaying over water but over large boulders. With tiny, careful steps I climbed higher, watching the support beam in front of me buckle a few inches more with each step. Suddenly, as I lunged for Aaron's outstretched hand, I felt the support beam crack, but with Aaron's help, I made it to the safety of a sturdy branch. Having escaped yet another brush with death, I allowed some time for the adrenalin rush to wear off and my fears to subside.

When the men returned with a freshly cut support beam, Stew and Aguy were glad to see that I had made it across. The old woman and Eabay collected and split some more tie vines, and before long, the bridge was fixed.

From the bridge we scaled another steep ridge. The dog, hiking along with us, had an extreme disadvantage with the leeches. As much as he whined when they sucked his blood, nobody paid him much mind or bothered to cut them off him. He wouldn't let Aaron or me near him. Every time we caught a glimpse of the little mutt, he had large, scrotum-like bags of blood hanging from his thin fur. We often found the blood-filled balls along the trail after they dropped off the dog, full, nearly to the point of bursting, and we exploded them with our boots.

By lunch time, I noticed extra weight under my arm and discovered, to my horror, a bloated leech preparing to drop off. By the time I finally got it off, it had injected so much blood-thinning serum into me that it took several hours for the bleeding to stop.

We understood the dog's usefulness late in the afternoon, when we heard it barking. The carriers went wild, running and shouting through the rainforest. The dog had treed a possum which sought safety out on a limb. Stew climbed the tree with his bow and arrows and got as close as he could to the cornered possum. With one shot, the possum fell from the tree top, the arrow buried deep in its chest. The impact from the fall took care of its last bit of life. Stew cut the belly of the possum open and pulled out its guts; he squeezed the intestines until they were empty, then tied them up and put them back inside the possum's belly. That seemed to be the only process needed to prepare an animal to be cooked.

After finding a run-down bush camp to sleep in for the night, they threw the possum—fur, guts, and all—onto the fire. While we listened to the fur sizzle on the hot coals, we feasted on some wild mangoes. The tart flavor of the mangoes tasted wonderful after eating bland rice and sago for so long.

After dinner, I left the camp in search of a nearby creek to take a much-needed bath. I found the creek suddenly, at the bottom of a deep trench. Not realizing that the ground I walked on ended sharply, I stepped through jungle growth hanging out over the edge of the trench, and fell hard, onto the rocky creek bed below. I managed to recover and bathe, but, by the time I made it up the steep, muddy bank and back to the bush camp, I was muddier than I had been before.

The next morning, in a desperate search for an escape from our misery, Aaron and I had tried chewing some beetle nut. Once we peeled away the green skin of the nut, we pulled a white pulp from its core and slowly chewed. Then, a strand of green mustard root, dipped in lime powder made from crushed shells was mixed with the beetle nut already in our mouths. The rather harsh, bitter tasting combination produced a red juice that demanded constant spitting. We chewed and spit all over the camp for nearly a half hour before I stood up to relieve my bladder.

The moment I got to my feet, the steady stare of the men quickly tilted in front of me. I grabbed hold of a hut pole to keep myself from falling over. Everyone burst into laughter as I swayed out into the dizzying jungle. Their laughter climaxed when I slipped on a log and landed square on my back. I pulled myself up and waded out into the vegetation; and holding myself up with the help of a tree, I managed to accomplish what I had set out to do in the first place. Because Aaron and I had enough trouble hiking in the jungle without being dizzy, we decided beetle nut was not a good choice for a breakfast food, especially if we were planning to be out on the trail all day.

The following morning was Christmas day. Aaron greeted me with a "Merry Christmas" and a weak smile. I returned the traditional greeting, though it lacked any merriness. We spent the rest of Christmas day hiking, trying not to think about all that we were missing back home: meals, laughter, joyous songs. It would have been the greatest Christmas gift of my life to be able to go home right then, even just for a few minutes.

I killed a Death Adder snake later in the afternoon, and Stew killed a long, red tree snake. Their cries of "Iiieeeeee" let us know that both snakes were indeed poisonous.

We hiked through several rainstorms before running across another run-down bush camp. Sogamoi was sick with malaria, so we gave him a cycle of pills. We tried to get him to stop and rest, but even in his sickness, he beat out a place with his bush knife for us to sleep.

As for me, I couldn't wait for Christmas to be over. It was the first Christmas I had spent away from my family, and I truly wondered if I would ever see them again in this life. It was lonely and depressing, a Christmas spent getting skinny instead of fat. The men cooked up the snakes along with several bland tasting bananas. In addition to snake and bananas, in celebration of the holiday and since it was Christmas dinner, we each had a military ration as well.

✳   ✳   ✳

The light from the hidden morning sun begins to leak through the dark canopy, causing the tarp overhead to glow light blue. My mind returns to the present. A brightly colored parrot waddles along a branch beside our camp. Aaron stirs, and soon we are up to face another day battling against all this island has to offer. After Sogamoi tells us he is all right to "walk about," we take down camp, swallow a half-cup of rice and begin the long day of hiking, feeling a little better now that Christmas is behind us.

We gain elevation throughout the day, ascending ridiculously steep ridges. The hope that we are finally topping the main ridge of the Centrals gives us the needed energy to push on.

Late in the day, we follow a finger ridge out into a garden clearing. It is the clearest outlook onto the New Guinea highlands that we have seen yet. The finger ridge ends, sharply falling away on three sides into a deep gorge. On the crest of the knoll is just enough room for a small hut, which seems to balance on stilts. A muddy path leads up to its black entrance. With blue sky surrounding it, it appears that the hut could slip off into nothingness. I peer down into the gorge across endless miles of ridges stacked close together. The folds of land rise higher to the west, giving way to massive rocky peaks that tower into the thick ceiling of clouds. Along the sloping, dark-green canopy below, a gentle mist hovers like the spray from an ocean wave. The garden-cleared knolls on high ridges, like the one we are on now, stand all around us and out into the distance, each one is complete with its own little hut.

The peaceful setting shatters as a high-pitched, dramatic wail rings out from the hut. Aaron and I startle, coming to an abrupt halt on the trail. To the right of the hut, the old woman and Agomi have dropped to the ground, rolling about in the mud with shrill screams. I take a frightful step back, and the carriers cry out in loud moans, dispersing themselves along the ridge. Their wails echo across the vast expanse of ridges stretched out before them. Aaron and I are stunned by such intense weeping, knowing something terrible has happened. My silence feels foolish; I feel awkward and out of place. With Aaron behind me, I step up and look into the hut. Within the shadows sits an old man who turns to look at me. A Bird of Paradise feather hangs from his pierced nose, strings of shells are wrapped around his head. His eyes hold a deep sadness. They reflect a sense of deep loss and grief.

"What is . . . ."

"Shhhh!" I cut Aaron off, thinking it best that we remain quiet in the commotion. A boy emerges from behind the old man, he looks around ten years old.His eyes squint in the sunlight as he studies us. The high-pitched cries of sorrow outside seem to reach a mournful climax. I nod "hello" to him. He nods back, but with no trace of a smile. The expression on the boy's face is like a hard-to-read poem. It hints of stoic acceptance of harsh reality, tragedy, but the whole story is unclear. Mowga approaches with tear-stained cheeks and notices our confusion.

"Father . . . belong boy die . . . Malaria." He acts out the story, letting the life drop out of him as his head nods back and his eyes close in death. Aaron looks at me.

"Iiiieeee," I screech, not knowing how to respond. The boy's shattered expression, and the sad eyes of his grandfather, makes more sense to me now. He has been robbed of his right to be a child. Left behind to fend for himself and his family, he seems up to the challenge. For though he has the body of a child, his face, I see more clearly now, is the face of a lion. His world has suddenly yanked him into manhood. In his vulnerability, I see strength rising to the occasion. He has already assumed his father's place.

Sogamoi is the last to finish mourning for the dead man. Within minutes, the mood shifts to laughter. The men tell stories in a circle of life; their smiles and laughs clash starkly with the mood they have just left behind. The boy leaves the camp with his bow and arrow, and Aaron and I sit down in the grass to rest our aching legs. Infection has sunk deep into our leg sores, causing the muscles to ache.

"Oh my . . . ," Aaron blurts out. He flinches and I spring to my feet looking for the source of his sudden uneasiness. A white ghostly form emerges from the dense undergrowth across the garden. Aaron presses against me, both of us straining our eyes. A large boar trots and snorts its way through the garden, following behind the whitish figure. It is a woman, her body naked, except for a tattered grass skirt. A light-colored mud is smeared from her head to her feet, dry and cracking with every one of her lonely steps. Gray ashes powder her hair. She lifts her head up, and her sorrowful eyes fly open wide when she sees us. Uncomfortable, both of us point to the hut where the pig has wandered. Tear stains streak the mud and ash on her face. She rushes past, quickly disappearing into the dark entrance of the hut. Once again, mournful cries come bellowing out. They last several minutes.

Aaron and I sit under our shelter within the protection of the netting. A black cloud rolls over us, engulfing the knoll in drenching rain and lightning. In the waning light of the setting sun, the form of a boy with a bow as tall as himself stands before us, the rain running in streams down his smooth skin. He holds a dead possum in his hand. He only hesitates for a moment before continuing on into the hut. Soon, men from another hut top our ridge, carrying several potatoes. After greeting us, they too enter the shelter of the hut. The rain pours hard against the tarp overhead.

"How many bags of rice do we have left?" I ask in a loud voice, noticing Aaron pulling out the stove to cook some dinner.

"Four." He starts pumping pressure into the stove.

"No, put it away." He stares at me in disbelief.

"We have to eat," he pleads above the pounding rainstorm.

"We have to eat possum and potato. We have four bags of rice left, and we haven't even topped the Central Mountains, much less crossed them." The rain grows louder. "If we eat that rice now, then believe me, the day isn't far away when we will be praying for possums and potatoes." Aaron thinks for a moment, looking towards the hut.

"What makes you think they'll give us any? They know we have our own food."

"Then we beg!"

He looks back at me. "Has it come down to that already?"

"Let's beg now, while there's food here to beg for."

He looks down for a moment before agreeing with a nod, then slips out from under the net. We dart through the rain and begin feeling our way into the crowded, pitch-black hut, for a place to sit. It seems that the entire village has gathered here.

My eyes adjust with the help of the flickering fire pit. The nasty aroma of burnt hair and skin fills the smoky room as the possum, along with several sweet potatoes, sizzles on the red-hot coals. My stomach churns. The old man throws more wood on the fire which quickly bursts into flames revealing the black lump of burnt possum. There are two possums. Lightning flashes outside, filling the hut momentarily with its bright light. The mud-covered ash-whitened face of the woman who had frightened us earlier flashes in and out of the darkness in the flickering flames. Her sad eyes searching for comfort; she is far away in her misery. Beside her sits her son, wearing the same mixture of bravery and loss as when I first saw him.

The old man pulls the two possums out of the fire and begins ripping them into chunks. He hands it out to all the men first, including the boy, but excludes Aaron and me. After the men begin eating, he starts handing chunks to the women. An old woman tries to get the dead man's wife to eat something, but she turns away from the food. She is caught in a trance, rocking back and forth, singing a low, mournful song, completely absorbed in her world of suffering. Next, the children come to the old man, one by one, male children first, then the little girls.

My stomach burns with hunger when the old man looks at me. He rips some meat from the carcass, turns away, and throws it to the dogs who begin fighting over it. He waits patiently until there is a loser before giving him a small piece of the carcass. Finally, he rips off two chunks and gives them to the mourning boy who delivers them to Aaron and me. We thank the boy and the old man. I put the meat into my mouth and bite down; it is soft like fat. I shut my eyes, rip off another bite and swallow quickly, coughing, gagging.

"I don't think this is meat," Aaron whispers to me.

"Don't think about it, just swallow." Someone begins an ancient tune on a juice harp in the dark corner of the hut. A man stares at me, his eyes fogged over with cataracts. I try to think about chicken as I continue to swallow whatever it is that I am eating. Guts, fat, bone— whatever it is, it's not meat. The potatoes come burnt, but at least I know what they are. By the time we leave for our shelter to sleep, I feel sick to my stomach.

When morning comes to the little camp on the garden knoll, my heart and stomach are troubled from yesterday's experience. We all need a rest, so we agree not to hike today. Instead, I make my way up to the highest and furthest corner of the garden. I lean over a log and throw up in a clump of grass, then again, followed by several dry heaves. I move down the log feeling better.

A thick wall of jungle stands at my back as I peer out over the ridges swept with mist below me. They look so heartless. I have a decision to make. Do we go on or turn around? We are running low on food and malaria medicine. We didn't take into account the possibilities of meeting other people dying from a disease that we have the power to cure.

It has been over a week since we left Rudy and Jay, and still there is no sign of the Central Divide. Things just don't look good at all. I look toward the peaks across from me, partially covered in clouds. The sun breaks through the clouds, spreading light out over the landscape. Dark shadows sink deeper into the ocean of green below. Movement catches my eye. A large flock of birds silently makes its way towards me. The sun causes their bright colors to gleam as their long tails swirl in the air currents, bouncing with each beat of their wings.

Birds of Paradise, I tell myself. Their graceful flight brings a peaceful feeling as they pass overhead. Then, I remember God's peace! God has been our ever-present help in times of trouble. Has He brought us this far just to desert us now? The flock of birds rises up over the southern wall of jungle, becoming specks before disappearing completely into the unknown land beyond.

I look back to the north from where they came. I can't see very far that way. I can't see Wewak where we first launched, nor the Sepik River. I can't see the river fork where we said goodbye to Rudy and Jay, not even our last camp. Fears return to envelope me: crocodiles and rascals, mosquitoes and disease, and the many other foes that have stood in our way. But our God has been faithful in conquering every one. I remember the blessings: Father Don, the Minters, Rudy, Jay, Sogamoi, and the rest of our carriers. All of them are blessings that we never planned on, miracles to help us along the difficult path. Never have we been given too much to handle, and our suffering has taught us how to trust God more. Confidence rises inside me. I know that His spirit will go before us into the unknown, just like the Birds of Paradise. He will prepare our way. I leave feeling that for some reason I cannot yet see, God himself is for us to cross this island. "Onward then . . . Onward to Daru!" I shout out over the expanse.

✳   ✳   ✳

A young man, named Libi, is chosen to accompany us across the mountains. He is thrilled with some worn-out socks that I give him. He immediately puts them on, and within an hour of hiking, has worn the feet completely out of them, something he doesn't seem to mind. We hike into the early afternoon before stopping for the night to make sago in a nearby swamp. This is the last chance we know of to stock up on food for the remainder of our long journey over the mountains. Aaron and I do our best through a long process of sign language and broken pidgin to explain to the men that we will share our rice with them at night, if they will share their sago with us during the day. Eventually, they seem to understand and agree.

This morning, my iodine-stained feet are covered in scabs and dried puss. I pull my stiff socks over the top of them, wincing in pain. The first steps hurt the worst, so much so, I can barely take them. Slowly, the pain begins to dull.

Between every ridge, the men wade across creeks and rivers. To protect ourselves from athlete's foot, Aaron and I must keep our feet dry, so we jump across the streams on rocks and logs, whenever possible. Otherwise, we are forced to take our boots and socks off, wade across, dry our feet, and repeat the painful process of putting them back on again.

Late morning finds us standing on the bank of a small river with a rock island twelve feet out in the middle. The men waste no time and wade across. I sit down on a boulder and start untying my boots.

"What are you doing? All we have to do is make it out to that island," Aaron pleads.

"We can't jump that far," I am pulling my boots off.

"We can build a bridge out to it." He starts looking around for materials.

"It will take too long, the men are already waiting for us." I begin pulling off my first sock. My body trembles as the dirt-stained cloth pulls away from my foot. Long strands of puss and ooze stretch out. When the sock clears my foot, they snap and dangle towards the ground. Splotches of blood mix with the puss, giving my foot a pinkish color. Aaron turns away in disgust.

"I am not taking my boots off again!"

"Do what you want. I'm wading across." I stand up and slip my swollen feet below the cool surface of the clear mountain stream. Refreshed, I carefully make my way out to the island and then across the powerful currents to the other side of the river. Sitting down on a boulder, I pull an old shirt out of my pack and sit down to dry my feet before putting my boots back on. Aaron has started building his bridge by throwing several large rocks into the water between himself and the island. The last rock splashes the boulder he is standing on as well as his pant leg.

The men are sitting together behind me, resting and enjoying Aaron's show. He picks up the largest rock that he can lift and starts to waddle towards the water. The rock begins to slip out of his hands, so he charges forward and leaps onto the boulder, tossing the large rock as far as he can. Not a good combination of movements when standing on a smooth, wet surface. His feet shoot out from under him. "Iiiiieeeee!" The carriers shout out their sympathy as he lands on his back, right on the crown of the boulder. One of his feet slips deep into the river, filling his boot with water. He jumps up quickly, in denial that one of his feet is now soaked. We laugh—out of control—while anger builds on Aaron's determined face. He picks up his walking stick and studies the rocks he has thrown in place. A hush falls over the small crowd as we sense he's going for it. He charges the river with a maddened expression. Leaping out over the surface, his foot lands dead center on one of the rocks. Quickly, he plants his walking stick into the bottom of the stream like a pole vault. It buckles in the middle as he springs from the small rock towards the island, and then a loud snap cracks through the air as the walking stick breaks in half. Suddenly, losing his momentum, he drops into the middle of the current, soaking himself up to his waist. We explode into laughter. Aaron rises up out of the river like a crazed serpent, water pouring from his legs. His face is bright red; his eyes hold the power to kill. He glares at me. I stop laughing. Then he glares at the carriers. They too fall silent. His body begins to tremble as frustration rises inside him. He lets out a cry of vengeance as he charges toward our side of the river, still twenty feet away. Water sprays up behind him as he reaches the main current, but it is too strong for his quick movements. He loses his footing again and falls to one side. For a moment, he completely disappears beneath the surface of the river. I glance at the men; their eyes are wide with wonder. Aaron emerges, pulling his defeated spirit up onto the bank. The men show no mercy, bursting into laughter until tears run down their dirt-stained cheeks. Even the old woman and Agomi are hysterical. Aaron stands up, keeping his eyes locked on the rocks at his feet.

"Go on!" He shouts. "Go on, and I'll catch up!" He sits down on a rock and pulls off his shirt to ring it out. His skin is pale white against the redness of his face. We have been trapped under the forest roof too long. I stand up to leave.

"You shouldn't laugh!" he scolds me. I turn around and approach him, feeling angry myself.

"It was your decision!" I shout back, trying to control my anger. "Maybe it's good that you're finally making your own choices. Maybe it's even good that you're not listening to me anymore! But if you choose to go your way, then you have to pay the price that comes with it. There's very little glory and always a whole lot of humility that comes with making your own decisions."

"You still shouldn't laugh at me!" He screams.

"Look at you, Aaron. You were trying to keep your boots dry and now even the top of your head is soaked. You're the one who wouldn't listen. If you want some of the authority that comes with leading this expedition, then I won't fight you for it. But you're going to have to take what comes with it! There are no mothers out here to dry your tears every time something goes wrong. If you choose wrong, then blame yourself!" I am yelling by now.

"Leave me alone then," he whimpers.

"That would be my pleasure." I turn around and begin to follow the freshly cut jungle left behind by the carriers.

For the next several hours, we work our way steadily up a steep ridge, using roots and vines to pull ourselves up. The men begin to chant as they climb ever higher, "Whooop! Whooop! Whooop!" (I have no idea why they do that.) By late afternoon, we are crossing a flat section of rainforest on top of the ridge, when suddenly a large Cassowary bird comes crashing through the dense undergrowth. Stew and Aguy mount an arrow and quickly follow after it, disappearing from our sight.

Launching from New Guinea's north coast on November 25th, with our kayak loaded down with 350 lbs. of equipment.

Our ocean paddling is done for now as we land at the village located between the North coast and the Murik Lakes.

Paddling up the Sepik River.

In Sepik tradition, the prows of dugout canoes are carved in the shape of crocodile heads. The people believe this protects them from the crocodile, their most feared enemy.

Too close for comfort to an aggressive "Puk Puk."

The first of two miserable days of pulling against the swift currents of the upper Salumei.

Self-portrait in an abandoned bush camp on the Salumei River, Day 19. I am on the left.

It had taken us over three weeks to reach the north side of the Central Mountains. This picutre was taken minutes before we started our attempt to cross them. Little did we know that it would take another 53 days to find the other side of New Guinea's rugged interior highlands. Left to right: Aguy, Aaron, Mowga, Stew, Joel, and Sogamoi with our kayak strapped to his back.

Aaron waking up to face another grueling day in the jungle.

Mowga shows off his pierced nose with a piece of bamboo while Sogamoi looks on.

Stew slowly hacking his way through the thick jungle with his bush knife.

One of the many poisonous "Lobis" snakes we encountered in New Guinea. This one is a death adder.

A man is traditionally smeared in mud while mourning for his dead brother.

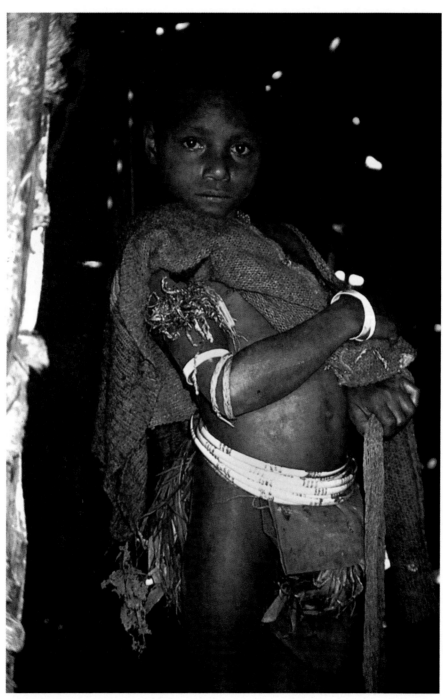

The dead man's son. His face shows the sorrow of a deserted boy and the strength of a man.

The great jungle hunter, Bushy man, whose wisdom saved our lives.

Aaron with the python which the Bushy Man caught on Day 42 of our expedition. We would all feast upon it later that night.

The controversial picture that Aaron took of the lost tribe's Big Man. Eagle feathers and Bird of Paradise plumes protrude out of his mushroom-shaped hairdo.

Two wild-looking women of the lost tribe who scared me and Aaron so much. They are decorated with belum strung hair, painted faces, pig tusks through their noses, shell necklaces, and red clay.

One of the lost tribe's women and her son.

Disaster strikes on Day 54. After our crash, Aaron stands in front of the wild Strickland River.

I am in shock after flipping the kayak and being swept through six-and-a-half miles of violent whitewater.

After climbing high above the Strickland, we fail to find a way around the torrent. We search the surrounding grassy slopes and valleys for any sign of a village, garden or bush camp, but miles of remote terrain is all we see. It would be another 36 days before we find a river we could navigate.

Finally the hiking is over! Aaron and I paddle our kayak, Amazing Grace, *down the Fly River, Day 95.*

A large "puk puk" hangs from the shore. When caught paddling at night in the remote swampland of the Fly River, we were frequently surprised and terrorized by crocodiles.

Getting hold of this powerful little crocodile almost cost me a hand.

Aaron with the old man who pierced his nose.

After 102 grueling days, our dream of being the first to cross New Guinea without motors is accomplished. We stand on the shores of Daru island and give thanks to God.

The Cassowary is one of the largest birds in the world, second only to the Ostrich. They are a flightless bird, sometimes standing six feet tall, and like the Ostrich, their claws are sharp daggers, known to kill hunters with a single kick. Their thick bodies are covered with shiny, black feathers, and they have beautifully colored heads, with long, slender necks. Their sharp eyesight and keen sense of smell make them the most wary animals on the island. Only the most skilled can hunt them success-fully. Thirty minutes later, Stew and Aguy return empty-handed. While they were gone, however, Eabay found the bird's nest and returned with two green eggs, larger than softballs.

As evening approaches, a storm's threatening roar echoes in the dark shadows. Aaron and I collapse with exhaustion as the shelters take shape in front of us. Without even a word, the men disappear into the jungle and bring back necessary parts for the shelters. Stew returns with support beams, and Mowga helps him thrust them deep into the soft ground. Sogamoi drags long, slender poles and fits them across the tops of the beams. Aguy throws the blue tarp over the structure and begins tying it down tight with the vines that Eabay and the women have collected. No talking, just work. Within minutes they have two shelters built, one with the blue tarp and another with a roof of leaves.

"Now that's teamwork," I tell Aaron who ignores me. We hold to our promise and give them a bag of rice to eat with their eggs. Our food situation is serious, with only a few small bags of rice left.

In the morning, we climb still higher on the endless ridge, until finally we find a flat shelf and on it a small clearing where we stop to eat some sago.

The men call out in unison, "Aaatiooo, whoop! whoop! whoop!" Stew suddenly throws his arms up as everyone becomes perfectly still. A voice, so faint I'm not sure it's real, emerges through all the bird and insect noises. The carriers jump to their feet, eyes wide with hope. It comes again, a chant, similar to the one the men have been calling. The men excitedly drop their packs on the ground. They form a circle and call out their song into the dense jungle surrounding us. Then, as quickly as their chant starts, it ends in dramatic silence. We listen for the distant reply. It comes again! This time louder and closer than before. I look at Aaron.

"Who would be living way out here?" he asks me in a low whisper. I shrug my shoulders. The men are trapped between the excitement of discovering another human life and fear of how this human will respond to us. All my attention focuses on some bushes that rustle in front of us.

I spot three large, white, eagle feathers with black tips above the brush. Then a white and reddish brown fur cap becomes visible beneath the feathers. I take a step back as two eyes peak over the top of a bush. The eyes hesitate on Aaron and me before a man cautiously emerges from the cover of foliage. Bird of Paradise feathers hang down from his furry, eagle feather cap. In the midst of a thick beard, as black as the jungle night, his nose is pierced with a piece of bamboo. He seems confused, trying to decide whether to stay or retreat. Libi speaks to him. The man glances Libi's way just for a moment before returning to stare at Aaron and me. The man's chest is bare, except for several strings of shells; his arms are wrapped with several vine strands, a symbol of honor to dead relatives. A long, tattered grass skirt hangs down from his waist, and he clutches a bow and arrows in his hands. Libi speaks to him again. He glances our way and takes a few steps forward. Then he speaks.

Relief sweeps through our group when he approaches us with a friendly smile, shaking the other men's hands but rarely taking his eyes off our white skin. He comes before me. He is a short man but strong. He shakes my hand, captivated with my looks just as I am with his. He appears ancient. He tells me his name, but I can't pronounce it. I look down and notice that his feet are gnarled with scars and his toes are twisted.

"Aaron . . . Joel," Aaron speaks to him, shaking his hand. He shakes his head and motions for us to follow him, then turns around. A large black cloak of animal skin, covered with tiny feathers so black they shine, lays across his back.

"Cassowary," Sogamoi says, seeing my interest. "Man belong. . . ." He pretends to shoot his bow in all directions to show that this man is a great hunter. I nod my understanding.

"Bushy Man. We will call him Bushy Man," I announce to Aaron.

"Why?" Aaron waits for me to explain.

"Because neither of us can pronounce his name, for one. And his beard is the bushiest I've ever seen, and he came to us out of a bush." Aaron laughs.

We follow our new friend for several hours until we come to a run-down bush camp. The Bushy Man's family is staying here while he hunts. We meet his two wives and several children, one a young man Libi's age. His wives have spent the day making sago and collecting potato, "kou kou", as the carriers call it. Libi seems able to communicate with them, and we all stay the night taking part in their feast.

The next day, the Bushy Man leads us all up a seemingly endless ridge. By the time we reach the top, in the late afternoon, I am completely exhausted. I stand on the crest of the mountain, looking down. A few hundred feet off the southern side, the ridge slopes down into a small valley covered in thick, dark-green grass. On the far side of this lake of grass rises the rest of the intimidating, yet majestic Central Divide. The steep slopes are covered in thick rainforest until they vanish into the cover of monstrous clouds. On the opposite side of the small valley is a river gorge. On the edge of the grass, nestled against this gorge, stands a small hut, insignificant when compared to its surroundings. The grass rolls in a breeze drifting down from the towering peaks which have already begun to cast shadows. The lower parts of the ridges form a bowl around the hut, and they are covered with fallen trees and speckled with banana plants blooming their heavy wind-shredded leaves.

I see the Bushy Man far below, his feet gripping a log lying across a ravine. The feathers covering his fur hat bounce with each of his steps until he disappears into the black entrance to his hut. The thrill of reaching the end of another miserable day of hiking is enough to bring me down the ridge into the valley. We take no chances crossing the logs that connect the lips of twenty-foot-deep ravines. Knowing that we are alone, Aaron and I straddle the logs and pull ourselves safely across, something the other men would definitely laugh at, if they saw.

I pull myself into the cool shadows of the Bushy Man's hut. A long hallway stretches out to my right with several openings leading into a large room with two fire pits. Allowing my eyes to adjust, I feel around for a place to sit. Some light pours in through the cracks between the poles that make up the walls. I look up. A vine runs beneath the ceiling, threaded with dozens of wild pig jaws. A small flame flickers up through a pile of wood in one of the hearths, illuminating the face of the Bushy Man as he blows life into it. The flame grows taller; his eyes look out towards me from beneath his furry hat. His black beard erases most of his face. Several vine-strung bows lean against the wall behind him among bundles of deadly-tipped bamboo arrows. Furs, skulls, and drying meat begin to glow in the orange of the fire as its flames grow stronger. The carriers go outside to work on a shelter for Aaron and me to sleep under because the hut is too small to contain all of us. Bird of Paradise plumes hang down from the ceiling. I stand up and gently pull them across my sweaty face. They feel so soft that I'm convinced even a gentle breeze would carry them away. I remember the flock that flew above the dead man's hut five days ago. It seems so strange that something so beautiful and peaceful was created to roam such dark places. The Bushy Man watches me intently from the other side of his fire.

"Thank you," he looks confused but gives me a smile and a nod.

"Another gift from God to help us along our way," I tell him, then leave the hut. The bright sunlight stings my eyes as I wade out through the grass.

Soon, Aaron and I lie down beneath our shelter in the waning light of evening. I sit up and stare at the mountains from within the protection of the net. They stand pitch black against a brilliant orange sky speckled with pink clouds.

"That's the Central Divide," I say to Aaron.

"If it's not, I would sure hate to see the real one," he comments.

"Just gotta make it across . . . Then we're home free." Aaron looks up at me, then to the mountains. I can't see any detail in the gloomy, black form of rugged peaks painted across the sky.

"Home free . . . or we'll drown in rapids," he says. All is quiet. Aaron pulls himself up to the edge of the net as we study our opponent together.

"They say that's the last place on earth where cannibals and headhunters still exist." I am whispering, as if some might be close by.

"God have mercy," Aaron prays, before lying back on his blanket. I scratch my lower legs.

"It's New Year's Eve tonight, ya know," Aaron says. I can hear him scratching as well.

"Do you itch too?" I ask.

"Around my ankles."

"Dang! What have we gotten into now? Getting off this island is my New Year's resolution." I search in the blackness for my flashlight. "It's been quite a year for me. Last year at this time I was digging a hole 18 feet in diameter, through six feet of snow in 30-below-zero temperatures, to get my tepee set up—from bitter cold to steamy jungles, grizzly bears to crocodiles. And from the depths of loneliness to the trials of hanging out with you all day." I turn my light onto my ankles to find them covered in red bumps. I examine them closer.

"I was in South Africa this time last year." Aaron remembers. I can see white tips on the new itchy sores.

"Looks like chiggers or something," I conclude. Aaron sits up. He has them all around his ankles as well.

"Must have picked them up in all the grass around here."

We scratch them together.

"Oooh, that feels good."

"Just don't rub the skin off, or you'll get a nasty infection," he warns.

"You mean *another* nasty infection," I correct him. We laugh. "It's almost worth having these sores just to have the pleasure of scratching them." I look at him. "I tell you what, if we can live through this year, what do ya say we take a vacation on the next New Year's day, or maybe we can just stay home and spend it with a beautiful woman." We're quiet for a long time.

"A beautiful woman," Aaron finally whispers. "What I wouldn't do just to talk to one."

The next thing I know, I wake up to an annoying beeping noise coming from Aaron's watch.

"Happy New Year," comes his groggy voice.

"Happy New Year." I roll over and go back to sleep.

The jungle begins to grow over the top of our shelter. The vines come twisting in as they turn into snakes embracing my legs beneath the net. I wake up, out of breath and sweaty. My body freezes when I feel something very real crawling down my leg. My hand carefully searches for my flashlight. It stops crawling. Don't move, I tell myself. It feels large, like a giant spider. It crouches on my ankle. I feel the net hanging across my right leg. I must have rolled my leg out from under the net while having the nightmare. It's going to bite me! I start to panic. Get it off! I think to myself. I clamp my eyes shut and kick my foot with a hard jerk. It doesn't come off!

"Iiiiiieeeeeeeee!" I scream, feeling a bite. My leg is kicking wildly in the air. Aaron springs up beside me as I pound at my leg through the netting. I pull it back under, still crying out with the pain that now shoots up my leg.

"What! What is it!" Aaron is yelling. I get my leg under the net slapping frantically at my ankle to make sure whatever just bit me is off.

"Find a flashlight!" I yell at Aaron. I hear him searching. I feel swelling in my ankle as I grip the throbbing tissue with my hand.

"What happened?" Aaron asks again, worriedly, flashing the light on.

"Something bit me!" We look. My ankle is swelling before our eyes; two little red needle-size pricks sit side by side. "Oh Lord!" Aaron says of the sight. "What was it?"

"Something bad! It was a spider or a centipede . . . I never saw it." Aaron springs onto his knees and starts searching the netting and blankets. "It was outside. I stuck my leg out from under the net." He glares at me. "Not on purpose—I was having a bad dream." He continues his search for several minutes until he is thoroughly convinced that nothing dangerous is in the net with us. I fall back on my blanket, moaning and writhing. I rock back and forth, searching for comfort. "Well, at least I lived for a few hours in 93," I laugh nervously.

"Shut up, dude! Don't you dare leave me alone in the middle of this dang island. Just hang on and try to be calm." Aaron's voice is not so calm.

"Just keep breathing. I can't die if I keep breathing," I try to encourage myself. I know one thing for sure. If I do live, I'm in for a long night.

CHAPTER 9

The Lost Tribe

High mountains loom on the morning horizon, daring me to try. It's the beginning of the third day since the bite, which has rendered my leg useless, wasting two important days that we could have been hiking. That first night of 1993, when I was bitten, is etched in my memory as a night of severe suffering, an unending throb of pain that threatened my sanity. I was still awake when the sun rose the next morning revealing my swollen ankle, poisoned by unknown fangs. Over the past two days and nights it has become worse, wasting no time getting infected.

The mountains continue to taunt me. I want so desperately to press on. Aaron walks up to the net and glances down at our only obstacle—the large, bloated lump of infected puss and blood, as big as my fist, protruding from the side of my right ankle.

"It's not getting any better."

"No," he agrees, handing me some sago, called "sok sok" in pidgin, for breakfast. He has done well taking care of me lately.

"If it's only going to get worse, we should move on," I suggest. Aaron studies my face as I look back towards the rugged horizon. "Better now than in a few days when it could be twice as bad."

"Good idea, I mean, hey, let's get as far away from Inaru as possible before we have to carry you back."

"Inaru is gone!" I point to the southern peaks. "We have to make it over to the Lagaip. It's the fastest way out of here now, crippled or not." I grab the medical kit and start searching for the pain killers. "Stop staring at me and pass the water bottle."

"You can't get your boot on," he pleads.

"I need a stick." He looks confused. "Trust me. I have a plan—all I need is a little stick about as big around as my finger." He walks off to look for a stick while I take some pills and pull out the bottle of iodine, cotton balls, and an ace bandage.

"All right, what's the plan?" He asks, throwing me a stick.

"If I'm going to get my boot on, I need you to squeeze all the gunk out of my sore." His face reveals the same horror that I feel in the pit of my stomach.

"You're crazy!"

"Have you got any better ideas?"

"And the stick?" he questions. I place it in my mouth and clamp down. "Do you really think that's going to help?"

I pull it back out of my mouth to speak. "I don't know. They always do it in the movies." I try to muster a smile. Aaron studies my ankle. "One more thing." He looks up at me. "Once you start, don't stop until it's all out." With that, I place the stick in my mouth, put my hands under my body, and lie back on them. I talk through the stick. "Just remember, do it fast and. . . ."

I feel his hands press in without mercy. My mouth clamps shut onto the stick. I sit up, wincing in pain, as he squeezes harder; gobs of bloody puss squirt from my sore all over his hands. He looks away when I bellow out a horrible scream. I begin to tremble in unbelievable pain. I need it to end. It has to end. And then, for a moment it does, until he starts pinching from a different position. I scream until he stops. I gasp for air, opening my eyes to find the bewildered faces of the carriers looking down on me. I sit up, feeling somewhat foolish.

"You okay?" Aaron's voice is shaky. I nod that I am, though I feel dizzy and nauseated. I realize my mouth is still clamped shut, so I release the pressure. The branch is stuck, deeply embedded in my upper teeth.

"I would keep that in," Aaron suggests, lifting up the iodine. I look down to find an empty crater in the side of my ankle. He pours the iodine in, filling the hole until it overflows. I tremble with the sting's intensity, and bite back down on the stick. After several minutes, I feel some relief. I wrap my ankle up with the ace bandage and reach for my boot. After loosening the laces, I pull it onto my foot with several loud screeches. Standing up, the blood rushes down to my sore, and it begins to throb.

With the Bushy Man and carriers watching me, I try not to show my pain. Limping forward, I put as little weight as possible on my crippled ankle. I take a step onto my right foot. Pain shoots up my leg, pushing a miserable moan out of my clamped-shut mouth. I feel the eyes of the men on me. I concentrate on smiling before turning around to face them.

"Walk about," I announce.

"Iiiiieeeee!" They cry out, shaking their heads while they tisk at me.

"You won't make it anywhere like that," Aaron comments.

"Just find me a walking stick, and I'll make it to wherever we're going."

"There's where we're going," he says, pointing to the mountains that loom on the horizon of steep jungle slopes and high rocky peaks.

"Please . . . just get me a walking stick." I'm standing with my weight shifted completely onto my good foot.

*   *   *

Lord, you are my God,
And I will ever praise you.

I stop singing for a moment to pull myself another couple feet up the muddy ledge. My foot catches on a root. I look up, the sweat stinging my eyes—nothing but more jungle, more climbing. I've been in last place all day, and now I'm feeling very alone. Grabbing hold of a vine, I heave myself up, dragging my limp foot behind me. I put some weight on it, then I pull my other foot up to a root. My leg aches as I move higher.

And I will follow you all of my days,
I will learn to walk in Your ways,
And, step by step, You'll lead me,
And I will follow you all of my days.

I sing to remember why I'm climbing this mountain of suffering. This morning is the second full day of working my way, slowly and painfully to the top of the Central Divide, the climax of our expedition. I am feeling every step! This morning we repeated the process of Aaron milking my wound so I could get my boot on. The first mile out of camp was the worst. There was dizzying pain as the blood flowed down my leg and put pressure on the wound that has become more infected. Aaron has done well, doing my load of the chores. He cooks, cleans, sets up, and takes down camp so that all I have to worry about is making it to the next camp.

"Iiiiiieeeeee!" I pull up my shirt and scrape off a large leech. I have learned the hard way that moving slowly through the jungle puts me at an extreme disadvantage. My handicap gives the leeches, ants, flies, and mosquitos more time to locate me and perform their merciless rituals of torment. I am caught between the misery of hiking and the torment of resting, the worst of both worlds. It makes sense to me now why the nationals have learned to move so quickly through their native terrain.

A vine dangles from the canopy up the ridge. It pulls tight when I get hold of it for a mighty heave, but a snap echoes and the vine drops, limp, to the ground. My hands panic in the air while the ridge slips away. The canopy becomes a streaking blur until it jerks still when my back slams hard against the ground. My sore ankle gouges against roots and rocks as I continue to tumble down the slope, my screams echo through the dense foliage. I have to stop, flashes through my mind; the bottom of the mountain is so far down it has taken me to days to get were I am. I forget the hurt for the moment and use my legs and arms to stop my out-of-control roll. With the world back in focus, I grab at a small tree to stop my slide. The tree quickly breaks from my grip, but I have slowed down enough to get hold of a vine that swings me across the ridge. Finally, I stop. Pulling my legs up to my chest, I gasp for air. Overwhelmed with pain, I cry out in hurt and frustration until enough of the throbbing subsides and I can think again. My shouts die down to moans, and I try to comfort my traumatized body with a gentle rocking motion. Finally, I sit up and slip my boot down to have a look. Blood is soaking through the ace bandage wrapped around my ankle. Ants crawl up my skin and flies prick at my back. Fury floods my heart and mind.

"Damn you!" I stand and shout to the canopy overhead, the dark shadows, the mountain. "Have you no mercy at all?" I feel something grip my shoulder and I wheel around with fright.

"You okay?" Aaron stands behind me looking concerned.

"Do I *look* okay?" I knock his hand off my shoulder and start back up the ridge. Enraged, I momentarily forget the pain as I storm up the same ridge I have already climbed. Aaron follows in silence somewhere behind. Before long, though, the pain comes back, shooting up my leg, making me even angrier. I put more weight on it. Tears flow from my eyes, and my jaw tightens. I look up into a never-ending jungle and push off three hard times in a row from my bad foot. Crying harder now, I move faster than I have in days

"Take it easy!" Aaron is beside me now. I'm dizzy and start to sway.

His hand grips my arm, and he lowers me to the ground.

"What are you doing?" His voice is confused.

"I don't care . . . I don't care anymore." I try to stand up, but he doesn't let me.

"Not until you calm down." We sit for a long time before hiking again. He swats at the flies on my back. I moan with every step; it's worse now, everything is worse. What choice do I have but to go on? Aaron hangs back for the next hour keeping me in sight. My moaning grows louder until suddenly he turns around, his face streaming with tears. He begins to cry harder as he charges me, throwing himself to the ground at my feet.

"God!" He screams in a hurt voice. "Please, please heal him!" His hand trembles on my sore ankle. He weeps out loud, his whole body shaking. "Why? Why won't you just heal him?" He cries in frustration. I reach down and place my hand on his shoulder.

"It's okay," I try to tell him, but it doesn't help. I realize my selfishness, that Aaron is more than a friend and a partner. His feelings are deeper than sympathy. I realize that everything I do, and feel, and suffer affects him. We are in this together. If I hurt, then he hurts with me! I realize the need to be strong for both of us. "It's all right, Aaron." He turns quickly around and starts back up the ridge.

My next steps don't seem to hurt as bad; it's not my ankle, but *something* has healed, something is different, something more important! I think of the ridge I am on, and suddenly know I can climb it, no matter how bad I hurt. I give thanks to God for His strength. Keeping my mouth shut, I climb for the rest of the day.

We are making our way up through a rock outcropping and come across the old woman sitting in a patch of grass. None of the other carriers seem to be around. The old woman notices our confusion and points to a large, black, gaping hole in the side of a ledge. Wild noises of beating wings and clanging metal blades striking rock ring out from the opening. I move closer, then flinch as a hurtling lump of skin and fur flies out of the blackness towards me, falling on the ground with a thud. A bat bares its teeth and hisses at me. Its wing bones are apparently shattered. Moist with blood, the broken ends of jagged bones are sticking out from the dark skin of its wing.

"Looks like it's going to be evil spirits for dinner," Aaron comments from behind. More clanging rings out from deep in the cave followed by several injured bats shooting out of the dark hole onto the grass. The old woman takes the dull end of her bush knife, and without even the slightest change of expression, begins breaking their good wings to form a squirming pile of hissing little mouths. She strikes the most lively bats on the head a few times with the broad side of the blade, being careful not to kill them. Then she begins to load them into her belum bag. The cave entrance produces about fifty bats before the Bushy Man and the others pop out onto the ridge with their eyes squinting in the sunlight.

In the search for a campsite, I fall behind again. Limping further, I notice the altimeter on Aaron's watch reads 10,000 feet. Throughout this day of climbing, the wet jungle has given way to pine trees. The wind picks up and begins to whistle; I look up at the tall pines swaying beneath a blue sky. It feels so strange to see the sky again. I take in a breath of air. The heavy humidity is gone; and the breeze is set free, whisking the dry moss that dangles from the surrounding tree limbs.

"Almost feels like the mountains back home," Aaron comments, turning around in front of me.

"Not really," I say, seeing the Bushy Man standing in a clearing waiting for us. He has come back to lead us to the camp. The air is cool, almost cold; my shirt is dry and no sweat pours across my face. I stop and wait for a moment, searching around me. No flies. No mosquitoes. Looking down, I search the ground for ants but only find a few. The thick undergrowth has vanished, leaving behind barren ground of dry dirt and rock—so much room to walk. The Bushy Man's bush knife hangs still at his side.

And then the ridge ends. I had all but given up hope that we were ever going to find the top. The wind picks up and moans an eerie sound—so ancient, so lost. Spheres of tree tops stretch out over us as we start along the crest of the ridge towards the east. How did I ever get here? I ask myself in the strangeness of this moment. Two large, rocky ledges rise up in front of us; a crack of air splits them in half. We enter the trench of solid rock and follow it until it ends in a flat area under an overhanging ledge. The smoke from a fire fills the camp. I drop to the ground from exhaustion. My ankle has been hurting so badly for so long that I have almost become used to the pain.

"I think I'm gonna like it up here," Aaron says, looking calm and safe from the usual array of attacking insects.

"Too cold for them . . . I just hope it's not too cold for us," I say.

The Bushy Man builds a cooking rack out of sticks while the others prepare a shelter on top of a small hill for Aaron and me. The overhang above the fire will be adequate for the others. The old woman starts handing wounded bats to the Bushy Man. He uses the sharp end of a vine to thread several wings before he ties the bats in place, on the rack over the fire. He ignores their tortured squeals as the flames rise up to engulf them.

Aaron decides not to watch this scene and goes to put up the net. With my now-throbbing ankle, I have no option but to stay put and watch. A heap of fifty bats now hangs over the fire, some already silent in the comfort of death, others just beginning the process. They look like "evil spirits;" their little mouths squealing in pain, revealing rows of sharp teeth. More wood is placed under them. The flames reach up, singeing the hair from their bodies. They screech, twisting and kicking on the vine as their ears curl up in the growing heat. Large blisters form and then quickly pop across the skin of their bodies and wings. I look down. If they were Birds of Paradise, then I would save them, I think to myself. Their noises of suffering finally begin to fade into the coming night.

With the absence of the gloom-and-doom jungle canopy, brilliant stretches of stars shed light on us. We are eating bat meat with men who still ponder the night-lit sky in the simplest of wonderings. I shut my eyes while I chew the dark, wild-tasting meat, trying to delete from my memory the gruesome scene of rising flames and squealing bats so strongly implanted a few hours before. The moss glows florescent green, performing a kind of ritual dance as the wind picks up. The air is cold, and even wrapped up tight in our blankets, the night is long and uncomfortable.

"Happy nun." I wake to find Sogamoi bent over our net.

"Nogat walkabout, Stew big pain," he announces, passing some burnt mummified bats under the netting.

"What's big pain?" Aaron asks.

"Me no suvey." Sogamoi replies. I take a bite of bat meat. It must have smoked all night, because it crumbles in my mouth like saltless jerky. Maybe it will keep for a day or so this way, I think. Aaron slips on his boots.

"I'm going to check on Stew real quick."

"Don't worry, I won't eat your bat," I tell him with a grin. Aaron returns as quickly as he leaves.

"I think you better come down," his voice is solemn. "Don't bother with your boots. We aren't going anywhere for a while."

"What is it?" I stand up, wincing with the pain shooting up from my ankle.

"I don't know. Just come down." He leads me down the small slope. Making my way down under the overhang, I realize the hurt in my foot has grown worse during the night. Stew is curled up away from the fire, his knees drawn up to his chest. He is shaking uncontrollably, with streams of sweat running down his face, even though the morning is cool. We are greatly concerned for Stew, and are stunned to hear laughter ringing out behind us. Aaron and I turn to find the rest of the men sitting in a circle enjoying one another's stories. Even Stew's wife, Agomi, sits by herself and smiles at us, seeming unconcerned.

"He's burning up with fever." Aaron has knelt down with his hand on Stew's forehead.

"Stew . . . Stew!" I shake him, but he shows no signs of comprehension; he continues severely trembling. Laughter breaks out again, eating at our distressed emotions.

"He's dying, Joel." Aaron's words quiver while tears start rolling down his colorless cheeks. Again, the laughter clashes against our fear, changing Aaron's expression to anger. Without warning, he jumps to his feet. "What is wrong with you people?" he screams. The laughter dies out. "Isn't Stew your friend?" With a red face, he turns to Agomi. "Isn't this man your husband?" His voice sounds desperate. They just stare at him, "Sogamoi, malaria, Stew gottam malaria? We twopella givem pills," he pleads in the midst of tears.

"Nogat malaria . . . big pain." Sogamoi breaks the shocked silence. He grabs his chest, "Iiiiiiieeeeee."

"Stew die?" Aaron asks. He shuts his eyes and drops his shoulders until Sogamoi understands the question.

"Me no suvey," he replies with a shrug. Aaron runs over and drops on the ground next to Stew's trembling body. "Stew! Stew!" He shouts, crying louder, but the only answer he gets is a low moan. The mountain people watch as Aaron stands and then storms up the hill to our shelter. I follow, limping my way up to the net. He sits down under the net and grabs the medical kit, pouring it out on the blankets. I look over his shoulder as he digs through the pile of worthless bandages, iodine, malaria pills, Lomatil, and stitching threads. Then, he breaks down. Holding his face in his hands, his crying turns to sobs. I crawl under the net and wait for him to finish, feeling the weight myself. Finally, he looks up.

"Have you ever watched a man die?" I ask him. He shakes his head. "Me neither." I hesitate for a moment. "These people have—it's a common part of their lives. Family, and . . . well, they just lost a friend less than a week ago."

"How can they just sit there and pretend nothing bad is happening?"

"Maybe they understand, deeply, that death is a part of life," I suggest. "How would it help Stew? How would it help them if they were depressed all day? They have to go on hunting and living, or else tomorrow they will get hungry and weak, and sickness will kill them."

"Stew was the strongest. I thought he was invincible, and now look at him. If men like him get struck down, then what chance do we have?" I look away, feeling his fear. He is right.

"It was the kayak, ya know . . . he carried it up here the last two days. That kayak is too heavy; everyone who carries it gets sick. Sogamoi got malaria twice when he carried it. Stew has carried it the last two days of climbing, and it looks like it is going to kill him, and for what? Twenty kina or less? It should be us, not him. And we have no medicine for him and neither do they!"

I look down at my ankle; it seems so insignificant now. "Maybe their medicine is to laugh." I pull myself back out from under the net. "Come on . . . let's go do the only thing we can."

Aaron follows me back down to Stew. I prop his head up, and we give him some pain killers with water. After gathering the men together, we lay our hands on Stew's trembling body. I pray. "There is only one Doctor in this place and one Medicine that can save our friend. Lord, our God, heal him! Thank you, Jesus. Amen."

"Amen," Aaron whispers beside me. We put one of our Gortex rain jackets on Stew and cover him with blankets before going back to the shelter to ration out rice. There isn't much food to hunt in this high country.

Surprisingly, Stew is able to sit up by morning and spends his day leaning over the fire. When his moans grow loud and more frequent, we give him some more pain killers. I find a stick for the daily "milking" of my wound, which has more gunk in it than usual. I bite down hard. As Aaron begins to squeeze, and puss starts to pour from my ankle. I turn away, trying to hold my emotions in. I know the days have been rough enough, but this is too much for me. I tremble in the wake of my moans. The stick snaps in my mouth, giving way to screams as I twist back and forth on the forest floor. Finally, the squeezing stops.

"Gross!" Aaron says in disgust. I look down to find a large pile of puss next to my ankle. It's black. Dark red lines travel in webs up my leg beneath my skin. "You have blood poisoning." Without warning, he pours in the iodine, throwing me back into a twisting tremor of agony on the ground. He puts fresh bandages on, while I recover, and gives me some pills to take. "You need to go on double antibiotics until it heals up." His eyes are filling with tears again. "I have to go." He picks up the little black Bible and quickly disappears into the woods behind the net.

I begin to worry about him in the late afternoon, but Aaron finally returns. We sit in silence, watching the men coughing in the background, spitting junk out of their lungs.

"They're all getting sick."

"It's too cold up here for them. Did you figure anything out while you were gone?" He nods. "I want to hear it." He looks a little shocked.

"It might be pneumonia that Stew has. This cold, dry air is making them all sick, so I say we need to get down to the lower altitude they are used to." He fidgets with his hair while looking at the carriers sitting around the fire below us. "It took these men eighteen days to get here from their village. Carrying Stew, it will take them longer to get back, so I don't really see that as an option. We need help. Our only chance is to find missionaries somewhere downriver. We need three men to help us down to the Lagaip River. Bushy Man, Sogamoi, and Mowga can continue with us. Libi, Eabay, Bushy Man's son, Aguy, and the women can help carry Stew down the ridge, back to the Bushy Man's hut. We can give them enough food to get them there. Then they have a garden. We make it to the Lagaip as fast as possible and then try to find a missionary for help. That's the best plan I could come up with."

"It's worth a shot," I agree. Again, Aaron looks somewhat shocked at my easy acceptance of his plan. "Good luck explaining it to the men." And that's what Aaron attempted to do—all afternoon until nightfall.

Stew looks better in the morning. We say a sad goodbye to him, Aguy, Eabay, and the women. We pray for Stew one more time before continuing our climb up the finger ridge, which takes most of the morning. We had thought we were right on top of the divide, but we had only topped a finger ridge connected to the main divide. By noon, the trees have completely disappeared, replaced by rock and grass. Within half an hour, we are on top of the island—an inspiring sight. The tips of pine trees point at us from below, gently swaying in a breeze rising up the steep slope into our faces. Below the pines, the thick green canopy falls and ripples across the ridges that go on until they disappear into the distant haze. The misty Salumei gorge cuts through the ridge tops in the far distance. Finally, we can see all at once the mass of ridges that we have crossed since the breaking konda bridge.

"Shhh! Listen!" I hear voices! A hand reaches up over the lip of the ridge, the knuckles whitening as it pulls, and the old woman's worn face pops into sight. Aaron and I look at each other, puzzled. Eabay tops the ridge, followed by Aguy, Agomi, Libi, and the Bushy Man's son, who turn around and pull Stew up over the lip. He looks at me, holding a walking stick in his hand.

"Stew?" Aaron questions.

"On top," he says in a weary voice with a weak smile.

"You truly are the toughest man I have ever met." I get up and walk to the other side of the ridge while Aaron tries to find out why they didn't go down to the Bushy Man's hut like they were supposed to.

From my vantage point, it doesn't look much different on the other side of the divide, just as thick and rugged. I call for Aaron. He comes and looks silently out over the vastness.

"Why did they come with us?" I ask him.

"No idea."

"See that gorge?" I point into the distance. A gaping canyon splits the canopy and the rugged terrain in the cloud-covered distance.

"Lagaip," Aaron says.

The carriers spend a lot of time looking out over their home-terrain from this radically new angle. They have spent their lives living beneath the dark blanket of rain forest, but now they get to see their world from on high, looking down.

"Onward to Daru!" Aaron shouts when we begin our descent down the southern slope of the divide.

The slope falls away so sharply that at times our lives hang by a tree branch or a root. Everything feels insecure. I face out into empty air, and gravity forces me to go much faster than I desire. The roots and vines that I had trusted as handholds on the way up are now behind, where I can't see. I think back to the many falls I have taken while descending smaller ridges, being unable to stop myself until having landed with a painful thud next to a creek bed. The pit of my stomach tightens when I search for the end of this ridge, but it looks bottomless. The ridges fanning out to the south seem miles away.

The way down is faster, but it is much more jarring on my bad foot than the slow climb of the past several days. Within a few hours, the tops of the pine trees grow closer together, casting shadows that grow darker and darker the more we drop in elevation. The first sign of the pesky, jungle foes is a leech I pull off the side of my neck. Soon, the usual cloud of biting flies returns along with mosquitoes and ants. I want to turn around and head for the high country again.

The jungle crowds me. Its canopy, falling sharply with the steep ridge, begins to shake with powerful gusts of wind, like being underwater during a terrible storm and looking up at the angry surface. I hesitate, watching the tree tops out in front of me fiercely jerk in the wind. The storm takes us by force when dark clouds collide with the ridge. Their grayish mist engulfs us, dramatically cutting down visibility. Stew is standing behind me now; I turn around and show him how to zip up the rain jacket that I have given him to wear. I pull the hood over his head as the rain begins to penetrate the leafy roof. It is important for him to keep dry.

As we continue to hike, a thin, slippery blanket of water and mud flows along the ground under my boots. I fall, sliding and tumbling down the side of the ridge several times until, battered, annoyed, and bruised, I catch up with Aaron and the Bushy Man. Aaron is also covered in mud from recent falls. We pass the carriers and the women who have taken shelter under a rock ledge to enjoy a smoke.

After a few hours, the rain dies down. Aaron and I continue to slip and slide our way behind the Bushy Man. Aaron lets out a loud cry of agony when he strikes one of his leg sores on a branch. Even Bushy Man flinches at the sudden and horrible shout. Then he suddenly freezes mid-stride, and his hand shoots up behind him. Aaron and I stop, not daring to breathe while we search the jungle. Slowly, the Bushy Man draws an arrow onto the vine stretched deadly tight against the hardwood tips of his bow. His flat, swollen feet move silently across the mud; then he crouches, placing the bow and arrow on the ground. His legs spring straight, hurtling him through the air as he clears a log and completely disappears in the green foliage beyond. He emerges moments later with a fifteen-foot python snake which he carries by the head. It twists its tail, trying to snare a leg, but Bushy Man escapes it.

The carriers have caught up with us now. Seeing the yellow and black-colored python, Libi cuts a branch from a tree and splits three fourths of its length with his bush knife. He slides the snake's neck into the slit, clamping down the open end with his hands while using a vine to tie it shut. Then he drops the squirming serpent onto the ground. A swollen lump in its middle makes it obvious that it has recently eaten something. Aaron runs over and picks the python up. "Joel, take a picture." He hoists the snake up while I dig for the camera. I am taking the shot when everyone bursts into laughter. Looking over the camera, I see that Aaron's excited look has turned to one of misery. With the snake on the ground again, Aaron looks down at his pants.

"What happened? Did he bite you?" Then, I see a big wet stain running down his pants and start to laugh. "Looks like you got pissed on by a python." Aaron does not find any of it the least bit funny. The strong odor of snake urine stings my nostrils as he storms past me to continue the hike. The old woman fills her belum with the night's squirming dinner. Libi has adjusted the stick on the snake's head to cut off just enough air to weaken it but still keep it alive and its meat fresh.

Stew is the last to make it into camp where he collapses on the ground. Aaron gives him more pain killers, then turns his attention to the reek of the snake urine still rising off his pants. He washes them with water and dirt, and, though it helps, it doesn't kill the odor completely.

Meanwhile, the old woman spills the mostly dead python out on the ground and goes to cut firewood as dinner preparations begin. The Bushy Man's son had killed a poisonous red snake when they first found camp. It's bush-knife-hacked body lies still next to the python who is now getting massaged by the hands of Libi and the Bushy Man. The lump in the snake's belly begins to move towards its mouth. I watch in horror. Libi unties the stick around its throat once the lump is close enough. I shut my eyes, hearing the snake gagging up its victim. The slimy, semi-digested carcass of a possum lies on the jungle floor. I start to gag.

Libi ties the stick back in place over the snake's throat. This time, he clamps it down as tightly as he can, cutting off the snake's air completely. He throws the snake aside to wait for it to die. About thirty minutes later the snake goes limp. Meanwhile, the three-day-old, partly digested possum is cooked over the fire, torn apart and eaten by the mountain people. Aaron and I pass when they offer us some.

However, the snake meat is white and juicy when it comes off the fire; its flaky consistency makes it fall easily from the hundreds of ribs. It is light, without a strong flavor. There is no fat or chewy toughness to it like some of the possum and pig we have eaten. Aaron slurps at the meat, eager for more. It's not that it really tastes good; it just doesn't taste bad! The Bushy Man sucks a piece of skin into his mouth. Then Aaron asks for more. Sogamoi hands over another piece, and Aaron catches my eye in the middle of scarfing it down.

"What?" he asks. His hair sticks out in all directions; his beard wet with snake-meat juices. I smile at him.

"We have been in the jungle too long."

Soon we finish eating and go to sleep; the night is filled with coughs, hacking, and spitting. Stew groans deep into the night until Aaron gets up to give him more pain killers. Then the rising sun wakes us to another miserable day.

After hiking all morning, we finally reach the bottom of the Central Divide. It is a good feeling to have it behind us, and now the excitement of being close to the Lagaip and the downriver stretch of our expedition gives us energy for the rest of the long day's hiking, energy I didn't realize I had, especially with the lack of food. We spend the rest of the day climbing and descending the buckling ridges that we had looked down a few days before.

The night overtakes us before we can find a camp, and we end up sleeping without a net or a shelter on a bunch of rocks next to a cliff. I pull my bag up under my legs so that most of my body is lifted up by the bag, a more comfortable position than lying directly on the hard stones. Needless to say, I don't get much sleep.

The sharp rocks which have dug into my back all night wake me at sunrise. Because there isn't a camp to take down and no breakfast for anyone, we start hiking earlier than usual. A wet-leafed branch slaps me across the face, the price I pay for following too closely behind the Bushy Man who makes his way quickly through the thick jungle wall. I step into an opening and look around. Bushy Man kneels down on one knee, studying a long muddy scar across the ground, slicing a path towards the south through the dense undergrowth. The carriers react in fear, their eyes wide and apprehensive as they stumble one by one onto the trail.

"What?" I ask Sogamoi, but he quickly warns me with his hand to be quiet.

"Belong man," he whispers, pointing to the trail.

"What man?" Aaron asks, looking worried.

"Me no suvey." The men chatter amongst themselves in quiet voices that are quickly swallowed by the jungle noises blaring at us from all directions. The women are nervous as we huddle together behind the cautious Bushy Man, creeping forward down the unknown path. He is listening intently with each silent step. Questions race through my mind while everyone scans the dark jungle surrounding us. Who made this path? What kind of people have been hidden in the dense interior highlands of New Guinea since the beginning of time? The fear in the mountain people only adds to my own.

A crude fence made from split wood woven together with vines pops into view. The tension rises! Wild pig tracks mark up the mud along the outside of the fence. Inside the fence is a garden which bursts into movement when some parrots take flight, sending panic through our group. I look to the Bushy Man. He moves on down the trail, leading us over the lip of the ridge. Suddenly, several huts, built high on stilts, appear just below us. We stand perfectly still. I hold my breath. When I look down, I see a village full of people.

My eyes focus on a woman whose body is smeared with red clay. Streaks of white, black, and red paint decorate her face. My heart begins to race as I realize that she is staring back at me. The large, white, pig tusk in her nose flips back when her mouth opens wide in a scream of horror. Belum strings hanging from her hair jerk as she makes a hasty retreat. The whole village explodes into movement.

Bushy Man drops his bow and arrows on the ground. The others follow his lead. Eerie screams quickly bring my attention down to several women snatching helpless children into their arms as they flee into the forest. The men come together in the center of the village, each one armed with bows and arrows. Tall, cone-shaped hair wrapped in snake skin and tree bark sways above their heads. Fierce war cries add to the shock when the men mount arrows onto the tight vines stretched across their bows. Huddled together, they rush towards us, their sharpened boar tusks swinging from their noses. They are a mass of red bodies, black foreheads, and violent faces.

I step backwards, and Aaron slips the bag from his shoulders. There's no time to think; it's all happening fast. The men are motionless, in shock. I think of running. Lord have mercy! I pray, when I realize I can't run. They are close now; the muscles in their arms strain behind the arrows drawn deeply towards their chests. Bushy Man takes several steps forward. The warriors cry out in fierce warnings. He falls on his face like a dead man in front of their arrows. Each deadly-sharp tip points in a different direction. One is pointed at me. I close my eyes in anticipation of being shot. It doesn't come, so I look again, down the shaft of the arrow at the face of the massive man behind it. His look shows me that he indeed possesses the power to kill. The laws that protect my right to live vanish. These warriors who stand before me have obviously killed before and are ready to kill again, if necessary. These are the ones who make up the laws in this land.

Bushy Man crawls closer. Lifting his head, he directs signs of peace to the one big man who stands out from the rest, stockier and fiercer-looking than his noble warriors. A broad boar tusk pierces his nose, its whiteness standing out in harsh contrast to the blackness of his thick beard and painted forehead. He alone loosens his grip on the vine holding an arrow that had been pointed at the Bushy Man. Unlike the cone-shaped hairstyle of the others, the big man's matted hair spreads out like a mushroom decorated with eagle feathers and the colorful plumes of the Bird of Paradise, which sway in the breeze. The warriors wait in perfect stillness. Then, Bushy Man carefully slides up onto the end of a log. The big man speaks to one of his warriors who immediately creeps over, hand still on his bow, and sits on the end of the log, opposite Bushy Man.

Bushy Man speaks, and the warrior lets some tension off his bow. They begin the struggle of communication with words and signs. The longer they attempt to understand each other, the closer they get to one another, sliding across the log a little at a time. When at last, Bushy Man establishes the message of peace, the warrior greets him by snapping Bushy Man's knuckles between his fingers. The sharp tip of the arrow which had been pointing at me throughout the whole ordeal finally drops. I take a deep breath of relief. At least for the moment, we are safe.

CHAPTER 10

The Crash

The jungle ceiling looks down on me with a thousand invisible eyes; the ground is hard, my mind uneasy. Drumbeats echo through the trees. I turn my head toward an orange, eerie glow which crawls from the Lost Tribe's bonfire into our camp. Red smoke swirls against the dark backdrop of leaves and vines. Aaron is beside me, and the other men are sprawled under the tarp of our shelter, but no one is asleep. Instead, we listen to the rhythm of several drums that rise and fall between slow but steady, hollow, deep-based blows. Ancient, mysterious voices visit us from the sacred fire circle—troubled voices, asking questions of the outside world that has so suddenly invaded. Two different worlds, both in shock, are colliding.

The rhythmic song seems to search for answers. Aaron and I search as well, lying still in quiet meditation. I look up to admire the canopy. It strikes me again just how thick and concealing it truly is. It has protected this culture and kept their world separate. I think of the technology at work outside, the complexity and power of modern civilization which swallows less-advanced cultures by force, leaving in its wake a disruptive mass of "progressive changes," and little memory of the way things were before its frightening touch.

The tribe where the man had died of malaria we had considered primitive. A few artifacts, however, showed that they had at least traded with the outside world. We had always found a trace of modern culture in the people we encountered: clothing, a lighter, a metal bush knife. Even the Bushy Man carried an axe slipped through the waist band of his grass skirt. But this tribe shows no signs of knowing about the outside world. They have no cloth and no metal. Everything they wear and use is indigenous. To start a fire, they use a piece of bamboo and a vine. Their tools are stone axes and knives, and their bodies are decorated with feathers, shells, furs, and snake skins. The jungle provides all that they have. Completely protected by miles of thick cover, they have stayed hidden from the rapidly changing world outside. They look at our rain gear, netting, and hiking boots, desperately trying to understand, trying to imagine the place from which we have come.

Again, I listen to their song and the wild tempo of drums. Maybe now they ask their gods, I think. I wonder about their secrets, also concealed from the modern world. It is chilling to think of Aaron and me as the first outsiders to visit them, the first white skin they have seen, the first link to something bigger. I try to fathom the responsibilities of such a position, and I wonder what their future holds. Lord, protect us from them, and them from us. Lord, we can go no deeper, no further back in time, than these people.

I fall asleep, still listening to the song continuing deep into the night. The chant of the hunt; the smoke's rising; stars shining above the jungle roof; high mountains, and deep, endless forests clash with my memories of home: rows of neat, stately houses, manicured yards, ringing telephones, highways crowded with cars, and airplanes flying overhead.

In my dreams that night, I go home again to visit my loved ones. "Where have you been?" my father asks.

"Far, far away," I say.

*   *   *

Feathery Bird of Paradise plumes swing with each jerk of the Big Man's head. His big hair casts shadows across the fierceness of his face. His warriors surround him in a cloud of smoke produced from the leaf-wrapped tobacco cigars hanging from their lips. Two six-inch-long beetles roast in the fire among red coals. Their black shells split in the heat, oozing out a bubbling white substance.

"I can't believe I want to eat a beetle," I tell Aaron, who looks up at me with hungry eyes. I am tired on top of my hunger. The tribe had danced, drummed, and chanted, deep into the night. Aaron turns to the warrior who crouches over the fire.

"Maybe, we eatem beetle?" Aaron brings his hand from the beetles up to his mouth. After shaking his head, the man grunts and points to the jungle. "Go find your own beetles," he seems to imply.

"You know it's bad when a man won't even give you a beetle," I say to Aaron, whose attention is grabbed by the squeals of a baby pig.

Sogamoi has traded several shell necklaces for the little rascal and is now tying him up with a vine.

"Do you eat pig?" Aaron points to the squealing beast and signs the question to the Big Man and his warriors. They nod and grunt in agreement that indeed they do eat pig meat. "Youpella's eatem bird?" Aaron asks. Bringing his hand from the feathers that protrude from the Big Man's hair, he places his fingers into his mouth several times. Again, they shake their heads, slapping their hands against their legs and repeat the signs to show that they do eat birds. The warrior reaches down and snatches one of the beetles from the fire, tossing it about in his hands to escape a burn. He breaks open the shell and allows the moist innards to slide into his mouth. He gulps them down before licking the inside of the shell clean. I envy his meal with my empty stomach. The Big Man points to the other beetle still roasting on the fire and repeats the signs of eating that Aaron has used. "Yes, eatem beetle," Aaron smiles. With the excitement of communication, Aaron goes on and on, flapping his arms and asking them if they eat bats, potatoes, lizards, and snakes. Each time, they repeat the signs with laughter and enthusiasm, assuring Aaron that they do eat all of these things. "Youpella's eatem . . . ," he starts to ask, then looks at me in a moment of uneasiness. The men wait. "You eatem . . . man?" I stare at him in disbelief as he pulls up the sleeve of his shirt and starts chewing on his arm! The men respond the same as they have with all the other foods. They shake their heads and laugh, slap their legs in agreement of the cannibalistic act.

"Aaron!" I warn in a harsh whisper. One of the warriors starts chewing on the arm of another, giving me a sick feeling.

"I just had to know," he tries to explain, his face quite serious. The carriers begin to fidget. The lost tribe falls quiet.

"Don't even bring up stuff like that!" I say sharply. "You might give them ideas."

Aaron nods and tries to change the subject, to ease the suddenly tense atmosphere.

The bush rustles beside me. Startled, I turn to find a striped, pig-tusked face staring at me through the thicket. Falling backwards, I catch myself on my hands and pull myself quickly across the ground in full retreat. Aaron jumps to his feet, running across the camp, not even taking the time to discover what has flustered me so badly. All of the men around the fire wail in laughter. Aaron gives me a sharp glare when the two women smeared in red clay emerge from the undergrowth. I shrug my shoulders, feeling embarrassed.

Long strands of belum string dangle onto the womens' shoulders, each string attached directly to their hair. They drop loaded belums from their backs before being swallowed again by the foliage. A large pile of sweet potatoes called "kou kou" in pidgin, is all that's left to prove they have been there. The men load down the fire as the patient wait begins for the food to cook. I pick up a raw kou kou, my stomach tight and desperate. Bushy Man cracks a smile when I take a bite and hand it to Aaron. I chew the moist pulp, and quickly swallow. Soon the potato is gone. It's enough to tide us over until the others are finished cooking.

After stuffing our faces with kou kou, Aaron pulls out the camera and begins to snap pictures of the warriors. A fierce cry of warning bursts forth from the lips of the Big Man when Aaron points the camera at him. "All right, no worries." Aaron snaps a few more of me and the warriors to show the harmlessness of the camera. When Aaron points the camera at him again, the Big Man shouts in anger and rushes towards him. Suddenly, Bushy Man is on his feet, pleading with Aaron to put the camera away. The carriers shout their warnings.

"Nogat! Lobis!" Sogamoi says to Aaron. Nobody rests until the camera is put into a bag, out of sight.

But the Big Man is much too magnificent for us to give up trying to get his photograph. Aaron hides the camera in the pocket of his rain pants until late afternoon when the Big Man finally turns his back. Standing behind the other men, I watch Aaron reach for the camera and snap a photo. The Big Man flinches in the sudden light from the flash. He wheels around to face Aaron before he has a chance to hide the camera. Aaron shies away from the rapidly approaching chief. War cries ring out in the jungle, bringing everyone to their feet. There is pandemonium. Aaron pleads his apologies, carriers yell warnings, and the Big Man looks at us as if he will kill. Even Sogamoi is angry and yells fiercely at Aaron who quickly retreats and hides the camera. The Big Man takes his warriors and women and leaves our camp.

Everybody is uneasy, restless; we are unable to sleep, not knowing when or how or if the Lost Tribe will return. Sogamoi makes his way up to our net in the cool night.

"Morning come, wepella walkabout. Walkabout Bosorio," he announces. "Wantem Kina." We feel uneasy and responsible for their fear as we pay each man the equivalent of fifty kina. Each face is afraid, even the Bushy Man's.

* * *

The Strickland River—rocks that line the shore slip past me in a blur. I study the topo map sealed in a water-proof envelope stretched out across my lap. Finding the fork from the Lagaip, I measure the distance. It is only the middle of our second day of riding the downriver currents, and already we have covered approximately seventy miles, and can average fifty a day if we can keep up the pace. The sun is warm on my face. I feel alone.

* * *

The morning after the Big Man got so angry with Aaron for taking his picture, we said goodbye to the mountain people . The Big Man's reaction had been an event that nobody seemed to fully recover from. The carriers and Bushy Man acted nervous all night and by morning, they decided to leave for their side of the Centrals. I feel a cold pit in my stomach now, remembering the sad goodbye, the large smiles of Aguy, and Mowga. We gave Stew more pain killers and prayed for him one more time before shaking his hand; he seemed to have lost so much life since the first time we shook it, 18 days before on the large boulder beside the Salumei River. We had come so far since that day when Eabay held back so we could follow. The old woman and Stew's wife, Agomi, were too shy to look at us; they giggled their goodbyes while looking out into the jungle. The hardest goodbyes were the last two. I will never forget Sogamoi and the deep eyes of Bushy Man. Tears well up in my eyes. I'll never see them again.

"Jesus . . . lives here," I had said, placing my hand on Sogamoi's chest, his smile larger than life. He had reached up and put his hand on my chest. "Jesus," he repeated.

I miss him, all of them, I think to myself. The jungle has retreated high up the slopes of the peaks, reaching for the sky on either side of the river. The ridges are covered in a rich grassland that traces the paths of wind gusts rolling from slope to slope.

* * *

Later, the Big Man had sent three of his warriors to help us carry our gear. From the village, it took four hard days to find the Lagaip

River: its currents were quick. It was quite a change to be moving faster than ever towards Daru Island, without having to exert much energy. The equivalent of a solid day's worth of hiking drifted past us in minutes.

∗   ∗   ∗

We are uneasy being alone now to face whatever lies ahead. The Old Man of Koup had told us to seek out the wise men along our way, but people are scarce. And now, our trust is scarred, having so recently stared down the tips of the lost tribe's arrows, and experienced the anger of their Big Man. We have no idea who owns the gardens that sometimes line the shore, or how the people would respond to us. After all, we no longer have the wisdom of Bushy Man to save us from danger.

In seventy miles of drifting, we have only seen one group of people, and that was yesterday. Five or six men, a band of hunters or perhaps a war party, crouched on top of a boulder with bows and arrows. They had remained completely still; leaves hung from their hair and grass skirts camouflaged them against the jungle backdrop. They never moved, never waved. I didn't even see them until we neared the boulder. I was so startled, I panicked and started screaming for us to cross the river. I suppose the surprise of seeing them, their quiet ambush-like postures, the piercing stares from their leaf-covered faces, the way they held their weapons, Aaron and me all alone . . . was why I didn't trust them.

We made it several miles downriver from them before camping. Ours wasn't as pretty a shelter as the mountain people had made, but it kept the night rains off us. Our bag full of cooked kou kou intended for dinner was rotten. By morning, my empty stomach growled in protest.

∗   ∗   ∗

Two hours have passed now since we forked off the Lagaip onto the Strickland River. I feel weak with hunger and helpless in my surroundings. Aaron's final words before falling asleep in last night's camp had been, "I'm afraid." Today, I am afraid with him. The river's distant shores would be a long swim if we found ourselves in trouble! The Lagaip had fought us with several class three and four rapids, not easy to maneuver in a twenty-foot sea kayak. But the Strickland River is much bigger, maybe four times the size of the Lagaip, with a swifter, unpredictable, and very powerful current. So far, the Strickland hasn't produced any rapids, but we know it's just a matter of time before she shows off her strength. Aaron and I are quiet, uneasy, sensing her nasty potential.

I look down and study the map. I see the fork and the high ridge lines that ride the horizons on either side. On the map, the grassland stretches out along either side of the river; then all lines, greens and browns, suddenly vanish into white. In a large blank area where the Strickland disappears, I read the fine black print. I have read it many times before: "Data incomplete." I look up at the ceiling of clouds hanging over our heads, said to dump between thirty and forty feet of rain on this terrain every year. With that much rain and so many clouds, it has been impossible to produce a complete map system from aerial photographs. I remember laughing about this section back home, the white splotch on the maps. In our ignorance the risk of it had struck us as funny back then. It's not the only "data incomplete" section that we have traveled through, but it is the biggest, and right on the most powerful river of our trip.

I turn around. Aaron is quiet. His lips have been sealed since we met up with the Strickland. So many questions whirl about in our minds, questions without answers, questions of waterfalls and rapids, drops in elevation and gorges. Where are the people? What are they like? It's been fifty miles since we last saw a garden! One thing is for sure, nobody is laughing now!

A low growl fills the air. The high cliff to our left suddenly falls away as we round a sharp bend. A mighty, thundering roar blasts us as the next stretch of river quickly unfolds into walls of spraying whitewater. The terrorizing scene rushes at me. The opposite shoreline is a distant blur.

"Keep her straight!" I yell. A sudden surge of cold water hurls me backward. The kayak rises to the top of a wave and turns sideways on top of a submerged boulder. I fall into a fourteen-foot-deep pit of churning power, am swallowed by the water's icy blackness. Violent, attacking torrents spin me out of control; my paddle is gone, my Teva sandals are ripped from my feet. All is thrashing, cold confusion. From somewhere the raging surface groans. I feel the magnitude of the water's power and stop my vain struggle. Helplessly spinning, I concentrate on holding my breath and wait. Finally, my lifejacket finds the surface as I gasp in air and choke on water. The current yanks me up through another wave. I catch a glimpse of Aaron struggling in the water, trying to flash me a peace sign before the white foam of another wave engulfs me. Again, I break the angry surface, searching desperately for air, coughing water out of my throat. I see the bottom of the kayak close by and swim to it, managing to barely grasp her ropes before the rapids suck us both under.

Somewhere in the darkness my knee cracks against a rock; pain shoots up my leg. I force my head between my arms for protection. The ropes burn my hands, but I don't let go. The kayak pulls me upward into bright light. As waves crash over the bottom of the overturned kayak, I search for a pocket of air to feed my starving lungs. Frantically, I pull on the ropes, using my strength and my weight, but I can't turn her back over. I am exhausted. The miserable darkness and spinning suddenly return. Then, I glimpse the surface and a moment of smooth, fast water allows me to grab the lead rope and swim for shore. The roar of the next rapid grows louder, but, the strength is gone from my arms, and the shore rocks are still far away. I can't make it! I fear. Too soon, the next rapid overtakes me.

I have to relax, I keep telling myself, clinging to the wall of the swirling kayak. A powerful desire to live overwhelms me when the surface comes back. I decide to let go and swim for shore. I can see downriver when I clear the end of the kayak. The sight of fifteen-foot waves fills me with new terror. It is the largest rapid so far. Intense fear and the sense of impending death, combine with the misery of shock and weakness as I race towards a mountain of pounding water. I quickly swim back and take my grip on the kayak. "I need a miracle, Father, . . . I need a miracle!" I pray out loud, then take several deep breaths. I hear the crash of the wave, feel a tremendous downward pull, and the kayak is now on top of me. The loud crashing of waves suddenly changes to a deep, mighty roar. I am pulled down, down, deep into violent darkness. The kayak jerks free of my grip, and I am alone. My tightly clamped eyes loosen; my legs and arms go limp. Turning over and around, amidst a power too strong to fight, my lungs begin to ache. The feeling worsens. I fight the urge to feed them water. All my hope slips away: Daru Island, friends, family, and home. The miserable feeling of drowning climaxes; my body tingles, even the desire to live becomes dull. My last glimpse of life begins to fade, buried deep beneath the muddy waters of the Strickland River.

And then, as if in a dream, darkness is flooded with light. I open my eyes to see the beauty of the sky, as my exhausted body hangs limp in the fast current. It feels strange to breathe again. Nothing seems real as I see the light green of the kayak drifting effortlessly towards a rocky shore. As I drift past boulders, I wrap my arm around one, coming to a stop. The kayak rests against the rocks in front of me, and I take hold of her ropes once again with my other hand.

I try, but I can't stand up! My hands and face tingle from lack of oxygen. Soon I manage to pull myself up onto mud where I can rest. Is this real? The rope from the kayak slightly jerks in my hand, as if trying to wake me. I roll onto my back, looking up. I feel dizzy, then sick, so I roll back over. Aaron? I think. Again, I am afraid.

Pulling myself up onto a rock, I begin to cough, nauseated. I see the wild rapids of the river and the strange stillness of the opposite shore. A sharp bend in the river sweeps in front of me. Desperately, I search for Aaron in the rage. I can't see upriver because of the waves colliding with huge boulders. Lord, please, please, save my brother! More time passes. How long has it been? I don't know. I feel strong enough to stand, but I grab at my swollen knee. I don't care about the pain. My legs tremble beneath my weight. When I still can't see upriver, an image of Aaron's floating, lifeless body flashes through my mind. Quickly, I chase it away.

Suddenly, a mass of red hair breaks the surface just in front of me, a mouth gasps loudly, tired eyes see me as they pass by. He holds one of our paddles in his hands. Aaron disappears into the rocks off shore. Relieved, I plop down on the kayak, finally enjoying the exhilaration of being alive. Several minutes pass without any sign of Aaron, however, and I start to worry again. Suddenly, his pale face, smeared with mud, pops into sight over some boulders. He crawls down towards me, the white of his shoulder protruding from a tear in his shirt.

"Let's eat," he says. Then we embrace.

"I thought I had lost you," I tell him. Quickly, he looks down.

"Let's eat the emergency rice." Aaron starts yanking on the kayak. I help him turn it over, only to find broken cords swinging free as it flips upright.

"We lost a bag," I say, reaching my hand under the spray skirt and feeling around. Another broken line is all I pull out. "Bush knife is gone." Aaron ignores me, digging like a madman into the green bag. I sit down on the soft kayak.

"We lost the bush knife," I mumble. I remember back, saying goodbye to Rudy and Jay. "Whatever you do, don't lose your bush knife," had been their wise admonition. An empty water bottle lands in front of me.

"There's a clear creek just over those boulders." Aaron's voice is shaky. I stumble up onto my good leg. He glances at my knee and then away.

"I cracked it against a rock." He doesn't respond. "We lost the bush knife, and a . . . ."

"I could sure use that water." He cuts me off, lighting up the stove. My knee hurts during the climb up the boulders, but at least I can put weight on it. I pause for a moment high on a pile of rocks. Although the river turns sharply towards more deadly whitewater; the currents from the turn gently lap against the shore in front of the muddy kayak. They are what pushed us to safety, the miracle I asked for. It still doesn't seem real. Bending down, I fill the bottle, then pour some of the chilly water across my face. I look around again, moisture dripping from my beard. The thundering river rages on; images of my struggle beneath its surface flash through my mind. Shaking the water from my head, I try to forget.

"Hurry up!" Aaron shouts. He seems so different. Taking the water, he focuses on cooking. I sit down on a rock and watch his hands tremble.

"Are you all right?" I finally ask, when the rice is done.

"I'm hungry." He pours half the rice into a bowl and hands it to me. Our emergency supply of two bags has dwindled to only one and a third—all the food we have left. I take a bite. It tastes good. Aaron shovels the white, fluffy flakes into his mud-stained mouth.

I look past the spraying water, up to a fifty-foot cliff and high, rolling ridges of light, waving grass, rows of trees following creeks, dashing their way down to the river. The grass rises for miles until it clashes with a dark green line of thick jungle, blanketing steep, mountainous terrain. Bold rocky peaks hang jagged on the cloudy horizon. I lean over the kayak, searching beneath the spray skirt again and again. Finally, I sit still, in a trance. My rice grows cold. I am staring at the broken line that once held our bush knife.

"I know we're in serious trouble," Aaron admits, as if he'd just come to his senses. "I got out."

His voice startles me. I turn to look at his hollow expression. "The maps are gone and our hats," I say. Aaron feels the top of his head. I wait for him to go on.

"I made it to shore with the paddle." He points to it lying in the rocks, the long blue pole dramatically bent. "I climbed up onto a boulder and saw you and the kayak still going downriver." His voice sounds weak against the echoing rapids.

"What did you do?"

He looks straight at me, his hands still shaking. "What could I do?" He looks out across the waves, breaking themselves against boulders in front of us. "I threw myself back in."

I finish the rest of my rice in silence, as the meaning of what Aaron has just told me sinks in.

"We lost our bush knife," I tell him again, breaking the silence.

"I know," he assures me, still staring at the river.

"It was the bend . . . the current sweeping over onto the shore, that's what saved us." I see a tear roll down his cheek.

"I'll bet when God made this river. He made it with that sharp turn just for me and you," he says. I think for awhile, remembering the horror.

"I've never felt so dead as I did then, or so alive as I do now," I whisper.

"How are we going to get out of here?"

"Same way we got here." I point to the Strickland.

Having eaten the rice, we have recovered some of our strength, but our nerves are beyond repair. We dare not get back into the kayak; so for hours we push her out and around boulders, tediously working her safely through endless rapids with the ropes. With only one bend of the river behind us, we discover another obstacle. We stand in awe of a fifteen-foot-high wall of surging whitewater shooting from the bank into the river, completely blocking our path. It is a tributary rushing down from the high mountains. By the time it reaches the bottom, it has picked up tremendous momentum and is shooting its mass of water thirty feet out into the currents of the Strickland. I shudder at the amazing display of power, realizing that we have no choice. "Front or back?" I ask Aaron, who holds the bent paddle.

"How can we tell what's on the other side?" he shouts. I steady the kayak in front of us before turning around.

"Front or back?!"

"Back."

My body is weak with fear as I climb in. Coiling the front rope, I place its end in my mouth and push off from the bank. Aaron steers us out around the constant blast. The moment we are clear of it, he struggles for shore. The water in front of us is smooth as glass, then it disappears altogether. Spray gushes up in the void beyond the drop.

"Waterfall!" I scream, wheeling around in my seat. Aaron loses strength, the paddle slapping at the water with each of his exhausted strokes. I turn and launch myself out over the water, my legs and arms pounding the surface, the kayak's tow rope clenched in my teeth. Fear pushes me from behind, because I know we can't survive another swim like before. Our only chance is to get out now.

I feel rocks under my feet and start to push off of them toward the shore. The kayak swings around, the rope still tight in my teeth. Soon we are both ashore. This second scare adds to our shock.

"This isn't going to work," I say, feeling defeated. "We've been pulling two hours and haven't made half a mile. We're gonna have to walk out." My stomach wrenches at the harsh realization. Aaron hangs his head; our downriver dream is over. I dig deep into the green bag and pull out our boots and dry, crusty socks. I throw them in front of Aaron, who doesn't move.

"We had four carriers helping us before. Now, with just the two of us, we're going to have to ding some gear," he says, looking up. I agree with a nod and begin dumping the equipment out over the rocks. We throw aside a pile of all our clothing, except one change each. The sacrificial mound grows with the pole spear, a snorkel and mask, extra parachute cord, an extra compass, repair tubing for the kayak, and everything but the essentials out of the kayak-repair kit. Aaron digs into the medical kit. Bandages, lotions, creams, and powders fall with a thud onto the pile. He takes our tube of toothpaste, and I watch as he squeezes all but a third of it out on the ground. Shampoo, soap, combs, deodorants—all of it must go.

Aaron, painfully, throws aside all that we have traded for: precious treasures from the Lost Tribe, belum bags and other artifacts. He takes a piece of parachute cord and cuts it with his knife. In silence, he threads the ends through the biggest pig tusk and ties it around his neck. I pick up the camera with the telephoto lens.

"No," Aaron pleads.

"It's heavy."

"No," he repeats. So, I place it safely back into the green bag with our film. We put all the rest that we can bear to part with into my yellow L.L. Bean bag. Aaron takes his Teva sandals and places them in the discard bag.

"You'll need those." He ignores me and blows air into the yellow bag and seals it.

"If you don't have yours, then I don't want mine," he says, throwing the bag out into the current. Our hope is that somebody will discover it downriver.

The muddy corpse of our kayak lies hissing out air, deflating like our hope. "Amazing Grace will be her name," I announce before rolling her up across the uneven rocks and tying her back in place on the backpack frame. It's been only two days and 80 miles since we got her back on the river.

I put Amazing Grace up onto my back. My knee aches with every step, my body shaking beneath the weight. I begin the climb up the deep, trenched, dirt ledges that hem in the river.

Within fifty-feet, Aaron collapses beneath the green bag, filled with the rest of our survival gear. I help him up, but it's not far before we both are forced to stop and rest. We look back out over the river. The waterfall turns out to be deadly rapids dropping onto overwhelmed boulders and arching down through the mist of thundering waves, dropping into a gorge hundreds of feet deep. The water funnels between narrow rock cliffs, sending us a message, ugly and clear: had we drifted another few feet, we would both be dead.

"I don't think our bag made it very far," I think out loud.

"Joel," Aaron says, staring down into the gorge. "No matter what happens . . . even the worst . . . I don't have any regrets for coming."

"Shut up!" He is shocked by my response. I look at my boots already covered in mud. "We're not dead yet!"

"Then what are we?" I don't have an answer. "We can't go downriver because of the gorge. We can't go up the side of the mountain with no bush knife. I don't know how we are going to get over that torrent we just nearly killed ourselves trying to paddle around . . . and even if we do get upriver, we haven't seen a hut or one living soul in the last fifty miles."

"We can pump up the kayak and try shooting through that gorge," I suggest.

"I'd rather starve than drown." His body shudders when he looks down into the vast chasm of angry water.

"Just wait until we start to starve, then the idea of drowning won't seem so bad." A long silence fills the air.

"I want to go to college," he tells me after a few minutes. His face is serious. "For the first time in my life, I want to go to college, get married and live in a nice house with a picket fence, and have two-point-five kids." His attempted smile is refreshing.

"Oh, come on, things aren't that bad yet." We laugh for a moment, but soon stop.

"Have you ever gone hungry?" I ask.

"No."

"Food is like gasoline: when you run out, you just don't go anymore. These packs are too heavy. I don't know if we have enough fuel with what's left of the emergency rice to even get our body weight out, much less these packs. If you ever want to get to college, then we're going to have to stash all our gear and look for help."

"Daru Island sure seems far away today, doesn't it?" Aaron is looking down on the river.

"Yes . . . it certainly does."

Sweat drips from my face, stinging my eyes. I rip my journal in half, throwing the blank half under the bundle of our gear which Aaron is tying onto a log. Our green rain gear is strapped over the top. Our desires have now changed—from crossing this island to escaping from it with our lives. To survive. That is the only goal, the only dream that we have left.

With the kayak, Amazing Grace, and the second pile of discarded equipment tied in place, we set out with only the green and blue bags. These bags hold just the essentials: the large blue tarp and the small ground tarps, the stove, the pot, the rest of our emergency rice, lighters, blankets, netting, two water bottles, malaria pills, antibiotics, Lomatil, iodine and a few bandages, our Swiss army knife, the small snapshot camera, the film we have taken, plus five new rolls, half of our journals, a pen, and a zip-lock bag with money, passports, and airline tickets.

"Will we come back for it?" Aaron asks, his depressed trance fixed on the heap of expensive, discarded gear.

"I don't know." The river purrs far below. Behind us, the lip of the gorge is covered in tall grass.

"He brought us here." I am remembering. "I mean, I hope I didn't just wake up one morning and decide to come here with you and cross this island. Please, let it be deeper than that. The sponsorship, the money, meeting you, it's all been a process." I feel faith stirring inside of me. "Don't we remember, Aaron, the waves of the north coast and the Old Man of Koup, how scared we were through the miles of crocodile-infested rivers on the mighty Sepik, Korosmeri, Kawari, and Salumei Rivers? Don't we remember the swarms of mosquitoes, Father Don, and the Inaru missionaries?" Standing up, I turn to face him. "They were sitting down, all fifteen of them, to eat Christmas dinner, the moment we pulled up. Remember Rudy and Jay as translators with the Bosorio carriers? Remember the compassion of Sogamoi, the time we ran out of food and into the wisdom of Bushy Man. We have slept with cannibals, hiked with headhunters, and swam through waters that should have killed us." I pause. "Can't we remember all that?"

"Yeah . . . ."

"Why would He bless us through all that to let us die now? I know it, I just know it! Somehow God is going to get us out of here!"

We climb up the fifteen-foot ledge of a square boulder to eat our small, nightly portion of rice. This rock fortress is nestled on the narrow knoll of a steep hill; western skies are on fire with the sunset. The muffled Strickland mumbles from the deep gorge to the west, reminding us of the day's events. On the other side of the gorge, the grassy slopes spread themselves out under the orange sky, and on top of the grass ridges sits a massive crown made up of dark jungle and several protruding, rocky peaks. Behind us, to the east, stand more high, rugged-looking mountains. The sky behind them is much darker. To the south, the walls of the gorge open wide, forming a gaping hole in the valley floor. In the far distance, as far as I can see, are more ridges and peaks. The shine of glimmering, orange water outlines the Strickland coming out of the north, and far away, I see the black silhouette of the dividing ridge where we sat only a week before with Bushy Man and our Bosorio friends. A thick line of trees marks the northern torrent which we paddled around earlier in the day. It falls straight as an arrow from a jungle-choked canyon, far above and behind us, into the river below.

"Trapped," Aaron comments after looking around.

"I've only taken five spoonfuls of rice and it's almost all gone."

"We have powerful torrents and rivers, thick jungles and rocky peaks surrounding us on all sides." Aaron is fidgeting.

I finish my rice and drop the empty bowl off the boulder. The tarp is spread out below for us to sleep on. For the first time, we have no trees to make a shelter.

"I say we go north," I propose, checking the sky for rain clouds. It looks fairly clear.

"It could take us two weeks to get around the gorge to the south," Aaron says. I hear his stomach growling.

"Have you noticed how quiet it is?" The river far below and the jungle far above our camp produce a strange silence that feels close, drifting into a distant rumble. Aaron turns around and looks up.

"East looks like quite a climb. Can't get through that jungle without a bush knife anyway."

"No mosquitoes."

"All the water is moving too fast around here, too fast for mosquito larva and too fast for us." He looks down at the torrent we paddled around. "The north is our best bet? With a wall of water as high as this boulder, moving faster than a train . . . and beyond . . . well, after paddling fifty miles, we haven't seen one person, not even an abandoned hut or a rundown garden." He looks at me. "I just can't believe north is our best direction."

"Believe it." The dark shadows crawl up from the roots of the grasses and blacken the night.

"I never got a chance to thank you for pulling the kayak out of the river after we flipped," Aaron says.

"I didn't pull it out."

"If you would have let it go, we would be sitting here in a pair of boxers and barefoot . . . nothing else."

"I did let go," I tell him, before climbing down to try and get some sleep.

The morning sun is hot without the protection of a canopy. Aaron and I are wearing sweat-soaked, long-sleeved shirts to protect us against grass cuts. Even something as minor as a grass cut can grow into a serious wound with all the tropical infection that floats everywhere in the humidity. We are somewhere in between ridges. The grass is several feet taller than our heads. Blindly, we push forward. We had a restless night. Hunger pains and spiders crawling on us prevented sleep, but the star-filled night had been brilliant. I looked for constellations, and when I couldn't find any, I made up my own.

Another rock catches the toe of my boot, hurling me through the wall of green until I hit the ground. I scramble to my feet, Aaron's trail of bent-over grass ends abruptly in front of me. I look about, confused. "Aaron!"

"I found some drinking water," he calls from somewhere below me. I drop down on my knees and pull the bent-over grass apart to find a cavern of empty space with Aaron lying at the bottom of it on a creek bed.

"You all right?" He rolls over and stands up, his head even with my boots.

"Hand me your water bottle," he says. He dumps out the muddy water from last night's torrent and refills it with the clear creek water. I thank him before jumping across the gap and pushing deeper through the wall of thick grass until I stumble onto a muddy vein riddled with wild boar tracks. The trail spreads the grass apart for some breathing room as it winds its way for a few hundred feet in the general direction that we are headed. Then it disappears altogether.

The grass angles steeply upwards until, finally, we reach the top of the ridge where the grass is short. Below is the line of trees protecting the turbulent waters of the torrent. We agree that our best bet of finding a way across is to go higher. So for two hours, we climb up the crest of the ridge leading us to a high plateau covered in boulders and surrounded by dark jungle. We wade through the grass, past an overhanging boulder with a large beehive to the edge of the plateau which falls sharply into the deep basin of the torrent.

Wild pigs scatter in the shadows as we slide down through thick mud under drapes of vines. The vibration of unleashed power reveals itself in a ridge of rushing water. I try to speak, but I can't even hear myself. All of my body vibrates. A gust of cool wind from the passing water blows against my sweaty face. I pick up a large branch at my feet and throw it into the torrent. Instantly, it is gone.

Aaron is shouting something. I point for us to continue up the slope. He nods in agreement. I need to go faster, but get tangled in vines. Ants bite my legs, cold wet leaves slap my face, and swarms of flies land on my sweaty shoulders. Unfortunately, I have no hat to swat them with. A sticker vine catches my unprotected hair. Aaron has fallen behind to pull leeches from his leg underneath his rain pants. A dizzy spell forces me to hug a tree covered with ants.

We continue to climb and fight, wrestle and pull, slip and get back up, get bitten but push on. Meanwhile, the torrent is losing none of its power. There are no breaks, no chances to cross. My stomach longs for food and my ears for silence; my body yearns to be delivered from the insects, to be set free from vines and enclosing undergrowth. The weakness of hunger strikes my head first with dizziness; then my hands shake and my legs get weak and wobbly. Aaron can't be doing much better since he hasn't caught up yet. I start looking for bugs, grasshoppers, anything for much-needed protein. Suddenly, a leech hooks me solid on my Adam's apple. I turn in circles, tripping over vines and crash to the ground. I pull it off and wipe my hand across the front of my neck to find it smeared with blood. Finding two rocks, I smash the leech between them, then throw its remains along with the bloody rocks into the torrent.

A large boulder stands in the middle of the blast, its peak rising above the white madness; beyond it, I can see the other side of the torrent. Aaron places his hand on my shoulder; I flinch, then point to the rock. We hike up the embankment to escape some of the noise.

"We really are trapped!" he shouts.

"I'm too weak to go any higher." He doesn't argue. "I say we find some fallen logs and build a bridge out to the top of that boulder and then across to the other side." Aaron searches my face for sanity.

"If we fall into that torrent, then . . ."

"What choice do we have!" I scream, cutting him off. I slap angrily at the ants crawling up my rain pants. "I'm going to at least try to build a bridge." I turn around to go back down.

"It won't work!" Aaron yells after me. I ignore him. I feel angry and frustrated, hungry and desperate enough to try just about anything. Aaron stares blankly as I approach the torrent with two large bamboo poles. Climbing a rocky ledge, I look down on the thrashing current beneath me. My hands tremble out of control.

I extend the first log out towards the peak of the boulder. It hits perfectly, the long slender beam hovering only inches above the rushing water. I take a breath, sliding the second bamboo beam across the first until it reaches the boulder; then I drop them beside each other and tie my end together as best I can with a vine. I push on the poles. They feel sturdy, so I stand up, taking hold of a tree branch jutting out above my head. Looking back at Aaron, I see him shaking his pale face back and forth, warning me not to try. Holding myself steady with the branch, I step out onto the beams, releasing some weight from my arms. I take another step. One more will take me away from the safety of the branch. I scoot my foot forward and press down with the weight of my body. The beam buckles in the middle and drops, touching the water. Spray shoots high into the air. I grip the branch overhead just as the poles slide out from under me. The ends of the beams drop from the boulder, then with a tremendous jerk and a blur of green, they smash into the rocky side of the water-filled trench. A loud crack rings out in the midst of the roar. An explosion of splinters spreads out into the foamy spray. Then, everything is gone.

My feet swing back onto the rock ledge. Everything in me is shaken and unsteady as I climb down, shrugging my shoulders at Aaron. He starts climbing tediously higher. I follow. Cat claw vines tear at our clothes. We grow weaker with every step. Aaron climbs away from the noisy water, coming to a stop under a clearing in the canopy. Towering mountain peaks stare down at us through the opening. Steep slopes and endless jungle rise higher than I ever thought possible. We give each other a blank stare; our little bit of hope vanishes at this awesome sight. Aaron starts forward, but I catch him by the arm.

"We're not going to make it," I tell him.

"We have to!"

"We have no bush knife and only half a bag of rice."

"What? You still want to build a bridge!" He shouts. I hang my head.

"No." I look away from the clearing towards the high ridges. "But to cross those mountains is just as unrealistic as crossing this torrent!" He sits down in frustration and throws his arms up above his head.

"We have to do something!" His face is turning red as he screams. "We can't just sit here!"

"No! What we have to do is relax, use our heads, and think!" I take off up the side of the ridge, angrily wrestling with vines. I feel trapped and claustrophobic as I rush forward. I need to see the sky, escape the ants. I need food. I'm out of breath and near the point of collapse, but my panic pushes me up, cursing vines, pulling. Dew falls from leaves, drenching my hair. I see the light of the edge, then blue. My eyes squint in the brightness. I wade into the grass, climb a boulder and sit down. The torrent is far away now, and the mountains are obscured by the wall of jungle. My head drops onto my knees, and sweat runs from my face, streaking my rain pants. I catch my breath and remain still. Sometime later, I sense Aaron near me.

"I know the way out," I announce. I point towards the Strickland. He shakes his head, respectfully.

"I'm not going through that gorge."

"Neither am I."

"What then?"

"We swim across, then hike upriver on the other side." He fidgets,

uncomfortable with my suggestion. "If we want to get out of here, we are
going to have to swim across our biggest fear."

"And if we don't make it across before the rapids?"

"You know the answer to that." I jump down from the rock.

*   *   *

The grumbling Strickland grates my nerves. The last of the rice
hasn't been enough to fill our emptiness. In front of us, the grassy ridge
falls sharply, and further on, the cruel waters of our foe lie in wait. My
eyes are heavy from a long, sleepless night spent under a beehive. This
morning a bee's sting woke me, bringing me out of another haunting
nightmare about drowning. Aaron is not behind me anymore. He has
chosen his own way down to the river bank. But I don't feel much like a
leader anyway—more like an animal, intent on survival. I nearly kill
myself sliding down the steep, dirt bank. A four-foot monitor lizard stirs
below me. I visualize eating him raw, but he disappears down a hole.

"My way was easier," comes Aaron's voice from behind me. I guess
he decided to follow after all. Kneeling down, I blow air into the blue
bag and seal it tight. "How are we going to do this?" Aaron asks. I start
towards the torrent, its wind blowing my hair as it shoots out across the
river. I turn to the river, slipping the bag strap around my neck.

"Joel!" Aaron calls out, but I don't want to talk anymore, or listen to
the river's power, or see the water drop downriver. If I have to do
something, if there's no choice, I'd rather just go! I run to the edge of
the river, launching myself from a boulder. Adrenaline rushes. My legs
and arms burst into action as I drop into the cold water. The only thing
I see is the other shore. Kicking and pulling with all my strength, I feel
the strap cut into my neck. Fear pushes me towards the far shore. The
rapids grow louder, closer, but fighting for every breath, I never take my
eyes from the rocky bank until I climb the rocks.

Aaron waits on the other side. After several minutes, he dives in
and swims with panicked strokes. By the time he makes it across, just
down from me, his energy is gone. I wait for him to recover enough to
walk to me.

It takes all morning just to make it to the first rapid where Amazing
Grace had flipped yesterday. It is over six miles of straight whitewater
between where we first fell out, to the sharp bend in the river that saved
our lives. This has been engraved in our memories as the longest and
most horrifying swim of our lives.

Sometimes the river sweeps the shore, forcing us high across piles of driftwood and numerous boulders. In the late afternoon, the river sinks, revealing a dark strip of black sand. Several hours ago, we were forced to swim back across the river. Even without threatening whitewater, the swim took its toll on our energy.

We walk on in a drained daze of hunger, around endless bends, searching for something to eat, insects, a beached fish, anything. My face is hot and sunburned; my head dizzy. Dark clouds flash with lightning in the distance as the river starts to rise.

"Joel! Come here!" Aaron shouts. He is kneeling on the sand. Some hope has found its way into his eyes. He points to tracks in the sand—the imprint of a human foot—then two fresh sets, side by side, one small, the other large. They lead upriver!

CHAPTER 11

Dark Jungles

The light of morning seeps in through the cracks of the hut. Several beads of sweat break loose over the top of my nose when I prop my aching head up against the wall. My muscles tense suddenly and paralyze me; the diamond-shaped head of a large snake dances before my eyes. Its silent tongue slithers in and out between venomous fangs; only my eyeballs dare move, staring in horror as the red body of the snake emerges from my stomach. I close my eyes, resisting the urge to panic.

"Aaron?" I call out, shrinking back from the pain in my head. His footsteps come to a stop beside me. "Is there a snake coming out of my stomach?"

The room remains silent. Aaron's hand is cool against my forehead. I open my eyes to see his concern, then glance down. The snake is gone. I feel stupid.

"Your fever is worse. . .I'll get your malaria pills," he assures me. My body explodes in cold chills. I pull my blanket tight around my neck. It is soaked with sweat.

The dark sandy shores of the Strickland River are a week old in my memory.

We had followed the meandering footprints for several miles upriver before stumbling upon their makers, an intimidated man and his boy. After using sign language, as best we could, to establish peace, they led us up to a jungle-hidden hut on the knoll of a hill. Squealing pigs, laughing children, and the bewildered stare from women stood in stark contrast to the loneliness of our prior situation.

Weak with hunger and fatigue, we laid inside the dark, cool shade of their hut. They offered us a bark plate loaded down with what looked like crumbly, overcooked fish. Without hesitation, we both took a handful, filling our starved mouths. A nasty, foul flavor overwhelmed my taste buds. Hungry as I was, I couldn't swallow. The taste was much ruder than bad manners. Pig crap! flashed across my mind, causing me to gag. Both of us spit the mushy, green gunk out onto the hut floor. Fortunately, the family found humor in our bizarre behavior, the children leading the way with an onslaught of laughter. Aaron and I weren't laughing at all. We ran out the door spitting and washing our mouths out with water. We felt sick the rest of the night, and it took three days for our fingers to come clean of the disgusting smell. Every time I caught a whiff, it made me nauseous.

"I think we ate pig crap," I said to Aaron several days later.

"Don't," he warned me.

The family also fed us plenty of kou kou, but our eyes flew open with delight and curiosity when they offered us a can of tinned mackerel. The preserved fish was the beginning of a delicious feast and several hours of attempting to find out where it had come from. The older man of the hut kept pointing towards the high mountains to the east. "Oksapmin," he said. Aaron had pointed to our white skin and asked about missionaries. The man nodded his head in full agreement that there were men like us in Oksapmin. We found it hard to sleep that night because of our excitement. We had finally regained the hope that had been stripped from us by the wild waters of the Strickland.

*   *   *

For a moment I return to the present, feeling nauseous. My stomach tightens; I roll to the side and find the bag. The morning's rice shoots from my mouth, filling the plastic bag that shakes in my hands. The pain in my head spasms; dry heaves follow my vomiting. Finally they end. Rolling once again onto my back, I wait for the pain gripping my head to release some of its fury. My water bottle feels cool against my feverish cheeks. Aaron helps me swallow some pills, but I have little faith in them. This is my third day of a three-day cycle of chloroquine, and I have gotten worse, not better.

It was four days ago, when we first looked down onto this beautiful, mountain valley. A break in the dark overcast sky had poured down bright sunbeams, illuminating a cluster of huts. For us it was the finger of God, pointing out the village of Oksapmin. But reaching it had been another cruel battle.

The hope of finding missionaries was the only reason we had foolishly left the hut of our rescuers. What we really needed was several days of rest. But the vision of another, Inaru-type crowd of friendly missionaries, fine foods, soft mats, and fellowship pushed us onward. The man and his boy led us over several garden-covered hills and onto a large, worn trail.

"Sisamin," he said, pointing down the path towards the northwest. "Oksapmin," he pointed up the trail to the southeast.

"Tank u tru. Oksapmin long way? Close too?" Aaron asked.

"Close too," the man assured us.

Aaron pulled out his water bottle. Mine was empty. He shows it to the man and again points to the southeast. "Lic lic water?"

"Plenty," the man said, with a big smile. We shook his hand and thanked him before emptying the bottle down our dry throats.

The trail led nowhere but up, crossed no valleys, connected no draws, and for most of the day, it steadily rose up the crest of ridges that joined higher, larger ridges, rising still higher to the tops of mountains. At times we climbed nearly straight up the trail, engraved like a ladder of mud and roots, up ledges that rose to such heights that they disappeared into misty clouds. Everything was up, everything ridiculously steep, much too steep to hold water. The symptoms of dehydration slipped in at first and then grew worse throughout the hours of constant climbing: splitting headache, lips that cracked and bled, a throat too dry to swallow food, dizzy spells. Eventually, in the hot afternoon, our sweating stopped. We cursed the words "close too" and "plenty" of water given to us by the man. We searched, we prayed, we suffered. I have never wanted anything so badly in all my life as I wanted water that day.

I cried without tears, crawling around on the jungle floor like a madman to lick the moist dew from leaves and rocks. Delirious as I was, I eventually recognized Aaron's voice calling that he had found water. I found him kneeling down over a creek bed. I stumbled up to him. Dry dirt and rocks were all I could see when looking at the creek bed, but Aaron told me to listen. A trickle of water rang in my ears; it poured forth like a tiny faucet from under a large rock and then, within a foot, disappeared again beneath the ground. From a miraculous rock, we drank the clear nectar of life. No doubt that day God was for us. Again, He had saved our lives that we might continue.

But now, right now, in a small hut in the village of Oksapmin, I feel as though I am dying again. The man in the jungle had told us there was water where there seemed to be none; what he said was "close too" was a ten-hour hike. But most disappointing of all is that we found no missionaries are in Oksapmin, nor anywhere nearby. Aaron sits by my side. He looks miserable. Behind him on the wall are penis gourds and the beautiful plumes from Birds of Paradise.

"You know what I have, don't you?" The beads of sweat spread across my burning face, like tiny ponds of cool water. He searches for the courage to speak.

"You have . . . cerebral malaria." He glances towards me, then away, itching the back of his neck.

"Tell me everything."

"It is a strain of malaria resistant to chloroquine, which is why the pills have done you no good. It seems every time they come up with a cure for one strain, then malaria comes up with another form of itself resistant to that cure. You might say it is an intelligent disease." He sighs deeply.

"There is no medicine for what I have then?" He begins to shake his head slowly, up and down.

"Quinine," he answers. He won't look at me.

"And we don't have any quinine?"

"No." Tears begin falling from his face; they drip against his rain pants. His chin droops to his chest. "I messed up, Joel," he admits. "That missionary back in Wewak flat out told me that we needed quinine. But just having finished my second trip to the infirmary, I was just too lazy to go back." He begins to sob.

"We have both made our share of mistakes." I try to comfort him. I should keep silent, but my need to know is stronger. "What happens if you have cerebral malaria and no quinine?" A long, uncomfortable silence follows. My cold chills attack again.

"You die," Aaron whispers, and quickly gets up to leave the room. "We need more food; there are more huts two miles from here near a rundown airstrip. Anyway, I will go down and try to find something different to eat than . . . ."

"Aaron," my weak voice manages to stop him from changing the subject. "My mistakes could have killed us just as easy," I speak softly, so as not to erupt the throb in my head. He hesitates in the doorway for a moment before leaving.

I see the little Bible across the room and remember my Scripture passage: "Though I walk through the valley of the shadow of death, I will fear no evil, for Thou art with me." The memory of my first sight of Oksapmin flashes back into my mind. A dark ceiling of clouds spread across all four horizons, with one break, one beam of light highlighting the village we had been searching for all that miserable day.

How was I to know then that I was looking down onto the valley of the shadow of death? I want to say now that I fear no evil, but the reality is that I do feel afraid. "Are you with me, Lord?" I ask out loud. "What got me this far? If me, then I am a fool! But if You, then I have followed well. If I started it, then I am dead. But if You, then finish what You've started. Lord, save me!" Drowsiness tugs at my closed eyes; a distant rumble grows closer until it passes overhead, shaking the hut. Then the familiar noise drifts away. Now sleep.

My eyes pop open with the sound of footsteps moving across the hut floor. My face feels swollen, cheeks hot, eyes stinging with sweat. Aaron comes into focus beside me. He's a puzzling sight. His clothes hang from his bony frame; his pale face is tired, in sharp contrast with his eyes, which are somehow alive with excitement and hope.

"I have the same thing you do," he announces, with a smile across his hollow expression. He walks towards the window. "Did you hear the airplane?" I shut my eyes to think; the rumbling hut comes back to me.

"Yes, after I prayed." Even my whisper irritates the ache in my head. Aaron wheels around, a big move for someone who looks like he should be unconscious.

"What did you pray for?"

"To live," I answer. He comes toward me, pulling something from his pocket.

"Quinine!" He jiggles the container of pills in front of my face. "God heard your prayer!" He poured three of the tiny white pills out into his hand as if they were precious diamonds. The bitterness spreads through my mouth before he can give me some water. "If I hadn't gone down to the airstrip looking for food, I would have missed the plane. It's a good mile hike. I got cold chills, nausea, and dizziness walking down there. The pilot was an Aussie, says he lands here maybe once a month for a load of vegetables to sell at a market in a mining town named Tabubul. He said it's several hundred miles away . . . ." He stops, reaches down and holds his stomach with an expression of misery. "I think I better go lie down."

"I hope these pills work," I think out loud.

"Ha! You mean to tell me that you're dying of malaria, with no medicine, out in the middle of the jungle, and you asked God to save you the moment a plane shows up, whose pilot gives me enough quinine for both of us, and now you're worried it's not going to work?" I try to smile. A loud groan comes from his stomach. He rushes out of the room. I close my eyes to rest. The gentle, lapping waves wash up the beach of Daru Island. Suddenly, it is real again, existing somewhere in my future. I can see my family and friends, feel their embrace, and hear their laughter. My future and hope had been stripped from me, but now God has given them back.

The jungle is always the same. The only thing that changes are the ones who pass through it, I think to myself, waiting for Aaron among the dark shadows. He stumbles into view, his pale, sickly expression standing out in contrast to the surrounding greens. His lifeless eyes are dull between strands of sweat-soaked hair. The village of Oksapmin is now mountain ranges behind us. I think back over the past two weeks of miserable trekking, since we had recovered sufficiently, regaining strength enough to leave Oksapmin.

On our first day back on the trail we had hiked over a high ridge to a nearby village. We hired some carriers to help us retrieve our kayak and equipment from where we had stashed it just above the rapids that had nearly killed us. It took two solid days to recover our gear which was still in good shape. From there we used several different sets of carriers to help us between villages.

Malaria, like a cruel, living being, has constantly pursued our efforts, stalking us throughout the long sweat-drenched days of blurred scenery, through dark jungles that just won't end, forging swift rivers, wading across the grass-blown valleys guarded on all sides by ridge lines. And through it all malaria patiently waits for our exhaustion to sink deep. It watches us from a distance, as we climb forever up through blankets of clouds. Each ridge takes from us the precious wages of energy and strength, causing us to collapse upon each crest. We stare out across a sea of clouds, towering ridges breaking the white misty surface. The mere sight of them sucks life from our souls. It seems too impossible to go on, yet too miserable to give up. It is a recurring cycle: first we wipe away the sweat, then control our breathing in order to gain the strength to stand and go on. And all the while our enemy, malaria, prepares to pounce on us in our weakened state after another day of

New Guinea crushing our spirits, and stripping our hope.

When darkness falls on our fatigued bodies, we are left vulnerable to malaria. The sting of its venom wakes us to ringing ears, aching muscles, a head full of hurt, a stomach of violent vomiting. In the heat and humidity, our bodies freeze; then in the next moment, we boil in a pool of sweat. Constantly fighting back, we battle with medicine that weakens its attacks, but we can't make it go away. As sure as we get better, it is out there somewhere, waiting for this island to break us down again. Since that long-ago village of Oksapmin, I have wrestled with malaria now three times. Last night Aaron started his third bout.

Now Aaron's legs buckle and fold, and he collapses on the trail. He moves his arms up from his sides, lifting his head smeared with mud. For a moment, he searches for footing before dropping helpless to the ground again.

"Nogat Walkabout!" I scream up the trail to our new carriers. I make it to Aaron and help him up onto a log. His head hangs limp between his knees.

"Ants," he says, in a weak voice. I start brushing them off his back. Alex walks up and drops his belum on the ground. We met him five days before in the high mountain village of Bimin, where a crowd of people swarmed us from the huts.

Aaron and I had been in the clutches of malaria. "Where you twos from?" a confident voice asked above the crowd noise and my ringing ears.

"Wewak."

"Iiiieeeeeee," the voice cried. Then Aaron and I both stopped to seek out the individual who could possibly understand such a thing. A young man who appeared to be around Aaron's age emerged from the group.

"Grade six," he said, proudly.

"Where youpella go school?" Aaron asked.

"Tabubul, speakem pidgin, lic lic English," he announced. Then his expression suddenly turned to concern. "Youpellas walkabout Wewak?"

"Yes." I was much too tired to explain about our kayak.

"Iiiieeee," came his sharp wail. He turned and explained to the crowd, and they broke out with loud cries of sympathy.

Alex lived with the village health worker named Gabriel, a small-framed man with a kind face. Over the next several days, Gabriel took it upon himself to nurse us back to health.

Now Aaron is down again. I look around. No village, just mean nasty jungle.

"Are you all right?" After some time, he still hasn't lifted his head.

"No," he mumbles. The other carriers return.

"Alex, Aaron nogat walkabout, sick malaria, sleepem belong this place, cook goodpella ki ki." Alex translates to the men.

"Man walkabout close too, close too bushcamp," he tells me.

"Aaron nogat walkabout, sick malaria."

"Men walkabout carry Aaron bushcamp, close too," he says. I agree with a nod. The men come to lift Aaron, but he pushes their hands away.

"Tell them to go ahead to the bush camp. I'll make it there," he says.

"You better let them carry you. You don't look so good." Finally, he pulls his head up.

"I came here to cross this island by my own power. Nobody's carrying me anywhere," he is looking me straight in the eye. Again his head drops. I send the men ahead. Alex and I stay behind with Aaron.

I start thinking of options: we could carry him back to Bimin; it would take a couple of days, but it wouldn't do us much good. Gabriel is no longer there. He fled into the jungle. Nobody really knows where he is.

*　　*　　*

Gabriel was a valuable friend. His compassion came with a deep medical knowledge and plenty of medicine. We had slept in his hut for two nights. We supplied the rice, and he and Alex did the cooking, though our sickness had robbed us of most of the nutrients. On the morning of the third day in Bimin, the peaceful setting had been shattered when an outburst of anger erupted outside the hut. When Gabriel came inside, he was in an awful panic, telling us that a crazy man wanted to kill Aaron and me. Gabriel said the man was after him as well because he was giving us shelter. After warning us to flee for our lives, he packed a plastic bag and rushed off into the bush. That was the last we ever saw of him.

*　　*　　*

Aaron stands to his feet. His clothes are rotting and torn; his bony frame is covered in irritated skin. His beard is now thicker than ever and his red, puffy hair longer. I have never seen his face so white. I can't even see his freckles. He looks so different than when I first met him, a young boy showing off for the girls, full of spunk and arrogance. Now he looks more like a ghost. He begins to walk with small, well-thought-out steps down the path. A hundred yards and he stops. Dropping down onto his knees, he begins to gag, mostly water and dry heaves. He lost his breakfast hours ago.

Alex starts to tisk. He is the most important of all our carriers—not for his jungle skills, because he is more of a city slicker of sorts. But with his education, we are able to communicate with the carriers better than we have in months. While he was off in school, the other carriers were just surviving daily life, and it shows. Alex is the first carrier we have had who actually falls down regularly while hiking. The insects bother him more than the other men; he carries no bow and arrows, and his load is always the lightest. But he can make conversation. For him, and us, that is enough.

Aaron rises once again, stumbling along behind Alex down the trail. As I follow, memories of better days fill my mind.

That bright, sunlit morning, now 65 long days ago, becomes a picture in my mind, when, soaring with anticipation, we had launched from the white sandy beaches of Wewak. I had felt so young, so alive and free, when I held onto the side of the kayak and rushed towards that first wave. It had smacked me good and hard. That very first blow, passing through the wall of water, jolted me from one world into another. That wave truly was the beginning, the first punch this island threw at us. There have been so many more since. I hadn't realized it at the time, but that first wave had torn open a hole in our energy, a slow, steady leak of our strength and endurance, spilling out over a hundred miles of rough seas, and five hundred miles of upriver currents. A little more was lost with every stroke of the paddle. We had made it all the way across the Central Divide only to nearly drown in the Strickland gorge, to become lost and hungry, struck down with dehydration and malaria. Every obstacle had been overcome, but each one had taken a little more from us. Now we feel empty, with nothing left for this island to take.

* * *

Fire smoke fills the lean-to as rain beats against the dried-leaf roof. The ants had made Aaron suffer for his slowness, and his legs are covered with bites. A hundred yards at a time, he had finally made it to the shelter. Fortunately for him, "close too," this time, actually meant within a half mile. He lies next to the fire, and I give him a drink with some more quinine. He props his head up on a log and looks at me.

"You feeling better?" I ask.

"A little." He watches a large spider work its way across the thatched ceiling.

"I was worried about you today. You should have let the men carry you."

Two of the carriers return from a successful hunt with a possum, barely alive. Building up the fire, they throw its kicking body into the sizzling, red hot coals.

"If I had died . . . what would you have done with me?" His question takes me by surprise.

"I don't know," I respond. A puff of smoke filled with the aroma of burning, wet fur blows gently into his face from the fire. He coughs a few times.

"If you die, I'll get you out of here," he says. I look at him.

"What do you mean?"

"I mean, your body, so you can have a proper burial back home." I am searching his face to make sure he's serious. He is.

"Shut up. If you die I'm leaving you out here." He looks offended. "You would do the same," I quickly add.

"No, I wouldn't!"

"Why do you think these hunters don't kill their prey until minutes before they cook it? Do you have any idea how fast our bodies would decompose out here? And you're telling me that you would carry my rotting, smelly, ant-eaten, maggot-filled body out to a river, put me in the front of the kayak and paddle me 700 miles to an airport so you could fly me home for burial! Get real!" He looks down, saying nothing.

A weird crunching sound comes from the fire. The carriers have cut the feet from the possum and are chewing them up, toenails and all. The largest of the men sits across the flames from me, eating the long, hairless tail.

"I would carry you out," Aaron insists again.

I shake my head. "If it happens, you have my permission to break that promise. I'm too tired to fight about it." I cook up some rice while the men share the possum guts and crack open the small skull to get at the brains. By the time the rice is finished, they hand over some of the meat for us to eat.

*   *   *

Never before in my life have I witnessed such suffering. The skeletal corpse of one of the village men hangs over the bamboo structure of the hearth. The bed of hot coals below his shriveled body is the only source of light in the blackness of the sick hut. After a night of rest and medicine, Aaron had felt good enough to hike. He made it through the long, steep hike of the day, but collapsed again only a hundred yards from this village. Since our arrival, fever and cold chills have once again taken over my exhausted body. We are lying in the darkness alone with a dying man, the sick separated from the healthy. Sputtering coughs jerk at his frail, black frame, his chest lined with protruding ribs sucks tiny breaths into heavy lungs. The coughs turn into loud hacks. He clamps his eyes in pain. Elastic strings of green and yellow phlegm shoot from his mouth and sizzle into the smoking coals. I turn away. From my compassion comes the desire to kill this man, and put him out of his misery. Alex says he has been this way for three months, that it's the "big pain," the same sickness that had plagued Stew.

Aaron is asleep beside me. My head hurts too badly to sleep. I pull my blanket up, shivering in spite of the humid night, feeling guilty that the dying man deserves my blanket more than I do.

It had taken Aaron several hours to make it up the last stretch of hill, an ugly sight, because once he stumbled into the village he fell on his knees, vomiting. The pigs rushed the scene, swarming him, devouring all that his stomach had rejected.

We are on our last cycle of malaria medicine, hopefully enough to overcome our present sickness. Unless we can find a health worker or missionary soon, the next bout of malaria will kill us. Somewhere nearby is a valley flowing with the Murray River. I remember it from our maps— our hope is cast on this river. Rapids or not, our days of being able to hike are quickly coming to an end. We need a way out, quick and easy, or else we will get exhausted and malaria will strike us down without any medicine to battle it with.

I fall asleep and dream of this river that I have never seen: quiet, peaceful waters flowing quickly but safely towards the south. While Aaron and I are asleep on the floor of our kayak, Amazing Grace, jungled shores sweep effortlessly past on either side.

*   *   *

The village of Tutimin is nestled on the side of a high mountain. Somewhere below us is the Murray River. Hope of her merciful currents is what pushes us onward. After two nights imprisoned in the "sick" hut, we have both finally recovered from our malaria. We hope now that the day's long hike hasn't brought it back since we have only a half cycle of malaria medicine between the two of us and our carriers. Our lives hang in the balance.

Twenty men now crowd into the largest hut of the village. Built up on rotting stilts, the floor is sagging towards the ground where the two fire pits are built. The walls are also rotting, letting in cool air. Hundreds of tiny cockroaches swarm in. The room fills with smoke from the two fires and several jungle cigars. Every time I start to fall asleep, I slide down the floor and wake up, worried about ending up with my feet in the fire pit. Cockroaches crawl across my body, their little legs getting tangled in my ratty hair.

We had rested earlier, down the hill a short stretch, next to a large abandoned hut used for a meeting place. We had walked up to this hut and found a boy swinging a vine and stick to produce an ancient, musical tune that rose and fell like ocean waves. Aaron and I sat outside, listening and peering off into the deep and distant southern horizon, brilliantly painted with streaks of orange, pink, and red swirling clouds. The dark shadows seemed to seep out of the canopy, swallowing the gray mountain peaks in the distance.

"Somewhere between here and those mountains is the Murray River," I had told Aaron.

He stared for a long time before speaking. "It's been a while, hasn't it?" I looked away from the intimidating landscape into his captured face. He looked so wise and bold. I could no longer see the boy I had started this trip with.

"What's that?"

"Since we've seen the Birds of Paradise?"

"Yes, it has." Giant bats begin to emerge from the canopy below us; they fill the sky with gloom.

"I could sure stand seeing one soon," he had said. It made me remember the peace that I felt when I saw something beautiful stand out in stark contrast to the rest of the jungle world. Aaron was right, it had been a long time since I had felt peaceful.

Aaron stirs beside me. I reach out and shake his shoulder. "Aaron," I say. He opens his eyes. "Let's go down to that meeting hut to sleep for the night. At least it's smoke free, with a flat floor, and there can't be any more cockroaches than here," I suggest.

"No."

"No? What do you mean, no?"

"I'm just going to sleep here." His voice is stubborn and makes me mad.

"That's stupid! Neither of us can sleep, and there is a perfectly quiet, flat place a couple hundred yards from here. Give me one good reason why we shouldn't go?"

"Because I don't want to." He rolls away from me.

"Fine! See you in the morning."

I strap my light on my head, grab my blanket, inform Alex of my plans, and make my way down the dark trail to the meeting hut. It makes me feel good to know that I am right. The floor is flat and large; there are no cockroaches, or smoke, or noise. I get a good night's sleep.

*   *   *

"Morning," comes Aaron's tired voice. He is cooking rice. I stand, stretching my arms above my head; my muscles ache. I drop and reach for my toes, stretching my sore back.

"How did you sleep?"

"Not good," he admits, with a weak smile. "I brought the rice and stove down to cook breakfast. Alex says we can make a village named Wenyabil by nightfall; the men told him that the Murray River is close to this village." The water is beginning to boil.

"I don't expect you to follow me like an idiot," I say. The comment catches him by surprise.

"If I'm ever going the wrong way, doing the wrong thing, or just plain have a stupid idea, then you should challenge me. I expect you to tell me when I'm wrong, but sometimes I'm right. So when I do have a good idea to make this miserable trip a little easier, then you should listen."

"You always think you're right, that you know better than me." He hands me a bowl of rice.

"All I'm saying is, don't defy me just to show your independence. That won't get either of us anywhere." The rice is bland and dry. "Why are you so angry towards me all the time?" I ask.

He picks at his rice for several minutes. "You were my hero. I trusted you to know the way and have the answers. This island has stolen or crushed everything that I believed in, everything but the power of

God. It has destroyed my religion and philosophies, my pride, and my heroes."

"You still haven't answered my question."

"I am angry because you haven't lived up to who I made you out to be in my mind."

"And is that my fault?"

"Some of it, yes. Some, no. You can't get us across this island. You never could. You have no power over the crocodiles, tribes, rivers, malaria . . . nothing. If it were up to your leadership, we would both have been dead a long time ago."

"So what are you saying?" I feel the blood burning in my face.

"That you hold no power over me. You're not now, nor have you ever been, more capable of tackling this expedition than I am."

I want to punch him. Instead, I close my eyes and try to relax. "I never said that I did have the power!"

"You let me believe it!"

"Well, you were stupid enough to believe it, then!"

"You talked of living in the mountains for four months alone, and of grizzly bears. You told me you were a great navigator . . . ."

"Are we lost?" I shout. "We may have a lot of problems, but knowing which way it is to Daru certainly isn't one of them!"

"You always think you're right! That you know better! You make me feel like a stupid, little kid! You've been telling me ever since we met that I had to take responsibility for myself; think for myself, and make my own decisions. But now that I am finally doing just that, you don't know how to handle it. If I had to learn how to take, then you're going to have to learn how to give and accept me as an equal. I will not be treated like a child any longer!" He stands up and starts to leave the hut.

"Aaron!" He stops in the doorway. My anger shifts to guilt. He is right, and for the moment I hate him for it.

"You can only have heroes as long as you don't have to get to know them," I tell him. He waits, silent in the door. "I'm sorry." I find it hard to say. "Your breaking away is a good thing, I know. Not long ago I was breaking away from men in the position I am in now. I felt the same anger towards them as you do towards me. I just haven't ever been on this end of the process. I am learning just like you." He turns around and faces me. I feel myself cooling off. "This jungle is changing both of us and our relationship. I'm just trying to keep up the best I can, so I'm sorry if I've treated you less." He comes back and sits down; we finish our rice together.

"I should have slept down here last night," he admits, after a long silence.

✻   ✻   ✻

We make it to the village of Wenyabil in the late afternoon. Huts rest on the edge of a deep river gorge. The waters are still too far below to hear, but the excitement of the Murray River's closeness awakens our spirits as we all rest in one of the huts before the next morning's journey.

"We twopella no walkabout. We twopella canoe bigwater," Aaron tells Alex. Alex doesn't like this conversation that we have had many times over the past several days. He talks of our plans to the men of Wenyabil. Their wisdom is important because they live so close to the river of our dreams. We try to ignore their negative reaction, their cries of "Iiieeeee," and their shaking heads. One old man, in the corner of the hut, shakes his head and tisks loudly at us.

"Nogat canoe big water, lobis bigpella waves," Alex translates. The old man raises his arm using his fingers to show water dropping to the floor.

"Waterfall?" Aaron looks worried. "We have been warned of bigpella waves before," he reminds me.

"You twos listen wise man. Canoe big water, you twopella die," Alex says, his face quite serious. I feel the hole in my soul open up again. I need to stop the leaking.

"Where youpellas walk about?" I ask Alex.

"Tabubul."

"How youpellas walkabout Tabubul from belong this place?"

"Walkabout Murray, walkabout, walkabout, walkabout, come big water canoe Tabubul," Alex explains.

"Youpellas have kina for Tabubul?" Aaron asks him.

"You twos givem kina," he answers.

"They need kina for Tabubul, so they don't want to lose their carrier jobs," says Aaron.

"So they tell us that the Murray River is too rough, and we have to stay with them," I add.

"What if there is a waterfall?" Aaron asks, after some silence.

"I doubt there is, but we'll be careful just the same, and if there are some rough spots, then we will carry around them."

"I've seen that plan go bad before," he says.

"We have to make it out of here. One more bout of malaria and we're finished." We are both getting uncomfortable. "Look, there is nothing we can do but hike down and look at the river tomorrow." We both agree and try to get some sleep. Several hours of restlessness pass on the hard floor.

"Aaron, you awake?"

"Yeah."

"I've been thinking about tomorrow."

"And?" He rolls over to face me.

"Tomorrow when we see the river, you look it over real good and think about what you want to do. I'll do the same. When we've made our decision, I'll count to three. Thumbs up, if we kayak, thumbs down, if we hike on," I suggest.

"What if it's a split?"

"Then we hike. The only way we kayak is if both of us vote thumbs up."

"All right," he agrees.

"And Aaron."

"Yeah?"

"Anything you vote, I'll understand."

* * *

"Get us to shore, Aaron, right now!" I yell from the front of the kayak. He starts struggling with our one bent paddle the moment he sees my face.

"What?" he asks, putting all of his strength into each precious stroke.

"Just paddle!" I shout. I feel so disarmed, so helpless. The front rope hangs in my clamped jaws.

"What is it?!" he demands fiercely.

"Waterfall!" He paddles harder. "Just the other side of the whitewater!"

The smooth, swift water turns white; the bow of Amazing Grace drops into a deep hole, and water rushes in. I grab a breath before I'm engulfed. Surges of water strike violently from all directions, and the fight for life has begun again. We hold on while the kayak shoots high in the spray. Aaron drops down behind me, disappearing for a moment beneath the angry surface. The force bends the kayak. Aaron is up; the bow folds as it crashes into a submerged boulder. The momentum flings me forward so that I roll out onto her pointed tip. Water pours over my head.

We are sideways when I crawl back in. We hit a dip, tipping the kayak up onto its side. Both of us counter with our weight. It is barely enough to keep us from capsizing. The river is suddenly smooth again, but quickly disappears into mid-air, out in front of us, with a bellowing roar. The shore inches closer. I dive out into the water, struggling for the rocks. The kayak passes me, but swings around as I gain leverage, my feet wedged into the rocks. Aaron jumps out, pulling on Amazing Grace from her rudder. I collapse on the rocks searching for breath.

Again, I feel the daze of exhaustion, the shock of terror, the world so unreal. We walk together only a few steps and peer off the steeply slanting river as it falls down the face of a boulder-choked mountainside at a forty-five degree angle. As far as we can see, there is no bottom to the violent falls of standing waves and rocks. What an awesome display of nature's raw power. The force of gravity pulls at tons of falling water which collide into boulders. Mountains of spray tremble the surrounding earth. Another few feet and we both would have kissed the lips of death. "Should have listened to the old man!" Aaron shouts, as we walk away.

"We'll have to carry around it," I tell him, when the roar dies down behind us.

"No. We've got to go back."

"We can't go back. Our carriers are gone."

"Then we have to find them."

"They're gone, Aaron."

"Do you see that!" He screams, his face red as he points to the falling river. "We should be dead! We didn't listen to Alex. We didn't even listen to the old man. We convinced ourselves this was the way and we almost died again! Now listen to me, we have to find our carriers. We need them." He stands tense, waiting for my answer.

It makes me mad that Aaron is right again. My pride wants to disagree with him, but time is precious. "All right, let's go."

Aaron and I pull the kayak up onto the rocks. Once again we release the air valves and stand there watching another attempted river escape deflate. How did we get ourselves in this situation again? I ask myself, as we stash our gear and start the search for our carriers.

We had spent the morning climbing down into the gorge amid a growing rumble of angry water. It was raining. The river was high and fast, its current declaring potential disaster. We had walked along its shores for an hour until we came to a konda bridge. Standing on two separate boulders twenty feet apart, I counted to three and both of us gave the thumbs up signal. We pumped up Amazing Grace and waved goodbye to Alex and our carriers in the midst of a downpour. We had taken the Murray for the same reasons we left the Strickland. No matter how dim, how risky, we were chasing hope in an attempt to escape our miseries.

*   *   *

"Maybe konda nogat hold man belong kayak," Alex says. His face is stressed, as his eyes follow the dangling bridge from tree to tree, steeply falling and rising between distant limbs.

"I will carry the kayak across," I volunteer.

Aaron glares at me. "Great idea, if you don't fall to your death. Then you're sure to get malaria by morning." I ignore his wise sarcasm.

Yesterday, while Aaron and I had been fighting another river, the carriers had fortunately stopped for the night in a nearby hut. New Guinea had made fools of us again. In our search for Alex and the others we had rushed headlong into exhaustion and a beehive. It took us many stings and several hours to make it across the konda bridge and up the hill to the hut of our humility. The weight of shame came heaviest from the wise eyes of the old man. We gave each carrier ten extra kina each to take us back, but more so to lessen our guilt.

I can't ever remember feeling more humiliated in all my life; so many signs warning us of danger, and we had ignored them all. The truth that we had hidden beneath our misery now seems so obvious. Aaron and I had different ideas about how to serve our penance. I refused to take part when Aaron lined up the men, asking them to slap him in the head. They carried out the plan with joyous laughter, all of them but the old man who refused to strike him.

The weight from the kayak cuts painfully into my shoulders; my penance has just begun. My legs shake beneath the strain as I climb to the lofty branches. I already feel tired with my first small step out onto the steeply descending konda vines. I come to a stick wedged between the vines. I grip either end of the stick in my hands because there is no way under it, not with the bulk on my back, and I'm too heavy to step over. So, I pull it out. Vines on either side collapse in on me. Beneath my dangling feet, I watch the stick fall, twisting until it is instantly snatched up by whitewater. I pull forward, the edges of my pack now catching on vines. The bridge begins to dance as I reach the sag. My feet move with the jerks, causing the weight to shift on my back. Another support stick. It's a scary moment to let go enough to rip the stick out. The bridge squeezes in on me. My eyes are stinging with sweat, and I feel the poison of exhaustion in my fight for balance. I start the steep climb, pushing through the gripping vines which become a little tighter with each stick I remove. My added weight begins to work against me with the angled climb growing ever sharper. I desperately need a rest, but can't. My legs shake out of control now; my arms drape limply over the vines. My mind drifts into a daze as I see the rocks below me and the branch not far away but nearly straight up.

"I can't make it!" I shout, out of breath, too tired to panic. But, leaning forward, I gather strength and give one more heave. As in a dream now, my worthless limbs wrap around the branch. Men are around me saying something, as I feel the crushing weight lifted from me. It's easier to breathe. Then many hands help me down to the ground where I collapse.

I open my eyes after a long while. My head is not so dizzy anymore, so I sit up.

"You should have just let them slap you in the head like I did," Aaron says.

"That one burnt potato I ate this morning just wasn't enough." I try to smile. "Where are the men?"

"I gave them the last of our rice, and they went on up to the hut to cook it."

"Iiiiiiieeee! How am I gonna get up that ridge?"

"One step at a time," Aaron says, helping me up.

My mind is tormented by flashes of butter and hot-syrup-smothered pancakes. I glance up at Aaron jumping onto a thick log. With the sweet image of chocolate ice cream, my mouth begins to water. A loud screech stops me mid-stride on the trail. The log is empty; Aaron is gone. "Aaron?" I shout. As I approach, I see a deep entrenched creek bed open up beneath the log. Something moves along its crest. Aaron's hand finds a root. His knuckles are pure white with strain, but he pulls himself up over the lip of the bank and rolls onto his back. Blood trickles in tiny streams down from his wounded head and across his pain-stricken face.

"You all right?"

He wipes his hand across his face, lying with a silent stare at his blood-smeared palms. "It's just too much." Rolling over, he gets up. He pulls his rain pants down to find a mess of blood and pus; the worst of his sores has burst open. "Just too much," he says again, stepping up onto the mossy log to carefully cross.

*   *   *

I lie in the hut, staring up at the thatched roof, though I don't see it. Three hours of grueling climbing got me here. Some plain rice and burnt kou kou for dinner gave enough substance to fill my stomach, but not enough flavor to satisfy my cravings. I can't shut off my tortured mind—pizza smothered in cheese and sauce, cinnamon rolls, donuts, chocolate chip cookies fresh from the oven. I feel suddenly anxious, out of control. Fear grips me. I'm going insane! My heart races; it's hard to breathe. I open my mouth to cry for help, but nothing comes out. "God help me!" I beg. My eyes focus on a section of the thatch where a gecko searches for bugs. I don't even blink as the emotions climax, colliding with one another.

I shut my eyes, trying to concentrate on my God and His faithfulness to me. A sense of comfort, weak but available, settles on me. I hold His peace in my mind and I grow stronger. The anxiety loosens its grip. I can breathe freely again as sweat drips down, stinging my eyes. My heart slows. I sit up to recover, knowing that I have just visited the gateway of insanity.

I write in my journal: Night 73,

> The jungle has completed its work of stripping us down to nothing. Of the three hundred and fifty pounds of expensive equipment that weighed down our kayak in Wewak, not much is left. Behind us is a 73-day string of lost or failed gear, now a trail over a thousand miles long. We now drink from the creeks like our national friends. Our expensive water purifier failed us long ago. I doubt Sogamoi and Mowga are getting much use out of the ripped netting of our old hammocks. Our shock, and the river currents have swallowed their share of bush knives, maps, clothing, and compasses. When we came here, we relied on such valuable equipment. Now, it means nothing. We never use our gas stove anymore; instead we just cook over the fire. With our military rations long since devoured, we graze on the same foods as the people who inhabit this land, and buy rice from every trade store that

we come across. Even our kayak has been rendered useless for these past months of hiking. Struggling for 51 days, to survive beneath the dark canopies of New Guinea's rugged interior jungles, has left us possessing nothing worth trusting in. Even the trust in our own abilities and the abilities of each other has long since died. God has taken from us all the things that we relied on. Now, after so long . . . so much, *He* is the only thing that we have left to trust.

Tonight we sleep barefoot, without blankets or netting, around a fire with our native friends. For the first time, there is truly no difference between us and them. They are the simple men . . . that we have become.

> I came to cross dark jungles
> as soldiers ride to war
> Searching not for death itself
> but life! . . . worth dying for.
>
> Home of comfort, I long for thee
> why did I ever go?
> Dreams in life; that I don't seek
> are the ones . . . I'll never know."

*   *   *

We stand in awe. Behind us the jungle siren, before us, silence. The grass lightly taps at my rain pants. The trees are broken up by a small grass patch on the side of the ridge, the last ridge. Before us, the view brings tears to our straining eyes, a breath of refreshment to our weary bodies. An ocean of flat green canopy, without a wave or ripple, stretches into the milky horizon. The sunlight glances from the smooth waters of a river winding its way south through the thick green carpet. No more mountains! Below us is a village spotted with huts, the reflection of a tinned roof speaks loudly of missionaries!

The men had told us last night, as they always do, that the next village was "close to," and that there were white missionaries there. But, this time we didn't believe them.

"This village belong canoe?" Aaron had asked, last night in the village of Goo Goom, a day's hike from the hut above the Murray River.

"Plenty, plenty canoe," Alex had replied.

"Village belong movie theater?" Aaron continued.

"Plenty, plenty," Alex had assured us.

"Pizza, village belong pizza?"

"Plenty pizza, plenty." But when we asked him what pizza was, he could give us no answer. All day, we had not believed in close villages, the end of the mountains, flat rivers, canoes, or white missionaries. We simply walked because we had no other choice. Our hopes were distant, not near.

Even now, with the proof stretched out before us, it is hard to believe. Aaron and I embrace and give thanks to God for the privilege of being alive, and for the most beautiful sight we have ever seen.

CHAPTER 12

Daru

Slowly I reach toward the bewildered face of a stranger. My fingers run gently over the cool, smooth surface of glass. Dirty blonde hair, falling in long curls onto my shoulders, stands out in stark contrast to the reddish-orange beard surrounding my mouth. Hollow, tired eyes sunk deep into their sockets stare back at me—I can feel their sickness. I search for something familiar, something comforting, but little is left of the man I once was. My ragged shirt hangs limp. I pull it off and run my fingers across my ribs, a bony frame stretched tight with skin, covered with red leech marks and ant stings. Fly bites riddle the back of my neck and shoulders. Out of the 75 days since leaving Wewak, 53 of them were spent crossing the mountains. I am deathly white after being trapped for so long within the coffin of canopy and jungle shadows. I pull the scale out from the corner of the bathroom with my toes and step onto it; the needle swings between my feet covered with infection. Slowing down, it comes to rest on 145 pounds. I shudder at the 40 pounds that New Guinea has eaten away from my body since the beaches of Wewak. In high school wrestling, I worked hard and starved myself to lower weight classes, but I could never make it below 165 pounds.

The door swings open and Aaron walks in.

"Oh, Lord," he whispers, staring over my shoulder.

"Get on the scale," I suggest, but he is too taken by his reflection to hear. "Aaron." I pull him onto the scale.

"Oh, Lord," he whimpers again, staring at his 139 pound reading. "That can't be right!"

"Take your shirt off and look back in the mirror. Then you'll believe it." He does, once again lapsing into a trance of disbelief.

"We have amoebas," he says, poking at his ribs.

"Dysentery? How do you know?"

His face turns slightly red. "Patty told me she can smell them on our breath."

"What else did she say?"

"She thinks we have worms as well," he says. A look of disgust comes over his face. "Patty has been working as a nurse here for fifteen years."

"Thank God He led us to someone who can help us."

I guess last night was fate. Alex didn't even know what pizza was, and yet he was right. There was pizza in the next village. The carriers had also been right, for once, about missionaries being in the next village. Fueled by the excitement of a tinned roof, we nearly killed ourselves this morning getting down that last ridge. This time we had not been disappointed. Despite the shaggy hair, dirty clothes, and muddy faces, the Woodyard family let us into their home. The father, Vance, and his son, Randy, led us down to the creek for a bath in an attempt to get us clean enough to take a real shower in their bathroom. Vance's wife, Patty, had lunch ready for us when we got back from the creek. We made absolute pigs of ourselves, scarfing down sandwiches like mad men in front of their children. Jonathan is their oldest, then comes Jessica, Randy, and Mary Ann who completes the Woodyard clan of six members. To hear crisp American English from somebody other than Aaron was a beautiful thing.

After lunch Vance and Patty had told us how they came to Dahamo some fifteen years before. It took them most of those years to build the airstrip so they could have a generator, food, and supplies flown in. "Life hasn't always been this good," Vance had told us. Patty has been working as a nurse in the village, treating the people for the island's wide variety of medical problems. She gave Aaron and me a handful of pills to take after lunch. Medicine for malaria, amoebic dysentery, and worms. When you are sick in so many ways, it's hard to keep track of which symptoms go with what problem. She also put us on antibiotics for all of our various infections, and helped us dress our leg sores. Last night, in the village of Goo Goom, we realized that we were coming down with malaria again. With only a half cycle of medicine between the two of us, we had once again prayed for God's help.

✳   ✳   ✳

The generator buzzes from beyond the screen door somewhere in the pitch black night. In front of me is a television and VCR in full operation. A large ship sails across the screen. I take a sip of Pepsi, letting it fizzle in my mouth for a moment before swallowing, then take a bite of hot pizza right out of the oven. My eyes close to concentrate on the pleasurable flavors which taste even better than I remembered. My eyes open to find my expedition partner laughing at me. Aaron shakes his head.

"My kind of culture shock," he says. I smile.

"Thank you," I say, after Patty puts more pizza on my plate.

I recall last night's sago cakes with bananas. We had been thrilled finally to be able to eat something different than burnt kou kou, even if it was as tasteless as sago. It had been over a month since we had eaten our last sago, made by Bushy Man's wives for our long trek over the Central Divide. I laid there in Goo Goom last night, just like all the previous fifty-three nights since leaving the company of Rudy and Jay on the Salumei River, hoping that tomorrow would be better. Maybe we'd find a village with missionaries, maybe a river to escape on, something to brighten our disease-plagued lives.

But pizza, and Pepsi, a wonderful American family, chocolate cake in the oven, and a movie? Once again God has blessed us above and beyond anything that we could possibly dream or imagine.

My stomach rumbles louder than the T.V. Everyone looks at me as I waste no time making my way to the bathroom. Within minutes I am flushing all my devoured pizza down the toilet. Aaron is on his way in as I make my way out. I hear the violent "hurling," then the toilet flushes before his pale face appears in the hall.

"It's about time we ate something worth getting sick over," he says with a grin. I laugh.

"Leaves enough room for the cake."

"I was worried about that myself," he agrees. The Woodyards look quite concerned as we come back into the family room, but we assure them that "hurling" has become a daily ritual for us, and it's no big deal. With that, we help ourselves to more pizza and then cake; it is absolutely delicious.

"If you guys get hungry in the night, help yourselves to some cake," Patty tells us as she and Vance bid us goodnight. We go into a back room where Patty had made some cushion beds for us to sleep on. The soft cushions and smooth sheets feel heavenly. Patty's tempting chocolate offer makes the next five minutes seem like an eternity. The moment the house-hut is dark and quiet, we sneak back into the kitchen and swipe the chocolate cake and a knife, then sneak back to our beds. With our flashlights mounted on our heads, we dig in piece by piece, swearing each time it will be our last. In minutes, the three-fourths of the cake left from dinner is reduced to a slice so thin it won't stand on the plate.

✳   ✳   ✳

The gentle breeze grows noticeably stronger; a towering wall of black clouds swallows up the jungle on the eastern shores of the Fly River. The kayak tremors at my rapid movements. Digging through the green bag, I throw Aaron's rain jacket up to him. Blankets of rain begin beating the far shore, and I see a line of bubbling whitewater moving towards us. I race to secure my jacket in time for the collision. Suddenly, the wind bursts into my face, ripping the hood off my head. The kayak swings left and, the river explodes into turmoil all around, splashing up into the boat. My back stings with its force. I pull my legs up under the protection of my jacket. Pulling the drawstring in my hood tight around my face, I look around but can't see anything but rain. I force my head down when the cold water begins trickling down my chest from my chin. My heart races as deep thunder rolls across the river. The thought of getting struck by lightning sinks me lower into my seat. The sky lights up. Amazing Grace crashes into reeds which bend beneath the surface as the wind drives us up onto them. I try to shout to Aaron in the back of the kayak, but he can't hear me above the groaning sky and thrashing rain. There's nothing to do but wait it out. Today is Day 89 of our expedition. With time on my hands, I reflect over the last eight days of river travel since the Woodyard's house in Dahamo and the Black River.

The Woodyard's oldest son, Jonathan, led the way to the river in his bare feet.

"Now, if you get bit by a Death Adder, clean the wound and have the men carry you back," his mother said to her son before we left. (After fifteen years in the bush, motherly caution turns from knee scrapes to snake bites.) It was hard to say goodbye to our new family, the fine cooking, humorous talk, and hospitality. Vance offered, one last time, to have us flown out; of course, we refused.

"Just had to offer it for conscience sake in case you get eaten by crocs somewhere downriver," he had explained with a smile.

Jonathan's leadership proved trustworthy after a few hours when we finally came to the friendliest currents we had seen in some time. The Black River flowed with beautifully clear, yet dark water, its coloring coming from tree roots along the shore. The high jungle walls on either side, casting shadows across the surface, also contributed to the name "Black" River.

We had no need to paddle at all as the current was swift and strong. When the river wound back and forth, we steered away from boulders and log jams; when the flow straightened, we floated outside the kayak with our diving mask on and checked out weird-looking fish hiding from the current behind rocks. We spent two days eating the popcorn Patty had made for us and drifting past large Cassowary birds standing six feet tall, covered in black feathers with blue and red rings around their eyes. Small crocodiles slid from the shore, while schools of fish darted under the kayak. Large Baramundi fish slowly swam their way up the stiff currents beneath the surface.

It was a poor-looking camp we made that night, put up hastily as ants bit at our bare feet. Our boots had worn out and our Teva sandals were somewhere beneath the Strickland River, so our feet were bare. We did manage to get the tarp up though, and that kept the night's heavy rains off of us.

On February 14, Day 83 of our expedition, the dark waters of the Black River poured into the milky-white currents of the Palmer River. We spent the night in the village of Drimski in the hut of a man named Koma. He and his family wailed in long "Iiieeeeee's" as we told them about our long journey. His wife fed us large, sago pancakes for dinner and breakfast. We were out on the river the next morning, Day 84, by 7:30 a.m.

The sugarcane shorelines spread out to the distant horizons. Our kayak twirled in circles as the waters from the Palmer collided with the southern-flowing Fly River, our tenth and final river of the expedition. We had kayaked the Sepik, Kawari, Korosmeri, Salumei, Lagaip, Strickland, Murray, Black, Palmer, and now the Fly. It felt strange to think that at the end of her currents, some seven hundred miles away, is Daru, the island of our dreams.

By late afternoon, we paddled into the mining port of Kiunga. Its harbor was filled with ships transporting copper down to the coast. These huge floating islands of steel seemed strange and out of place. Natives in dugout canoes fished with nets on the opposite shores with their familiar and friendly smiles and waves. However, the men working the ships were too busy earning their wages to even look at us.

We stayed in Kiunga that night, with the Taylers, an Australian missionary family. Bill and Rosemary Tayler had been expecting us after hearing about us on the radio from their friends, the Woodyards. I came down with my fifth bout of malaria, so we ended up staying in the midst of their friendly hospitality for three days.

Aaron had gone to the stores in Kiunga to resupply us with enough food to get us to Daru. When I asked if the bread that he bought would go bad in the humidity, he blew up in a rage, defending his choice with hostility. However, with my malaria, I just didn't have the energy to fight about anything.

By Day 87, I was well enough to say goodbye to the Taylers and sit in the kayak while Aaron slowly paddled us a stroke at a time towards Daru. The current was still strong, allowing us to make good time.

That evening, Aaron and I spied a hut that we hoped we could sleep in for the night. Approaching it, I realized it was full of women and children, and they were screaming and crying, sounding terrified. Quickly, men appeared, coming to the rescue. They were able to explain to me that their women and children thought I was a ghost. After assuring them I was no such thing, they let us sleep in their village.

Day 88 was an uneventful, hot and humid thirteen hours of paddling to a village on the western side of the river. Once there, Aaron had pointed to the opposite shore. "Irian Jaya?"

"Yes, yes," the villagers chattered excitedly. Aaron gave me a look of pride over his communication skills.

So I pointed again to the far side. "Michael Jordan?" I asked. "Yes, yes," came the reply. Aaron's face turned red with anger.

"Well, I think that's Irian Jaya!" he snapped.

The rain finally begins to let up. I look at Aaron peeking out from under his soaked hood. After 89 days of expedition together, he seems so far away, even though he is sitting in the same kayak with me. Everyday it seems our anger towards each other grows. Every argument places a little more distance between us. I am beginning to hate him, as he is me. I wish I could make my feelings vanish, but as hard as I pray and try, they just won't go away. Aaron points to a canoe ahead of us, hesitating in the currents, with two men in it. Several minutes pass. The men seem afraid, but they finally approach with extreme caution. After greeting them, the two men tell us we can stay the night with them in their village. We follow them downriver as the day begins to fade into night.

I remember the warnings of Bill Tayler. "When you reach the

region where the Fly River borders between Papua and Irian Jaya, make
sure you stay on the Papua side of the river." I am suspicious of the two
men in the canoe out in front of us, leading us into the night. One of
them wears a green military-looking shirt. I feel uncomfortable. Unlike
Papua, Irian Jaya is not an independent country, though they are fighting towards that goal. At present, the country is owned by the Indone-
sian government against which Irian rebels have been fighting for years
using guerrilla warfare. "The freedom fighters have set up camps along
the river. They have been known to take American missionaries hostage
in an attempt to gain publicity for their cause." Bill's warnings begin
ringing in my head again. "Don't underestimate them. They will kill
you!"

"I'll bet these two are leading us right into a rebel camp," I say.
Aaron doesn't respond. "Let's ditch these guys and go on downriver and
camp," I suggest.

"We'll be all right."

"What makes you so sure?"

"God will protect us," he says with coolness.

"Maybe He wants us to use our common sense this time, or maybe
that is something you know nothing about."

"Don't shame me!" he snaps. A sudden urge to smack him in the
back of his head with the paddle comes over me. I resist.

"What?" I am disgusted.

"You heard me." He turns around and looks straight at me. "Don't
blame *me* for *your* fear." My mounting anger is distracted when the lead
dugout pulls to the bank.

"This is the Irian side of the river," I whisper with urgency.

"So?"

"So, Bill Tayler said to avoid this side at all costs. Let's get out of
here." But Aaron steps out onto the shore.

"I'll be back," I say, seeing Aaron begin to untie our bags. I want to
check this village out for myself to decide if it's safe. I follow the two men
down a dark path and stumble on some roots. The jungle grows louder
as we penetrate deeper. Soon, several high-standing huts appear in the
blackness lit up by firelight. Their long stilted legs reach down from
large platforms that disappear into the undergrowth. We come to a
ladder and the men insist that I climb up first. This adds to my suspicion,
but I climb up and stand on the platform. Several men sit huddled
around a large fire. They turn and listen to the voices of the two men

behind me, explaining my presence. I begin to count them but can't finish as one offers his hand in greeting. His shake is firm, but his eyes seem cold. Looking down, I see a black machine gun laid across his lap. My body goes numb. The other men begin greeting me, but I don't see their faces, just their laps filled with more machine guns and shot guns. I start to leave, but the two men are still behind me blocking my way.

"Me go big water, helpem Aaron plenty plenty gear," I explain. The first man who shook my hand snaps his fingers at the two men standing somewhere behind me.

"Youpellas go helpem," he says. They go down and vanish in the darkness. I turn and start down the ladder just as one of the rebels stands up. He hides a sawed-off, double-barrel shotgun behind his back and approaches me with a strange, guilty look on his face. The thought of him shooting me races through my mind with a hot flash of panic. I jump from the ladder into the blackness below, hitting the ground hard, but am still on my feet. I rush towards the river, faster now. I start to run, convinced there are several guns aimed at my head. I hear the sound of footsteps behind me trying to keep up. Soon the moonlight shimmers off the river's surface and the dark silhouette of Aaron tying down Amazing Grace. He finishes and meets me on the trail.

"We have to get the hell out of here!" I tell him, taking him by the arm and continuing towards the river.

Aaron resists. "What's wrong?"

"Just come!"

"Tell me what's wrong!" He insists. I think of leaving without him.

"This is a guerrilla camp!" The two men catch up from behind.

"What happened?" he asks.

"Youpella come," one of the rebels demands, taking a step closer. I check their hands for guns . . . none that I can see. I start back down the path but stop again when I realize that Aaron isn't following.

"Are you stupid? Come on!"

"Let's go in peaceful," he suggests.

"They have guns!"

"Youpellas come!" the man demands louder.

"If we run, they'll find us. Our best chance is to seek peace," Aaron suggests. My fear turns to rage.

"Fine! Why not die tonight!" I shout at him, and storm back towards the huts. "You sure did pick a whale of a time to defy me," I say as I pass him.

"Lord, save us," I pray, climbing the ladder once more. The guerrilla fighters shake hands with Aaron. He too is intimidated by the sight of so many weapons. We sit down. A strong urge to face the facts comes over me.

"Youpellas belong Irian Jaya?" I come right out and ask them, feeling Aaron stare at me. All the men agree with several grunting head shakes.

"Youpellas fightem Indonesians?" I ask.

"Plenty! plenty!" they shout in excitement.

"We twopella no likem guns," Aaron says, pointing to their weapons.

"No worries, no worries," their big man assures us.

"Wepella shootem pig, possums, shootem Indonesians, no shootem you twos," is his comforting goodnight promise. It's enough for Aaron who falls right to sleep after we set up the netting. I pretend to be asleep, wondering why it is necessary for them to check on us every few minutes with their flashlights. An hour passes before Aaron stirs.

"Do you think they will let us go, if we try to leave?" I ask him.

"No."

"Fine jam you've got us in," I say, coldly.

"Me?"

"We should have left when we had the chance!" I snap at him in a harsh whisper.

"All right. They're rebels, but he promised he wouldn't shoot us, and I believe him."

"All I know is, we're at their mercy now. The next time I tell you to do something, you'd better damn well do it!" I say.

"I'm not your boy!"

"Did we agree from the beginning of this expedition that I am the leader?"

"Yes."

"Did you or did you *not* sign a piece of paper stating that you agreed to give me that authority? And did that paper not say that I am to have the final say in decisions if the need arises?"

"It did."

"And did you not sign it?"

"Screw your piece of paper!" he snaps, and rolls back over to sleep. I lie in anger for several hours, still unable to sleep. Suddenly, the men stand to their feet. My heart begins to race. One by one, they climb down the ladder, their quiet voices disappearing into the jungle noises towards the river. I check the watch. It's 3:00 am.

In the morning, we make our way down to the river worried that they might have stolen our kayak. It is still there, once again living up to its name, Amazing Grace.

"They went through our bags," I say. The seals hang open with our clothes and equipment strewn around the inside of the kayak.

"Looks like it's back to eating plain sago," comes Aaron's depressed voice.

"Oh, please no, not my hat." It's missing from the bow of the kayak.

"They stole all of our canned food from Kiunga." His stomach growls in protest. I look up, concerned about the sun beating down on my unprotected head.

"Look at it this way, there will be a guerilla fighter running around shooting at Indonesians with a hat that says in permanent ink: "Though I walk through the valley of the shadow of death, I will fear no evil."

*   *   *

Aaron charges the river, launching himself from the high bank into an acrobatic somersault. The villagers of Manda fill the misty air with cheers as Aaron pulls himself from the muddy currents to impress them once again.

"How deep is the water?" I ask, as he walks past.

"Deep enough."

"You didn't know that the first time. I thought we agreed not to show off and take undue risks on this trip," I complain.

"I'm not."

"Anybody knows it's stupid to horse around from high places into unknown, muddy waters."

"You're just jealous," he says.

"Jealous? I have nothing to prove to you or these people. You're breaking the rules, so cut the crap."

"And if I don't?"

"Then I will hurt you myself." My fists are clenched. Aaron's face is flushed with anger. He turns around and storms off to the murmur of a disappointed crowd.

The war between Aaron and me has grown bitter since being robbed two days ago by the rebels. Last night we stayed in an abandoned guerrilla fighter camp. A sign on one of the trees read "Rebel Camp 3." The place had a spooky atmosphere, because we were never sure when or if the armed inhabitants would return. Men become violent and edgy in war. The rebels we had already met had eyes so cold we knew they had killed many times before. Maybe killing us wouldn't bother their consciences.

As quiet as we should have remained, we got into one fight after another, about who could start the fire faster and better, who could cook his meal tastier and in a more creative way, and on and on. We have been torn apart like a rebellious son from his father. I desperately try to hang onto the old idea, clinging to the authority that I once had. Aaron takes hold of the new. He doesn't listen; he doesn't care anymore. I know that I must let him go, but it is easier in my mind than in reality. His respect for me has turned to bitterness and hatred. I return his spoil with more poison of my own.

I follow Aaron through the village of Manda to a large hut. The afternoon fades to night. Tomorrow will be Day 92. Several men enter the hut to trade with us. They have brought what we want most, several crocodile teeth.

"I want this one." Aaron quickly snatches the largest tooth from one of the men.

"I want it too."

"He gave it to me!" Aaron demands.

"He was showing it to both of us. You just took it."

"I saw it first."

"You already have a pig's tusk to wear around your neck. I have nothing," I plead. The fighting goes on until we buy all the teeth and agree that nobody can wear any of them until the trip is over and they are all divided equally.

The morning leads to a fairly routine day on the river, long, hot hours of paddling with the usual scenery of swamp grass, sugar cane, and bamboo. A man gives us some sweet bananas along the way, which we enjoy. There is little or no talking between us—it's the old rule that if you don't have anything nice to say, don't say anything at all. We stop for the night in a rundown bush camp, something Aaron takes a lot of pride in spotting for us.

The coming of night releases the usual swarms of mosquitoes with their high-pitched, annoying whine. They cover our net like gray dog hair.

"Dang! I forgot to bring in my can from dinner," I say, disgusted.

When the outside world is ruled by millions of foes that like to suck your blood and carry disease, then you don't leave the protection of your net for any reason, not even to take a leak, which is the reason for bringing our empty dinner cans into the net at night. I dig up a zip-lock bag.

"Don't use that; you'll spill," Aaron warns me. I ignore him. Besides, it is my only choice.

The night has cooled off when my aching bladder wakes me. Aaron is sound asleep. I search for my flashlight but can't find it. I get up on my knees and begin filling the bag. Soon, to my horror, Aaron's prediction comes true. My urine runs over onto the tarp and my blanket.

Anger comes quickly and with a power I cannot handle. I feel hate towards New Guinea and all of its suffering. My body begins to shake in fury as flashes of rough waves, rugged mountains, and fierce rapids shoot through my mind. I feel my heat rash and insect bites itching, the infections covering my body. I am hungry, thirsty, and tired. And now there is urine all over my only blanket, my only possible bed. I explode into a scream of madness. Aaron flies up beside me, looking around confused. He grabs me, desperately holding down my arms, as I start tearing down the net. I hear him shouting at me to "Calm down!" I curse the island! Completely out of control, I begin shouting the Lord's name in vain. Aaron panics, trying to cover my mouth with his hand, but my rage cannot be leashed until I burn up all my energy.

I feel stupid and childish this morning. I am mad at myself because I could not control my temper. Hanging my head in shame, I remember how I dishonored the God who has blessed me so many times on this awful island. If only I could take the words back. Aaron's silence also eats at me. His pride is painted thick on his face, about how he can keep his cool, and I can't. I hate him this morning more than ever before. I can feel it like a lump of ice buried in my chest. My heart is cold.

"Make sure you get everything this time," Aaron breaks the silence.

"What's that supposed to mean?"

"It means you always forget things at our camps." If he's trying to get me steamed, he's doing a good job.

"Shut up!"

It's my turn to paddle, so I take the back of the kayak and push us off, while Aaron begins preparing breakfast in the front of the kayak. I am watching him carefully because I no longer trust him to divide between us evenly.

"Throw me your hat," I say, with the sun shining in my eyes. We have agreed since the rebels stole my hat, that Aaron's hat now belongs to the one paddling. Aaron begins desperately searching for it and then becomes still.

"I think we left it behind." His face is bright red.

"We?" I am not in the mood to show mercy.

"Yes *we!*" he yells, in defense.

"So do you have any ideas where *we* . . . left *your*. . . hat?" I ask, rubbing my sarcasm in his face.

"It's hanging on the side of the bush hut," he finally admits. I put in left rudder, turning the kayak towards shore.

"I don't see why I should have to suffer from your mistake." I am beginning to sweat as I battle the current. "You should have listened to your own advice."

"Just paddle," he says in a miserable voice. I feel the boat flinch and look up. Aaron is crawling back towards me. In front of him something large charges the kayak just beneath the surface, water sprays in its wake.

"Crocodile!" Aaron screams, falling onto my feet. Both of us are in a panic. The spray hits the boat; a long gray body passes beneath the surface. I stare in disbelief.

"Catfish," I say, catching my breath and calming my nerves.

It takes thirty hard-fought minutes to retrieve the hat. Back with the sturdy current, we eat a late breakfast. We finish eating some sago and bananas; then Aaron pulls out a little devotional book.

"I'm going to read a devotional that I think you need to hear," he says in a self-righteous tone.

"Why me? Why not you?"

"I seem to have more control over my tongue," he responds, his pride intensifying my anger.

"Look, I got mad last night and said some things that I shouldn't have, I'll admit."

"You always get mad," he insists.

I raise my voice in defense, "God makes people different—some are fast to anger, others slow, but it doesn't make either one any better."

"You used my God's name in vain!" His face is red with hate.

"He's my God too!"

"He is the only reason we're still alive. He is our protector and provider. You'd have to be insane to dishonor Him out here; I would never use His name in vain."

"I *was* insane last night!"

"You just lost your temper, like always!" He yells. I want to punch out the smart look on his face.

"You're losing your temper right now." I tell him.

"Only you can make me like this," he claims.

"So your imperfection is my fault?" I snap, losing control.

He is up on his knees now, his face bright red, eyes furious. "You used the Lord's name in vain! I can't! Don't! Understand that!"

"Christ died for me! . . . because I do stupid things and need His forgiveness. If He was as slow to forget as you, then we would all go to hell!" I shout back. "God made us different; my impatience eats at you just like your slow patience eats at me. I hate it that you're slow, and you hate it that I'm fast."

"Then I hate the way God created you." His words cut me like a knife.

"And I hate you," I slice back at him, sliding down into the kayak. I stare at the water. After 93 days together has it come down to hate? It doesn't make sense. I think back over all the things we've been through together, all the experiences that we have shared and that we will remember. Only us, nobody else. For the first time in a long while, I remember that we are floating downriver, actually living what most only dream. The memories flood my mind: Aaron's wide-eyed expressions the first time I met him. He had been so young and alive, cocky and ignorant, yet so willing to listen and to follow. He was a boy. I look at him again. He holds a fierceness about him now; his eyes are far away. The waves, the long hot days of paddling, mountains of endless jungle misery, deadly waters, and disease have hardened him. This island has crushed his boyhood. I remember his fears in the beginning, how the crocodiles controlled his every waking moment. I search his face now. His fears control him no longer. I remember him sleeping the night away amongst rebel machine guns. He has stared down the shafts of arrows, begged for food in dark huts far from home. I have not seen anything that he has not seen, nor felt any greater pain.

The tears well up in my eyes. He sees them trickling down my cheeks and looks away.

"I don't hate you, Aaron, I can't hate you . . . ." My voice chokes up. "I have been through more with you in three months than with anyone. We have seen things together that few will ever see, gone places that men like us should never go. We have trusted God together for our very lives. What greater thing can two men do than that?" Aaron's anger melts away. He too begins to cry. "You are a man, Aaron."

"I know," he says.

"God has called us to walk together. How could I hate you? If I had been a good leader, I would have desired that you become better than me, more than me . . . ," I am crying too hard to speak. "I love you!" I blurt out. The moment those words leave my lips, I know them to be true. We rush to the middle of Amazing Grace, embracing one another in violent sobs.

"I love you!" Aaron whispers in my ear. We continue to weep, floating in the gentle current.

"It's gone," I whisper, of the bitterness.

Aaron nods his head. "All of it," he agrees. A sudden gust of wind causes me to open my eyes. The sky is black.

The race for our rain jackets begins. In minutes the storm hits with ferocious winds whipping sheets of rain into our backs. There is no visibility, only flashes of lighting as the river surface boils white with rain drops. Overhead, are the deafening rumbles of thunder. Suddenly, a powerful gust of wind threatens to capsize us. We sink down low into Amazing Grace, to stabilize her, before slamming into a wall of sugar-cane and bamboo. They buckle and slide beneath the kayak. Deeper and deeper, the wind drives us until we are surrounded by bending stalks. My back stings in pain. Water trickles down the front of my jacket from my beard. I am curled into a ball as the storm rages on and on. But, I am at peace; the bitterness in my heart is finally gone.

By early evening, the cloudy sky is bloodshot red, reflecting orange off the river's surface in front of us. The day has been filled with joy since the morning's resolved conflict and the storm. We have passed the hot hours in talk. Everything seems so different. We paddle with new vigor even though our desires for the shores of Daru has faded. I feel content with our life in New Guinea, on a wilderness river surrounded by swamp.

We entered the Fly River Delta late this morning, a place of vast swamps and canals surrounding the winding river. We have been told that there are no villages through this stretch, no land to build them on, nor for us to camp on. The swamps stretch for miles in all directions making it one of the most unpopulated places on earth, infested mainly with mosquitoes and crocodiles. We have no idea where we are going to sleep tonight, and the darkening sky makes us edgy.

"Grab the camera!" I shout from the bow. Out in front of me a dark object ripples through the orange glow. "It's another swamp deer . . . Looks like a doe this time."

Earlier we had spotted a large, six-point buck, swamp deer swimming to the western side of the river. We had taken out the camera and burned up most of our energy chasing after it, trying to get close enough for a good shot. One snap, at sixty yards, of a water-logged buck jumping out of the water and quickly disappearing into tall swamp grass was the best we could manage. We have been waiting for another opportunity ever since.

Both of us are paddling at full speed. The dark head of the deer grows larger. Our kayak glides smoothly across the surface. I strain heavy on my paddle. We close in, and I put down my paddle to reach for the camera. Aaron also stops paddling. Everything is quiet as our kayak drifts steadily closer. The water is darker now. The deer stops swimming. His head turns to face us. An alarming sensation rises from my gut. What I had thought to be a small furry, deer's head is now, plainly, a huge, scaly-skin-covered head. Yellow, glowing eyes glare up at me. A long snout begins to open, revealing large, dagger teeth. I drop the camera onto my lap.

"Crocodile!" I scream at the top of my lungs. The kayak still glides forward. My panicky hands search wildly for my paddle. Desperately, I slap the water in an effort to stop us. We slow. The croc is close now. His massive body twists in the shadowy water. He approaches us head on. Aaron is screaming from behind me as we paddle, back-stroking with all our strength.

A quick splash, and the crocodile is gone beneath the dark, murky surface. My head jumps from side to side, searching for the beast. We stop paddling for a moment. My body tenses with horror, anticipating the attack. I realize I am screaming along with Aaron. We switch directions, paddling forward again, water spraying from our paddles.

"I think we lost him," Aaron says after several minutes of hard paddling. We slow our pace, trying to catch our breath and calm our hearts.

In the setting sun's final minutes of light, we see more crocodiles moving from the swamp reeds into the river to hunt for the night. Desperately, we search for some place to make camp, but there is no land at all, just swamp on either side. The warnings from all the nationals begin to sound off in my head.

"Daytime, you twos paddle paddle . . . belong night Iiiiieeeeee, nogat paddle, puk puk Iiiiieeeee." I chase the voices away.

"Steer closer to the reeds," I say. The last pink has faded from the sky. The night becomes pitch black. The only way I can tell where the river is going is by watching the contrast between the starry sky and the black shadow of grass cutting across it. Suddenly the reeds begin to shake violently. Our kayak, picks up speed as both of us lean into our strokes.

"It's just a swamp deer!" I shout, just as an explosion of water sprays us from a thundering crash. Adrenaline races through my body. Both of us are screaming from the fright. We move away, and to my surprise, there is no attack.

"That was no swamp deer, Joel. It was a big . . . ."

"I know, I know," I cut off Aaron's shaky voice behind me. He is steering us out into the middle of the river now. "They're out here, too." I look down into the black water. My whole body is tense. "I say we stick close to the reeds."

"No way. I'm not going back over there."

"If they get one of us out here, the other will just be floating along in this current waiting for the inevitable," I complain.

"Please, don't talk about it," Aaron's voice pleads. I wrestle with my imagination: large jaws clamping down on my leg, pulling me down into the cold, black water, then the twirling and drowning. It all seems too close to reality. I shiver.

Lord, You are my God,
And I will ever praise You,
Lord you are my God,
And I will ever praise You,

Aaron begins to sing. It seems to help to focus on the mercy of God. I join in.

I will seek You in the morning,
And I will learn to walk in Your ways.
And step by step You'll lead me,
And I will follow You all of my days.

I turn to look at Aaron. His face is pale with fear. "Paddle. The worst thing we can do is drift like bait," he says. Suddenly, the water ripples beside him; a dark object shoots across the side of the kayak striking Aaron in the side. My body flinches; I see a catfish slide along the rubber wall before splashing beneath the surface. My face feels hot. Aaron is in convulsions, almost falling out the other side of the kayak.

"Ohhhh man . . . I thought that was it!" He is out of breath. "Paddle!" he shouts to me. I remember and begin stroking the water again. "What's another song? I need another song." His voice is panicky.

Amazing Grace how sweet the sound,
That saved a wretch like me.
I once was lost, but now I'm found,
Was blind, but now I see.

He sings on. The hours pass by. We have been paddling for fifteen hours straight, and, exhausted, my paddle strokes are powerless. Still, the fear of drifting among twenty-five foot, man-eating reptiles does not allow me to rest. Aaron is silent behind me, too tired even to speak. I hear his paddle strike the water, a little slower with each passing hour. I have given up hope that our energy will last until sunrise, still a few hours away, when a light breaks through the darkness in the far distance. We come to the village of Obo.

The next morning, Day 94, after a good, solid breakfast we push on from Obo and by evening come to a small bush camp. We are working great together now. Camp set-up and take-down has been reduced from a one-hour ordeal to a matter of minutes. By the time the sun is up on the morning of Day 95, we are already back out on the river, cooking breakfast on the gas stove which sits on one of our paddles. We have learned to utilize every minute of the day to move us closer to the end of our expedition. We cook, clean, organize, and plan while the current pushes us onward to Daru!

The sun sets on our 95th night with no land in sight to make camp on. We are horrified at the thought of spending another night on the water! When we paddle too close to the reeds, we hear giant crocodile bodies slide into the water. Out in the middle of the river, jumping fish keep our nerves on edge. Sometimes, while paddling in the dark, we hit moving animals with our paddles—fish we hope. Soon however, and luckily, we see the firelights from a village ahead, the village of Kawatangwa, where the Suki tribe lives. These people, until recently, were the most feared headhunters on the island. Now most of them have converted to Catholicism.

In the morning, having gotten a restful night's sleep, with extra fish hooks that we still have, we trade for baskets, tusks, a wooden paddle and a giant crocodile tooth. Comparing this tooth to the others that we have traded for, it must have come from a croc measuring well over twenty feet. We ask the man who gave it to us to tell us the story. He excitedly gathers all the men from the village who were on the hunt. Together they put on quite a show for us. Three men swing back and forth on the powerful tail, while other men hack at the animal's head and spear its body, until the invisible "puk puk" lies dead on the hut floor.

Aaron and I are finally enjoying each other's company without conflict, as we float farther down river on the last day of February, Day 96 of our expedition. It has taken almost one hundred days to adjust to life in New Guinea. We both agree that we now feel at home here, so alive and so free. We stop on a small island for lunch. The tall treetops above us are speckled with thousands of white parrot-doves. Aaron reaches into a bag and pulls out the huge crocodile tooth we traded for. It is twice the size of the one we fought over in Manda last week.

"I want you to have this," he says.

"You take it."

"No, it's yours. You've led this expedition well. I know that now. If it wasn't for you, we would never have even come here," he says.

"But. . . ."

"Please," he cuts me off. "I want you to have it. I want you to wear it around your neck . . . you've earned it."

"Thank you."

We paddle deep into the night again before hearing the strange sound of music blaring from a radio. Lights begin appearing around a long bend. Two small ships are anchored side by side. We paddle up to the biggest one and shout "hello." A white man appears on the edge of deck and peers down on us.

"Get out of there!" he shouts in a panic. "Are you mad? Get out!" He continues to yell until we are safely aboard his ship. "You can't paddle at night. The crocodiles will eat you for certain," he warns.

"I'm Aaron and this is Joel," Aaron introduces us.

"Pleasure. My name's John . . . work for the copper mine. I build water catchers for the villages since they can't drink from the river anymore." He shakes both our hands firmly. "I have heard about you two on the ship radio. Everybody is keeping track to see if you make it.

Which you won't, if you paddle at nighttime. Is it true you've come all the way across from Wewak?" He asks.

"It's true," I say, happy that others have been watching our progress.

"Yep . . . by the look of you, I believe it! Now, follow me," John says. He leads us to an aluminum dinghy in the stern of the ship. "Do you see this?" He points to a large, deep dent smashed into the side of the dinghy. "A huge croc did that when I lost my motor one late afternoon and had to paddle back in the dark." I feel goose bumps cover my arms and legs. Aaron looks at me with wide eyes.

"We get the point," he says.

The next morning, after spending the night on board the ship, Aaron and I go into a small nearby village and take a translator with us who speaks some broken English. We are searching for someone who remembers how to perform nose piercing, a New Guinea ritual of manhood. Within a few hundred miles of the coast, we are finding that the village cultures are greatly influenced by the western world. The only person we find who seems to understand what Aaron seeks is an old man who is sitting in some shade under a hut. According to the translator, there was a time when this old man used to help in ritual initiations. Through the translator, Aaron communicates that he wants to have his nose pierced, and the old man agrees to do it.

"Are you sure this is what you want?" I ask. We sit down on the ground.

"I am," Aaron assures me. Behind us the old man sharpens the end of a bone from the leg of a Cassowary bird. "His eyes remind me of the Old Man of Koup," Aaron says.

"Yes, they do . . . It's gonna hurt like hell, ya know," I say, staring at the sharp-tipped bone. Aaron is looking at me.

"I just want something to remind me of the change . . . am I ready?" He asks. I look at the confidence on his face.

"You're ready." I place my hand on his shoulder. "Lord, though You have used an island, it is You who changes us . . . we ask that You bless this initiation into manhood."

As word spreads, other villagers gather to witness this painful ritual. The crowd of about thirty hush as the old man instructs with his hands for Aaron to lie down. I am next to him. "Iiiieeeee," the crowd moans in sympathy. The old man gently places the sharp point against the cartilage separating Aaron's nostrils. Aaron closes his eyes.

The old man speaks to me in his dialect. "He wants to know if you are the one who has walked with this boy?" our translator asks.

"I am." I nod my head. Again the old man speaks.

"Has the boy died?" The translator repeats the old man's question.

"Yes," I say.

The old man grips the bone tightly, grabs the tip of Aaron's nose, and in one powerful shove thrusts the bone through his nose. Aaron's eyes fly open wide, his whole body trembs with pain. Blood trickles down the wound and spreads out over his lips. Tears stream down his pain-stricken face. His mouth, clamped shut, suddenly opens with an awful scream. "Iiiiieeeee," comes the moans of sympathy from the villagers. They do not understand. They have already forgotten the old ways of their culture that Aaron has come to understand.

We spend a second night on board John's ship before traveling on downriver to the village of Dewala-Gesubada. As payment for our lodging and food there, we tell the men stories of our journey, and act out our crash on the Strickland River. It has become our little play, and Aaron and I are the stars. We perform each night in a different village.

The next afternoon, we stop at a village to ask for the distance to the next village downriver. After seeing the dent in John's dinghy, we do not want to get stuck paddling in the dark again. The entire village comes and stands before us on the western shore of the Fly.

"How far belong next village?" Aaron asks.

"One hour!" one of the villagers shouts.

"Yes, one hour," agrees another.

"One hour, five minutes," comes a younger voice.

"Five, six, seven, day something," another man says.

"Sun belong sky," Aaron tries to explain by pointing to the blazing ball of heat. "Where sun belong, we twos paddle paddle come next village." A man steps forward proudly.

"Yesterday," he announces. The crowd agrees with him.

"One, maybe two months," says another.

"Thank you. Happy nun," we say, and paddle away much more confused than before we asked the question.

By nightfall, we arrive at the village of Tapila. It is the 100th night in our crossing of New Guinea.

"We twopella wantem speak Big Man belong Tapila." I tell a small crowd of villagers. They lead us up the side of a hill and call out to a hut.

An older man, a national, walks out into the falling darkness and greets us with a handshake and a friendly smile.

"Pastor," one of the villagers says of the man. We tell him of our long journey as he gives the traditional wail of sympathy. Then he makes sure that our bedding is set up, that our favorite meal of sweet banana and sago is prepared, and later that we are left alone to rest.

In the morning the pastor and the rest of the villagers escort us out to our kayak. The tide has gone way out overnight, leaving in its wake over a hundred yards of knee-deep mud. We wave goodbye to the crowd and begin pulling our heavy kayak across the mud. I feel some of the load lighten. Looking behind me, I see the pastor pushing at the end of our kayak.

"Oh, no. We twopella make big water," I tell him. He ignores me and keeps pushing. With his help, we soon make deep enough water to paddle. I pull myself up onto the edge of the kayak, my legs and feet reeking with smelly mud. I feel something touch my feet and jump! The pastor has begun to clean them with his hands. "Oh, no, please." I grab his hands and try to stop him.

"Me washem feet belong youtwos," he insists. He takes my hands and places them in my lap. I look at the crowd. From the bank, they all watch in silence. Aaron looks uncomfortable sitting beside me on the kayak.

"I can't let him do this!" I whisper to Aaron. He shrugs his shoulders sympathetically. Then, I know in my heart that I must. Tears well up in my eyes as the pastor carefully cleans the mud between my toes. This washing begins to reveal to me the mistakes I have made as the leader of this expedition. I feel ashamed. Have I been a servant to Aaron, the one I have been leading? I look to the bent-over man washing my feet, then to the crowd of people. His entire village stares at his humility.

With each of his cleansing strokes, he teaches me, all of us, about true leadership. I begin to realize that leading is not about being in control, nor is it about people giving you authority because you're qualified. It is about who you are. I suddenly know that this man washing my feet is a leader of leaders because he serves from his heart. If I could have been like him back in Wewak, I never would have tried to control Aaron. I never would have felt insecure about my position as the leader of this expedition. I would have desired, with a powerful thirst, that Aaron become more than me, greater than me. I would have rejoiced when he exceeded my abilities. But, instead of letting go, I had defended my honor with hostility. I had claimed my position of power, and when Aaron challenged it, I turned to insecurity and hate.

The man finishes. My feet are clean, and tears are rolling down my cheeks. He begins to wash Aaron's feet now. I listen to the silence of the crowd. Aaron fidgets in discomfort. It looks like it is a strange feeling for him to be served. I certainly was not strong enough to serve him.

"I'm sorry," I say.

"For what?"

"For not being more like this man . . . I was afraid of you!"

"Afraid of me! Why?" He asks.

"Because you're 19. God is teaching you what He is teaching me, only for you, six years earlier." Aaron looks confused. The man finishes cleaning his feet. "I've been afraid because I always knew that God would make you greater than me. But, that's all right now."

"No man is great in this world . . . only God," He says. I smile at him. It has touched us both, deeply, having our feet washed. We thank the man, and bid everyone goodbye. I feel free, like a burden has been lifted from my shoulders as we paddle from Tapila. I know that I am no longer the leader of this expedition. I never really was. Aaron and I paddle together towards Daru, a team now, and somewhere out in front us, and deep inside of us, is our true leader: God, who has protected us from so much danger over the past 100 days.

"I can't imagine what it must have been like for the disciples to have their feet washed by Christ," Aaron says after awhile. His comment leaves us paddling silently for much of the morning.

Five days and four nights have passed since Aaron's nose was pierced. It is still causing him pain, but the swelling has gone down. The river is too wide to see across now. We are at its mouth, where it spills into the sea, and it is forty miles wide. We have been riding the tides for the past week. When the tide goes out, the ocean sucks the water out of the river at eight miles an hour, allowing us to make good time. As the tide changes, the river current becomes still. At this point, we have to get out and wait for the incoming tide to pass us by. If the tide is big enough, the new level of water travels upriver in what's called a tidal bore. More like a giant wall of water, rather than a wave, a tidal bore can reach heights of twenty-five feet and travel for hundreds of miles upriver, at eight miles an hour, destroying everything in its path. Even the large mining ships wait out at sea until the bores move upriver, which takes about eight hours. Then again, the current stills as the tide changes direction. At this point, we get back on and ride the tide out towards the coast.

The sun is setting now, giving birth to the night of March 5th, night 101 of the expedition. Last night we slept in a coconut plantation called Madira. Tonight we have tied our kayak, Amazing Grace, to a pole emerging from the water. The tide is forcing a strong current upriver. We cook some dinner, waiting for the current to change so we can go on. Daru is nearby, and we are much too excited to sleep. Even our fears of saltwater crocodiles is dulled with the anticipation of the journey's end. Our stove is fired up and boiling rice as it rests on the wooden canoe paddle that we bought from the Suki tribe. The long kayak paddle holds the pot in place over the fire as Aaron and I hold either end. All of the stove support wires have snapped off somewhere along the way, but we have become masters at improvisation, utilizing whatever we have to get the job down. Still sitting in the kayak, we eat and rest a while, slapping at mosquitoes in the dark. The moon rises above clouds, full and bright. When we drift past the pole in the water, we know the tide has shifted. We untie and begin to paddle.

"Onward to Daru!" I shout. It is exciting to be so close. We see on the star-covered horizon a large island covered with tall, steep hills. Between this island and the mainland is the Torres Strait, and just beyond the strait lies Daru.

We spend several troubling hours trying to enter the strait. Sand bars force us farther and farther out to sea. But, we finally make it and have land on either side of us. A gentle current helps to push us through. Tiny, phosphorescent organisms twinkle a brilliant green with each dip of our paddles. Bright moonlight falls down from a dark sky of silver clouds. We talk of sharks now, but they seem so tame compared to crocodiles. It's 3:00 in the morning when we finally exit the strait and get grounded on a sand bar near shore. We have been paddling for fifteen hours and are feeling the exhaustion, so we decide to sleep. We hear a large splash in the distance as we curl up in our blankets to protect us from the mosquitoes.

"Did you hear that?" I ask Aaron.

"What, am I deaf?" he responds, but we are much too tired to care.

I wake up. Lifting my drowsy head, I see that we have drifted out to sea with the tide. I wake Aaron, who reluctantly gets up to help me paddle us back in towards shore. The huge dark back of a crocodile breaks the surface just in front of me, then in an instant disappears with a splash. This wakes me up! We paddle in until we beach ourselves on another sand bar. Then, we sleep again.

My eyes pop open to pitch blackness. I pull my blanket from my face. There is a cool, refreshing breeze. The sky is brilliantly painted in pinks with flares of orange. I roll over towards the east. The sun peeks at me over the wavering horizon of reddish water. My eyes find a dark spot just beside the rising sun. I tilt my head up straight for a better look.

"Aaron," I whisper, "Aaron," a little louder. He stirs.

"What time is it?" he mumbles. I can feel him looking at me.

"Daru," I whisper, as if we are both still sleeping. He hesitates for a moment before facing the east. For a long time we just lie there wrapped in our blankets in the silence of morning, watching the finish line of our journey rise and fall in the gentle waves.

Our minds are flooded with the memories of 1700 miles of paddling and hiking, 102 days of unceasing adventure. I look at Aaron. I can honestly say that I love him in my heart. I remember the faces of wise men like the Old Man of Koup, and the Bushy Man, the faces of suffering and strength like Stew's. I remember the faces of the warriors of the lost tribe, and the warm, loving smile of Sogamoi. I think of Alex and the miles of jungle we conquered together and the pastor who washed our feet. We have made many unforgettable friends along the way, men we will most likely never meet again. I remember raging rivers we rode, the wild music we heard, the dark jungles we crossed, the high, rugged peaks we climbed.

We get up and paddle towards the tiny island, which slowly grows larger and more real. But the silence stays. Within an hour we near her shores, shores that at many times along the way I thought we would never reach.

"Now that the end is here, I don't want it . . . I don't want it all to end." Aaron says.

"I know." I feel deeply sad.

We paddle closer. The town's people of Daru gather on the beach, staring out at us.

"There is no power in it . . . is there?" Aaron whispers. I turn to find his face far away in meditation.

"In what?"

"In being a man," he says, staring at the near shore. I turn back around towards Daru.

"No," I say. "The only reason we are here is because God allowed it." Aaron nods his head in agreement as Amazing Grace runs ashore on the beaches of Daru Island.

EPILOGUE

Two years have now passed since running ashore on those white sandy beaches of Daru Island. Out of money, Aaron and I washed our best pair of shorts and shirts. We flew back to America with bare feet, wild hairdos, and bones and crocodile teeth around our necks. A piece of bamboo stuck through Aaron's pierced nose. Our fellow passengers started asking us questions of where we had been. But neither Aaron or I could figure out how to explain such things. Each time the stewardess brought us a meal we would just about start crying from pure joy! My family met us at the airport with hugs, kisses, and three different kinds of homemade cookies. I can't remember my mother ever looking so relieved. Her anger, for what I put her through was to come out later. Aaron's family joined the celebration as soon as they could from overseas. Within three days of our return, I began a challenging three-month bout with Hepatitis A. But being sick in a hospital with nurses, food, and a real bed just didn't seem that bad. To date Aaron and I have no lingering medical problems from our expedition.

Aaron has spent the past two years completing what he promised on the shores of the mighty Strickland River. He recently graduated with a two-year degree from Phoenix Community College in Arizona.

I have spent the two years giving a multi-media presentation about our New Guinea experiences, writing this book, and falling in love with a beautiful woman. On May 27, 1995, with Aaron by my side, I launched my next major expedition by taking Catherine Elizabeth Cole to be my beloved wife in a small non-denominational Christian church—an expedition that will last a lifetime, full of adventure, hardship, and joy. For me, a much nobler task than crossing an island!

The name Israel means "to wrestle or to struggle with God." What an appropriate name for God's chosen people. There is good reason why the Bible is the most read book of all time. It is an accumulation of the greatest stories ever told, true stories about how God seeks out relationships with mankind. It is a rugged book of turmoil, slavery, wilderness, prisons, and martyrs. Its pages are filled with bloody battles, persecutions, deep sufferings, and intense hardships.

The stories are portrayed by a wide array of characters who continually defeat staggering odds, conquering impossible mountains in their quest for a Kingdom that is not of this world.

God matches boys against giants, shepherds against champions. By the sound of trumpets fortresses fall; by the charge of a few, armies are defeated. Characters who spend the night with lions are not devoured. Men thrown into furnaces are not burned. A handful of soldiers are sent to war, armed only with torches and trumpets, stories where the touch of a hand heals the sick, in a word the dead are raised.

The magnificent tasks of these Bible stories are never handed over to the experts. God passes by the professionals, despising those who claim to be qualified and experienced. Instead, God sets the impossible before ordinary people, choosing the least to become the greatest, the weak to become strong, and the last become first. So that when ordinary men like Aaron and I stand on the shores of Daru Island, we can know without a doubt, "That He is God."

The Old Man of Koup was right. Without the wisdom of the people of New Guinea we would have surely perished. Such knowledge was worth God sending a storm to wash two fools ashore. But God did not reveal the secrets and mysteries of an entire island to one individual. Each wise man we encountered only understood a portion of the whole. The people along the coast helped us through the waves. The tribes along the rivers warned of crocodiles. The Bushy Man led us over the Central Mountains, yet he knew nothing of the Strickland rapids ahead. When Aaron and I stood, alive, on the shores of Daru Island, we could say without a doubt, "That with man it is impossible, but with God all things are possible."

Though there may be times when we are not afraid, there is no such thing as "No Fear." If you don't listen to your fears enough, then you will lose their protection. There will be nothing to tell you to get off the river of death! And if you listen to your fears too much, then will you lose the hope that they protect? There will be nothing to tell you to get on the river of life! As for Aaron and me? We shall fear the Lord! For He is our protection, and He is our Life!

To learn to know the island of New Guinea, we had to wrestle with it. The wisest of Teachers taught Aaron and me on this difficult journey to know the lesser so that we might understand how to know the Greater.

As I sat down in a muggy motel room in Port Moresby, Papua New Guinea, having accomplished my dream, my heart was sad. I knew the day would soon come when Aaron and I would have to part ways. I end this story with my letter to him. Journal entry, March 10, 1993:

Dearest Aaron,

To know God we must be smashed by the waves of His spirit. Like the mosquitoes we must be swarmed by evil until we learn to protect ourselves beneath the shelter of the Almighty. We must battle and overcome the strong currents of this world that ever try to wear us down, pushing us backwards towards the sea of souls where there is eternal fire. We must cross the mountains of God's Kingdom no matter how high, no matter how rugged. When the jungles become dark and thick, then we must pull out the sword of His word and hack our way through; when we grow weary, we will eat from the Bread of Life to regain our strength that we may continue. As we travel, the leeches of this life will cling to us; they will suck our blood, but we must cut them off. Throughout our journey, we will realize our sickness and misery. At that time we must seek healing from the Man who was wounded for us, that our health might be restored. For He is the One who is able to give eternal medicine to even the weakest of travelers.

Once we have conquered one impossible mountain with all of its dangers, then we must climb down the other side with caution, for the slopes of pride are slippery. And as we put mountains behind us, there on the horizon will be another, this time larger and with more hardships. But we must press on no matter the depth of our suffering, for the prize which we seek is eternal. As we gain ground and learn, as our faith is strengthened, and our relationship with the Big Man grows, then our mountains of hardship will spring forth into rivers flowing towards our treasure. Float in humility, lest we find more mountains to cross. Though we will travel on the currents with Amazing Grace towards the finish line, fear will try to strike us down. But like the crocodiles who lurk in the night, pass them by, one by one. When it grows too dark to see, we must search for the beacon of truth, for this is the guiding light. And when we have endured, fought the good fight, finished the course, then we will stand before our Creator and it will be like a small island. For it will be isolated, just you and Him. His face we shall recognize and He will say to us, "Well done, good and faithful servants."

Aaron, seek God in this life through your experiences. For you are more than a conqueror. You once thought like a child, reasoned like a child, and spoke like a child. Now that you have become a man, you have put these childish things behind you. Therefore, as a man, be responsible to seek after God with all your mind, soul, heart, and strength. And love your neighbor as yourself. Then you will be a man among men. That is, A MAN OF GOD!

AS FOR MYSELF:

My dreams are huge and growing fast
I will listen for their calls
I will pursue them across oceans and mountains
Through jungles and swamps
I will track them across all terrains
Hunting them down like wild animals
Searching for them like a sacred treasure
Longing for them as a true love
And if they should spread their wings and fly away
Then I will soar after them
For to lose sight of them
Hope of them is to dig my grave!
I must be more than a man who ponders
But a man possessed with the chase
To one day capture the greatest treasure on earth
The very heart of God!

ACKNOWLEDGMENTS

First of all, for the success and completion of this expedition, I would like to thank my God for His ever-present love and faithfulness to me; my partner and friend, Aaron, not only for his perseverance but also for his patience with me; and my family for all their love and support.

I would also like to express my deep gratitude to all those in New Guinea who helped us across the "Land of the Unexpected." A very special thank you to all the nationals we encountered and\or traveled with whose wisdom literally saved our lives. Also, a heartfelt thanks to the missionary families and Catholic Fathers who provided a "safe harbor" to us and shared their homes, their food, their medicines, and their lives with us as we journeyed: the Woodyard's, the Minter's, Rudy, Jay, and George, the Tayler's, Father Don, Father Liam, and Father Joel.

Also, more thanks goes to AIRE (for our most valuable piece of equipment—our kayak), L.L. Bean, Vasque boots, and R.E.I. for their durable and dependable equipment.

And finally, in the long, hard struggle to complete this book, I would like to thank my editor, Diane Kulkarni, my brother, Aaron, my parents, Barry and Joan, my wife Cathy, my sister, Heather, and my friends, Sharon Hanson, Georgia Herod, Dave Ewing, Jinx Vesco, and Evan Hanson for their comments, support, and encouragement.

In all things, to God be the glory! Amen!